PLATO'S FABLE

NEW FORUM BOOKS   *Robert P. George, Series Editor*

A list of titles in the series
appears at the back of the book

PLATO'S FABLE

ON THE MORTAL CONDITION
IN SHADOWY TIMES

Joshua Mitchell

PRINCETON UNIVERSITY PRESS

PRINCETON AND OXFORD

Library of Congress Cataloging-in-Publication Data

Mitchell, Joshua.

Plato's fable : on the mortal condition in shadowy times / Joshua Mitchell.

p.   cm.   — (New forum books)

Includes bibliographical references (p.   ) and index.

ISBN-13: 978-0-691-12438-4 (hardcover : alk. paper)

1. Plato. Republic.   2. Political anthropology—Greece—History.   3. Philosophical
anthropology—Greece—History.   4. Classical literature—History and criticism.

I. Title.   II. Series.

JC71.P6M56 2006

321'.07—dc22   2005016653

ISBN-13: 978-0-691-12438-4

ISBN-10: 0-691-12438-8

British Library Cataloging-in-Publication Data is available

This book has been composed in Sabon

Printed on acid-free paper. ∞

pup.princeton.edu

Printed in the United States of America

1 3 5 7 9 10 8 6 4 2

If man were wholly ignorant of himself he would have no poetry in him, for one cannot describe what one does not conceive. If he saw himself clearly, his imagination would remain idle and would add nothing to the picture. But the nature of man is sufficiently revealed for him to know something of himself and sufficiently veiled to leave much in impenetrable darkness, a darkness in which he ever gropes, forever in vain, trying to understand himself.

—Alexis de Tocqueville, *Democracy in America*

The wisdom of Plato is not a philosophy, a search for God by means of human reason. Such a research was made as well as it can be by Aristotle. Plato's wisdom is nothing but an orientation of the soul toward grace.

—Simone Weil, *Intimations of Christianity*

CONTENTS

PREFACE

A N APOLOGY, of sorts, would be in order if I were here offering yet another "interpretation of Plato." Perhaps in an earlier age—say, in the aristocratic age—further justification for what I have done would not be required, since this offering, small though it may be, would be received under the category of "commentary" rather than "interpretation." And while that would not hallow what I have provided here, it would certainly authorize it.

We do not live in such an age, however; and so a warrant of a different sort is required, one that vindicates a project such as this one on more imaginable grounds. "Commentaries," which presume a durable tradition, within which the conventions of scholastic conduct remain tacit, hold little sway in an age that has no enduring interest in tradition. And "interpretations," at their worst, fall into the category of mere personal opinion, for which no one concerned with science in its fullest sense should have patience. Knowledge is not soliloquy.

At their best, of course, "interpretations" are far more than mere personal opinion, as a perusal of the secondary literature on the history of political thought demonstrates. At their best, such works warrant our attention less because they are perspicuous articulations of the original author's intention than because they provide a *resume* of a coherent, even if deeply troubled, moment of history, when for a time thinkers labored under a set of prejudices that set the boundaries of their generation. In their more distinguished expressions, the fecundity of a original text, and the light cast on it by its interpreters, unwittingly cooperate to divulge the contours of a historical moment that is fleeting—as all are. Here, contingent interpretation is correlative to canonical authority. Together they issue that *third* thing: an authoritative self-understanding that holds sway for this or that community, here and now. Somewhere between the accidents of personal opinion and the Timeless lies "interpretation."

While "interpretation" of this sort is certainly more than mere personal opinion, its compass remains more restricted than our aspiration, hushed though that might be. In the terms of Plato's fable, such "interpretation" corresponds to the passing shadows in the Cave that are first identified by the cleverest of the prisoners below. For a time, a coherent world is brought into focus by their efforts, and then shifting light and the transience of all things conspire to wreak havoc with their labors.

Suddenly, to look at their work is to *look back*; for now new shadows loom, which call forth new "interpretations."

This melancholy of knowledge, which always seems to reach beyond its grasp, is dignified, even if not redeemed, by historicism's allegation that 'the owl of Minerva flies only at dusk,' that wisdom *is* the purchase that *looking back* grants. Theologically, the loss of innocence is a retrospective affair, known only in hindsight, on the occasion of being thrust into the world of time and of death. Hegel, the first systematic architect of historicism, built upon this theological foundation, and so it seems fitting to bring it to our attention here. And in fairness to Hegel, the contribution of historicism is not the relativism of all knowledge, but rather the hazard that the historical moment in which we dwell gives us the only purchase we will ever have on the shadows that have *already* passed before us.

Alternatively, the melancholy of knowledge may be averted by philosophy, which begins with the passing shadows in the Cave, only to leave them behind. Philosophy is, after all, *para doxa*: against opinion, against the timely. Philosophy ascends through timely opinions, unsullied, to the Timeless. As such, it knows nothing of mere personal opinion, "interpretation," or the wisdom that comes only at dusk—all three of which are species of timeliness that grant only fleeting satisfactions, and then quietly succumb to the sting of death.

So specified, however, philosophy altogether evades the central problem of the *Republic*, namely, the respect in which dimly lit reason is *incapable* of ascending to the Timeless; for if anything is evident throughout this fabulous account, it is that none of his interlocutors have really understood what Socrates has said. In this fable in which there is incessant agreement—"Yes, I concur," "You are right to say that justice is the better course," "How could one think otherwise," and so on—no one really understands Socrates. What are we to make of these misunderstandings about which nothing is said?

It will be noted that Plato wrote esoterically, cognizant that only "the few" can come unto knowledge. True though that may be, however, this insight has provided a warrant for a kind of Bolshevism of the mind, by which the inevitable and intractable situation that the *Republic* sets up is bypassed by a sleight of hand that separates the stained from the redeemed, those caught in time from those who purport to hover above it. In Plato's great fable, the light of unaided reason is dim, and remains that way unless illuminated by the Good. The claim that "the few" can understand what Plato is *really* saying, while "the many" cannot, while perhaps true, emboldens the honor-loving, noble, soul (about which more in due course) who knows nothing of the Good—and who pretends to have no need for such knowledge. Nobility, and the associated calculus by which the few are distinguished from the many, is, at best, ancillary, to philosophy proper, which takes the measure of things higher still. Nobility searches for the "hidden truth" of the *Republic*, which must be protected from the many. The *Republic*, however, tells a different tale, namely, that *truth hides itself* from dimly lit reason. The mantle of esotericism, eagerly donned by the noble soul in order to distinguish itself from the many, does not fit as that soul imagines. The melancholy of knowledge cannot be averted if philosophy is, indeed, a cloak by which nobility bestows upon itself the title reserved for a type (the philosopher) that is higher still, and confuses participating in a dialogue "across the ages"—and so with the only immortality with which the noble soul will ever be familiar—with the Timelessness that alone is the antidote to the melancholy of knowledge. Philosophy is the antidote for just this sting; the noble soul remains yet poisoned by it.

If my words seem harsh, it is not because I find pretentious the aspiration of philosophy to the Timeless, nor because I have an aversion to nobility. Nobility has been much maligned of late, and we scarcely know how to render it its due. My objection is rather that under the auspices of nobility, the ascent to the Timeless is a victory too easily won: Nobility presumes that dimly lit reason is *someone else's* problem, and so it misunderstands what is at issue, and how it may be addressed. The noble soul, as we shall see, believes that truth—a "teaching"—is passed down generation to generation, perhaps through initiation. The *Republic*, however, nowhere involves truth-telling, but rather everywhere involves story-telling. Philosophy, moreover, is not passed on generation to generation. The philosopher's task is not to *hand down* a luminous and unspeakable "knowledge of the Good"—Socrates makes light of those who claim to possess such a thing as this—but rather to awaken souls that yet slumber. Not by mortal generation is philosophy born; the midwife to *this* event comes prepared with palliatives of a different sort.

Anyone who has tried to awaken young children from a deep sleep will have discovered that the best way to steal them away from their dreams is to tell tales that gently insinuate themselves into their shimmering world, until they stir. Herein lies my reason for entitling this work *Plato's Fable*. If the mortal situation is indeed akin to sleepiness, as the *Republic* suggests, then the manner in which philosophy proceeds must involve this telling of tales. Dimly lit reason, like sleepiness, responds not to "teachings," but rather to fables. The aspiration of philosophers to the Timeless cannot bypass this undertaking that is made necessary because of our drowsy condition and made perilous because the fables that abet our education are not themselves the education we finally need. They inaugurate the journey from childhood to adulthood, but are not to be confused with what is proper to adulthood itself. The *Republic* is a fable, then, in *this* sense: Forever trapped within the confines of the shadows from which there is no escape, Socrates tells tales to those who dream of a world they cannot as yet verify, to the end that what is brought forth through such telling is not stillborn. I will be satisfied if I succeed here in conveying this double possibility: on the one hand, that Plato's fable is a provocation unto birth; and on the other hand, that *qua* fable, it cannot escape from the dream into which it enters, and so may never awaken souls that slumber. While both possibilities receive attention here, the burden of what I have provided concerns the provocations that emerge from Plato's fable—the questions *for* thought, as it were, that are occasioned by a tale that is not, properly speaking, an object *of* thought.

Since nobility has already been mentioned, it would be appropriate here to note that my subject has not easily lent itself to the current conventions of academic writing. The matter of manliness (*andreia*), to use a rather unconventional term, is one that cannot simply be glossed over in the *Republic*, especially in light of the fact that manliness, which in the Homeric world corresponds to a proximity to death of the sort that only the warrior knows, is a precursor to philosophy. This raises a host of questions, of course, which I think best to bring into relief rather than to flatten out with language that might suit the sensibilities of our own age, but at the cost of obfuscation. I have therefore used the terms "man," "men," "mortals," and "human beings"—the list is not exhaustive—in the context that seemed to me most fitting. That it will be possible to quibble about this or that usage, there can be no doubt; that the univocal term "human beings" would have been inadequate is no less obvious. The matter becomes doubly complicated in the conclusion, where I have occasion to discuss what I call the "fable of liberalism," out of which, arguably, emerges the univocal terminology that I have elsewhere found wanting. There my usage shifts frequently, though not, I hope, because of muddled thinking on my part, but rather because the subject at hand admits of the complexity that such usage implies.

A few words, finally, about the duration of this project and of the debts it has accumulated. Some ten years ago I began what I took to be a relatively short project involving a comparison between Tocqueville, about whom I had written in 1995, and Plato, with a view to examining their thinking about the instability of democracy and the manner of its amelioration, if any. While Tocqueville plays a significant part only in the conclusion (in the second section), he lurks in all that I have written about the *Republic* here. I believe now, as I did then, that Plato and

Tocqueville have more to say to us than any other two authors from the history of political thought. Juxtaposing them has allowed me to see questions that I could not have seen had I considered them separately. My good fortune has been to receive generous support throughout this period, from a number of sources. Among the more prominent are Georgetown University for a Junior Faculty Fellowship that allowed me to begin this project in 1995; the Earhart Foundation for a Summer Grant that encouraged me greatly along the way; and finally Georgetown University again, this time for a Senior Faculty Fellowship that allowed me to make significant progress on this project in 2002. Beyond the inestimable assistance they provided me stand the many colleagues who have helped in thinking through the issues I have raised here in manifold ways, most notably Peter Berkowitz, Todd Breyfogle, Jean Bethke Elshtain, Jill Frank, Tim Fuller, Ralph Hancock, and Gerry Mara. Without their thoughtfulness, this project would have been even more flawed than it already is. I would be remiss not to note the labors of two quite extraordinary graduate students whom I have been fortunate to count on during this lengthy, and at times painful, period of gestation: Joanna Bache Tobin and Richard Avramenko. Without their originality, tirelessness, ongoing conversation, patience, and subtlety of mind, this project would have been the poorer. Since philosophy is not something that is passed down, I cannot claim to have been their teacher. But because philosophy is the occasion for abiding friendship, I can claim to be the richer because of their proximity.

A NOTE ON THE TRANSLATION

FOR PLATO'S *Republic*, the ostensible subject of much of this book, I have largely relied on the translation by Richard W. Sterling and William C. Scott, which is itself in no small part a compilation of earlier translations. It should hardly require mention that the art of translation is a difficult one. At one extreme, a translation may provide a literal rendition of the text, missing much of its spirit; at the other, a version that aims at conveying a work's spirit may fall prey to exaggeration. After evaluating several of the standard English translations of the *Republic*, I have concluded that Sterling and Scott largely avoid either of these extremes. In the few instances where I believe they deviated somewhat excessively, I have amended their translation with a version I believe to be more trustworthy. In addition, to avoid any potential confusion in regard to key terms and phrases, I have inserted a corresponding word or phrase in transliterated Greek where I thought it might be useful. I ask the reader, should any differences of opinion arise, to bear in mind that fidelity to Plato in written English requires attentiveness to the things to which Plato directs our attention in written Greek. In this regard, on his own account of the relationship between Truth and what can be written, both languages fall short. Finally, the Greek text of the *Republic* against which the English has on occasion been compared is the recently published: *Platonis, Rempublicam*, edited by S. R. Slings (Oxford: Oxford University Press, 2003), in the Oxford Classical Texts series.

Chapter 1

INTRODUCTION

Unless philosophers become kings of our cities or unless those who now are kings and rulers become true philosophers, so that political power and philosophic intelligence converge . . . there can be no end to troubles, my dear Glaucon, in our cities or for all mankind.[1]

THE PREVAILING opinion about the character of reason renders this Platonic paradox quite unthinkable today. Philosophers, we learn in Plato's fable, are ruled by reason; yet in what sense could it possibly be true that reason is necessary to *save us*? As a fantastic artifice we may perhaps be entertained by this bald assertion, but to understand it as something more useful requires resources that we scarcely possess. Why this is so, and what those resources might be, is the question that concerns me here.

Wishing to defer for a time even more vexing problems, and in order to begin to understand just what might be at issue in the claim that reason is necessary to *save us*, let me offer a few thoughts about what will turn out to be a central concern of my analysis here, namely, the significance of imitation in mortal life. By way of anticipation, I suggest here that the problem of imitation turns out to be what reason saves us from; and that we are well served by reading Plato's fable in that light.

Imitation in Mortal Life

In light of the scant attention imitation receives today, and in light of the predominant contemporary understandings of Plato's *Republic*, it may well be asked why imitation need be invoked at all in an exposition of this sort. Among most political scientists and many political theorists, for example, imitation is scarcely a subject of serious debate, because human beings are considered first and foremost to be rational beings, not imitative beings. Yet this prejudice is a relatively recent one, as a perusal

[1] Plato, *Republic*, trans. Richard W. Sterling and William C. Scott (New York: W. W. Norton, 1985), Book V, 473c–d.

of the writings of Plato, Aristotle, Augustine, and Tocqueville, to name only a few of the more prominent, attest. Reason is, of course, a central concern in all of their reflections; but whatever their conclusions may have been about it, fidelity to their subject matter as a whole entailed a consideration of the significance in imitation in mortal life as well. Today, the need for this conjoint attentiveness to reason and imitation has not been the starting point for political theorization. Indeed, the two most prominent devices in political theory during the past quarter-century—Rawls's veil of ignorance[2] and Habermas's ideal speech situation[3]—deliberately rule out imitation altogether, since all things inherited purportedly sully reason's acumen.

Fortunately, however, Rawls and Habermas are not our only resources. With a view to exploring the alternatives to this one-sided emphasis on reason, what I do in what follows immediately below is provide a synoptic historical overview of two contemporary tropes—namely, "socialization" and "identity politics"—that concern themselves with the theme of imitation. I should note right at the outset that my purpose in exploring these two tropes is specify how, as "ideal types," socialization *underestimates* the problem of imitation, and "identity politics" *overestimates* the problem of imitation. Said otherwise: The former is too optimistic, and the latter is too pessimistic.

To be sure, there have been attempts, especially in the last decade, to invoke "identity politics" in such a way as to suggest that the difficulties implied by its typological expression are not fatal.[4] It is not by accident, however, that such treatments of "identity politics" achieve the purchase they do largely within the Anglo-American world, which has a long history both with pluralism and with absorbing emigrants from different nations and which, consequently, invites the conclusion that "identity politics" need not be characterized in the stark way I describe it here. This dubious conclusion has given rise to a strategy, adopted largely by the Left, of *leveraging* an already intact pluralism, with a view to elaborating new criteria for political inclusion, since relying explicitly on

---

[2] See John Rawls, *A Theory of Justice* (Cambridge: Harvard University Press, 1971), Part 1, ch. 1, sec. 3, p. 12.

[3] For an early iteration of this idea, see Jürgen Habermas, *Theory and Practice*, trans. John Viertel (Boston: Beacon, 1973), p. 17, where he invokes the phrase, "the logic of undistorted language communication." The clearest statement of the idea occurs in Jürgen Habermas, *Moral Consciousness and Communicative Action*, trans. Christian Lenhardt and Shierry Weber Nicholson (Cambridge: MIT Press, 1990), pp. 86–94.

[4] See, e.g., Charles Taylor, *Multiculturalism: Examining the Politics of Recognition* (Princeton: Princeton University Press, 1994); Will Kymlicka, *Multicultural Citizenship* (Oxford: Oxford University Press, 1995); and Iris Marion Young, *Democracy and Inclusion* (Oxford: Oxford University Press, 2000).

the liberal paradigm of interest alone would render "this" or "that" political "identity" invisible. Historical good fortune, however, should not be confused with theoretical clarity. That pluralism may be leveraged through the invocation of "identity politics" for the purpose extending the franchise in novel ways is a tribute not to the happy implications of "identity politics," but rather to the robustness of pluralism itself. If recent disaffection with the Democratic party platform of the 2004 election is any indicator, the attempt to leverage pluralism in this way may well have already reached its apogee; and the Left, in order to recapture its position of political prominence, may be better served, as Rorty has suggested,[5] by returning to the category of rhetoric and thought that is native to the Anglo-American world and that underwrote the Progressive era, namely, pragmatism.

The Disappointments of Reason

Against the backdrop of what notion of reason can we understand the tropes of socialization and "identity politics"? A good place to begin is with the early progenitors of the liberal paradigm, who were usually nominally or once-removed Reformation Christians—a fact that will become relevant as our discussion proceeds. By the liberal paradigm I mean nothing more complicated here than the sort of thing elucidated by Madison,[6] which persists under the rubric of pluralism. Most important for our purposes, reason is taken to be a faculty of preference formation,

[5] See Richard Rorty, *Philosophy and Social Hope* (New York: Penguin, 1999).

[6] See James Madison, "Federalist No. 10," in *The Federalist Papers*, ed. Robert Scigliano (New York: Random House, 2000), p. 60: "The smaller the society, the fewer probably will be the distinct parties and interests composing it; the fewer the distinct parties and interests, the more frequently will a majority be found of the same party; and the smaller the number of individuals composing a majority, and the smaller the compass within which they are placed, the more easily will they concert and execute their plans of oppression. Extend the sphere, and you take in a greater variety of parties and interests; you make it less probable that a majority of the whole will have a common motive to invade the rights of other citizens; or if such a common motive exists, it will be more difficult for all who feel it to discover their own strength, and to act in unison with each other." So imbued is Madison with this liberal paradigm that he renders landed property in terms of "interest" (ibid., p. 56) rather than the aristocratic term "rank," on which Tocqueville surely would have relied. See also Federalist No. 51, p. 334: "Whilst all authority in [the federal republic of the United States] will be derived from society, the society itself will be broken into so many parts, interests and classes of citizens, that the rights of individuals, or of the minority, will be in little danger from interested combinations of the majority. In a free government the security for civil rights must be the same as that for religious rights. It consists in the one case in the multiplicity of interests, and in the other in the multiplicity of sects."

which deliberates among goods that are *scalar*—that are sufficiently commensurable so that by some evident or liminal calculus "this" can be *preferred* over "that." Politics works because these preferences, when represented in elected assemblies, with the appropriate checks and balances, can be mediated without the sometimes enduring acrimony that arises when differences of language, race, ethnicity, religion, and, more recently, sexual orientation obtrude and overshadow the scalar logic of preferences.[7]

There has, of course, always been a measure of dissatisfaction with this pluralist model. In the last generation, this dubiety clustered in domains of research that sought to address the pressing domestic issues of the Cold War period. While the civil rights era might have been the occasion for the emergence of "identity politics," at the time the idiom of preferences and interests largely prevailed, because there was optimism that if the federal government successfully supervened over the "coarser elements [in local communities],"[8] as Tocqueville called them, then the pluralist model would be vindicated. Had this occurred, race would not have shown itself to be an intractable problem to which the scalar logic of preference had no answer. Needless to say, the subsumption of much of the contemporary research on the politics of race within the category of "identity politics" confirms that pluralism has, on this count, largely failed.

It was, however, feminism, rather than race, that raised the first serious philosophical questions about pluralism in mainstream, secular political science.[9] If women were not just another interest group, with differing preferences, then the justification for this would have to be that the difference between men and women was not scalar, but rather incommensurable. Women would have to be *different* in a way that the deliberative faculty of reason could not mediate. The use of the term "sex" seems rather out of place, I recognize, but replacing it with "gender" specifies the problem in a much less contentious way, and indeed

---

[7] It is worth noting that whatever fault may be found with quantitative research in political science in America, its methods are eminently applicable to a polity of citizens who evince the sort of scalar preference formation that liberal thought supposes. Quantitative research endures because the political world it measures is based on the measured and measuring deliberations of reason.

[8] See Alexis de Tocqueville, *Democracy in America*, ed. J. P. Mayer (New York: Harper & Row, 1969), vol. I, part I, ch. 5, p. 62.

[9] An important reason why race did not immediately raise the sorts of questions that sex did was that the problem of race in America was comprehended by many not only in terms of pluralism, but also, significantly, in the religious and covenantal terms. Not so with feminism, which, when pushed up against the limits of the liberal paradigm, turned toward the alternatives provided by the Continental tradition. The rhetoric of feminism did not, in other words, draw on religious resources.

partially masks the difference, since a difference that is merely "socialized" is one that is much more readily altered—and subsequently mediable—than one that is always-already-there, as sex is.[10] Feminism occupies the space between the always-already-there character of sex and the always-alterable character of gender. From the former, feminism derives its leverage *against* pluralism; from the later, it derives its leverage *within* pluralism. As such, feminism is located in the boundary between pluralism and "identity politics." Because there are respects in which men and women are completely alike *and* respects in which they are completely different, this liminal position is inevitable. Feminism verges on "identity politics," but does not wholly arrive there. It straddles two worlds.[11]

Hegel and the Origins of "Identity Politics"

"Identity politics" may not immediately seem to oppose Madisonian pluralism, but it bears no family resemblance to it, and that fact itself is telling. Madisonian pluralism emerges out of the Anglo-American tradition; "identity politics" is of Continental origin and can trace its proximal roots to Hegel's claim that in the course of the march of world history, Absolute Knowledge subsumes all "difference."[12] *Religiously* expressed, this is a claim that God uses the oppositions between good and evil in order to redeem a fallen world,[13] at the end of history. "Dif-

---

[10] See Luce Irigaray, *I Love to You*, trans. Alison Martin (New York: Routledge, 1996), p. 47: "Sexual difference is an immediate natural given and it is a real and irreducible component of the universal."

[11] The ambiguous status of feminism in the current debate around identity politics has brought forth, among others, responses by Seyla Benhabib (*Democracy and Difference: Contesting Boundaries of the Political* [Princeton, N.J.: Princeton University Press, 1996]) and Nancy Frazier (*Justice Interruptus. Critical Reflections on the "Post-Socialist" Condition* [New York: Routledge, 1997]).

[12] See G.W.F. Hegel, *The Phenomenology of Spirit*, trans. A. V. Miller (Oxford: Oxford University Press, 1977), para. 808, p. 492: "This Becoming [in history] presents a slow moving succession of Spirits, a gallery of images, each of which, endowed with all the riches of Spirit, moves thus slowly because the Self has to penetrate and digest this entire wealth of substance. . . . In the immediacy of [any] new existence the Spirit has to start afresh to bring itself to maturity as if, for it, all that preceded were lost and it had learned nothing from the experience of earlier Spirits. But recollection, the inwardizing, of that experience, *has preserved it and is the inner, and in fact the higher form of the substance*" (emphasis added). For Hegel, all residual historical antecedents are incorporated into the current incarnation of Spirit. Nothing is lost or left incomplete.

[13] Cf. Augustine, *City of God*, in *The Fathers of the Church*, ed. Roy Joseph Deferrari (New York: Fathers of the Church, 1950), vol. 7, book XI, ch. 18, pp. 213–14: "God would never have created a single angel—not even a single man—whose future wickedness He foresaw, unless, at the same time, He knew of the good which could come of this evil. It

ference" and historical existence are coterminous here, though with the important addition that a promise of a *final* unification is held out as the substance of faith.[14] Philosophy, however, has no place for either God's providence or for faith, since such religious notions are merely the "picture-thinking" version of what unmediated thought can know by and in itself.[15] In Hegel's thought the insight about the relationship between historically inevitable difference and final unification that Christianity proffers is appropriated, though purportedly on the higher ground of pure philosophical thought. What Christians relegate to God, Hegel relates to *Geist*. At best, this is dubious theology; at worst, it is a theory of historical meaning that all but invited the response it received.

It would not be an exaggeration to say that "identity politics" is the response of the Hegelian Left to the notion that difference is subsumed by the Absolute. "Don't be a chump" may be the highest ethical imperative of rational choice theorists; "let the different remain different" is the call of those who champion "identity politics." Difference can *never* be subsumed; identity remains intransigently self-same.

We should not be confused about what this intransigence means for the prospect of mediation across the boundary that separates differing identities. "Identity politics" supposes not only difference, which pluralism acknowledges, but also difference of a sort that is not mediable through the scalar calculus of preference. Said otherwise, *identity is not a preference*. Preferences, because scalar, can be quantified; "identity" must be qualified.

By this I do not mean that identity can be comprehended by a *constellation* of empirical attributes which, taken in sum and properly configured, serve as a ready indicator of "this" or "that" identity. Quantitative research has certainly sought to proceed in this manner, but this method

---

was as though He meant the harmony of history, like the beauty of a poem, *to be enriched by antithetical elements*" (emphasis added). Throughout this work I will first cite the more authoritative Deferrari edition (as *City of God* in *Writings*), and subsequently cite the page or pages to which it corresponds in the more readily available Bettenson translation (New York: Penguin, 1972) as *CG*—in this case, *CG*, p. 449.

[14] Augustine, *City of God*, in *Writings*, vol. 6, book I, preface, pp. 17–18: "[The future security of the City of God is that] goal for which we patiently hope 'until justice be turned into judgment,' but which, one day, is to be the reward of excellence in a final victory and a perfect peace. The task, I realize, is a high and a hard one, but God will help [us]" (*CG*, p. 5)

[15] See Hegel, *Phenomenology*, para. 765, p. 463: "*This form of picture-thinking* constitutes the specific mode in which Spirit, in [the religious] community, becomes aware of itself. This form is not yet Spirit's self-consciousness that has advanced to its Notion qua Notion: the mediation is still incomplete. . . . The *content* is the true content, but all its movements, when placed in the medium of picture-thinking, have the character of being uncomprehended" (emphasis in original).

seems rather blind to what identity involves, since those who claim to be members of an identity group purport to speak authoritatively not on the basis of a constellation of empirical attributes, but rather on the basis of a *constitutive experience* that outsiders cannot know. The scalar preferences acknowledged by pluralism are, in principle, capable of being deliberated over by any and all citizens. Identities, on the other hand, are *confessional*, monological. About identity citizens cannot really deliberate, since the locus of its authority is not the faculty of reason. Identities are their own authority and provide their own authorization. They are self-same, immune from the possibility of appropriation and, therefore, incorporation; and bequeathed by the accidents of birth[16] or the calamity of violence.

This harsh picture will no doubt be contested. I provide it, however, with a view to the original problem for which it was an answer, *viz.*, the subsumption of all difference, the elimination of any *remainder*, in the system of Hegel's thought. Comprehended politically, "identity politics" is a strategy of resistance, a manner of declaring independence from a corrosive and dehumanizing logic of history. Indeed, that was its place in the anti-Colonialist literature.[17] That is, perhaps, its virtue. Its cost, however, is precisely the mediation of difference that the liberal paradigm purports to make possible. The very strategy of resistance that is at the heart of "identity politics" yields a stubborn intransigence whose imitation assures that patterns of human thought and action are unlikely to change—or to be overwhelmed from without. "Identity politics," in sum, *overestimates* the problem of imitation, and this because it is a response to the impulse toward totalization that is at the heart of Hegel's project, and not his alone.

Rousseau's Gentler Form of Imitation

You will recall that the subject before us is the proximal source of the two tropes by which imitation is understood in contemporary thinking about politics. "Identity politics" is a particularly strong version, since its claim is that differences whose warrant is the always-already-there character of identity, and which are imitated from generation to generation, are not amenable to conciliation—or usurpation—by reason and its cognates, "preference," "choice," and so on. Identity remains what it is, not because of reason, but in spite of it.

---

[16] Nietzsche's rejection of the idea that the faculty of reason hovers without connection over the body—a thought that suffuses all of his writing—led him at times to offer the rather chilling formulation that the vitality of a people is predicated on their blood line. See Friedrich Nietzsche, *The Genealogy of Morals*, trans. Walter Kaufmann (New York: Random House, 1967), first essay, sec. 5, pp. 28–31.

[17] See Franz Fanon, *The Wretched of the Earth* (New York: Grove, 1963).

A much gentler trope through which imitation is understood is found in the idea of socialization. The idea of socialization is not to be confused with Aristotle's account of the formation of character (*hexis*),[18] which presumes that man has a "nature" (*phusis*) that establishes the boundaries of such formation at the same time that it establishes man's end (*telos*)—considerations that have no unambiguous equivalents in the literature of socialization. Aristotle has no direct bearing here.

The idea of socialization, like "identity politics," emerged *in opposition to* another idea, the pedigree of which we scarcely remember today. Curiously enough, both ideas emerge out of the Reformation tradition, though from different wings of it. "Identity politics," I noted, emerged in opposition to Hegel's philosophical project—which Hegel himself thought was perfectly consonant with Luther's own religious reflections.[19] The idea of socialization, however, emerged in the thought of Rousseau, which is notable, among other reasons, because of Rousseau's opposition to the conclusions of that other citizen of Geneva about whom we know, namely, Calvin.

To put the matter succinctly: Hegel's reworking of Luther's incarnational and eschatological theology, on the one hand, and Rousseau's response to Calvin's ruminations on the depravity of man, on the other, are the occasions for the emergence of "identity politics" and the idea of socialization, respectively.

Let us briefly consider the theoretical relationship between Calvin and Rousseau, with a view to illuminating the question for which socialization—*rather than original sin*—is the answer. In Calvin's *Institutes*, we find one of the clearest formulations anywhere of the contested

---

[18] See Aristotle, *Nicomachean Ethics*, trans. W. D. Ross, in *The Complete Works of Aristotle*, ed. Jonathan Barnes (Princeton: Princeton University Press, 1984), vol. II, book II, 1103a34–b6: "[M]en become builders by building and lyre-players by playing the lyre; so too we become just by doing just acts, temperate by doing temperate acts, brave by doing brave acts. This is confirmed by what happens in states; for legislators make citizens good by forming habits in them, and this is the wish of every legislator."

[19] See G.W.F. Hegel, *The Philosophy of History* (New York: Dover, 1956), part IV, sec. III, ch. I, p. 415: "Luther's simple doctrine is that the specific embodiment of the Deity—infinite subjectivity, that is true spirituality, Christ—is in no way present and actual in an outward form, but as essentially spiritual is obtained only in being reconciled to God—*in faith and spiritual enjoyment*" (emphasis in original). The inner truth of Christianity, for Hegel, was subjectivity. In his introduction to G.W.F. Hegel's *Early Theological Writings* (Philadelphia: University of Pennsylvania Press, 1971), Richard Kroner notes, "[The] philosophic decision [to deny knowledge of things as they are in themselves] and the method of reflective subjectivity which it entailed are, according to Hegel, fruits on the tree of Protestantism. The reformers made an end to the confident rationalism of the Scholastics. They cut the bond between knowledge and faith, between human intellect and divine revelation, between the temporal and the eternal. By denying philosophy the power of penetrating into the essence of things, Kant and his disciples gave their blessing to this separation" (p. 37). Kant and Hegel are the outworking of Lutheran categories of thought.

issue on which Reformation Christianity has taken one side, and Rousseau and his heirs have taken the other. Consider the following remark, which is found in a section entitled "Original sin does not rest upon imitation":

> Adam, by sinning, not only took upon himself misfortune and ruin *but also plunged our nature into like destruction*. This is not due to the guilt of himself alone, which would not pertain to us at all, but because he infected all his posterity with that corruption into which he had fallen.[20]

What Calvin understands is that in order to account for sin in the world (or, if you wish, wickedness), there are really only two alternatives available: Either it is "original" or it comes by way of what he calls imitation. Either it is always-already-there in everyone by virtue of Adam *standing for* all or it is passed along, now here, now there, by imitation—in our contemporary idiom, by socialization.

On the imitation hypothesis, wickedness—not sin—is carried forward by socialization. On the original sin hypothesis, sin is anterior to any occasion for socialization, because while socialization occurs *in* time, if sin is "original," then it is already present "before" any and all descendants of Adam live out their lives. Sin is a constitutive condition of human life in time, not an accident of socialization. When Calvin calls sin a "hereditary depravity,"[21] he cannot, in other words, mean what Darwin meant some three hundred years later by the term "heredity." Sin is hereditary not by imitation—not by the transfer of genotypic and phenotypic configurations and markers from one generation to the next—but by virtue of being, again, "original." When Calvin says of children that "they descend not from their parents spiritual regeneration but from their *carnal generation*,"[22] and hence are suffused with original sin, he does not mean by this what immediately comes to mind for us in the post-Darwin era, *viz.*, that it is "genetic." That would be imitation, not *original* sin.

Rousseau, whose turbulent history with Calvin's Geneva is well known, recurs instead to the category of socialization in order to understand the origin of wickedness. Indeed, he seems to have the idea of original sin very much on his mind when he takes this other path that Calvin lays out, the path of imitation.

Rousseau, in fact, offers a vivid explication of this path in two distinct idioms: phylogenically in the "Discourse on the Origin and Foundations of Inequality among Men" and ontogenetically in his *Emile*, a passage from which is provided below.

---

[20] See John Calvin, *Institutes of Christian Religion*, ed. John T. McNeill (Philadelphia: Westminster, 1960), vol. I, book II, ch. I, sec. 6, p. 249 (emphasis added). The entirety of secs. 5–9, pp. 246–53, is worthy of careful study.

[21] Calvin, *Institutes*, vol. I, book II, ch. I, sec. 8, p. 251.

[22] Calvin, *Institutes*, vol. I, book II, ch. I, sec. 7, p. 250 (emphasis added).

[When a child cries at] one time we bustle about, we caress him in order to pacify him; at another, we threaten him, we strike him in order to make him keep quiet. Either we do what pleases him, or we exact from him what pleases us. . . . Thus his first ideas of are those of domination and servitude. Before knowing how to speak, he commands; before being able to act, he obeys. . . . It is thus that *we fill up his young heart at the outset with the passions that we later impute to nature and that, after taking efforts to make him wicked, we complain about making him so.*[23]

The child is not born depraved, he says, but is rather *made* so by the wicked patterns that we impute to our children—in short, by our socialization of them.[24] The project of *Emile*, therefore, is to educate children in such a way that the corrupting patterns are not imputed in the first place. Similarly, the project of the *Second Discourse* is to trace out the historical lineaments of our defection from nature, the source of which defection is purported to be the establishment of the institution of private property[25]—a thought not subsequently lost on Marx.

In Rousseau's thought we have all the trappings of the now familiar response to Calvin's understanding of original sin: first, sin—or rather wickedness—is not original, but comes by way of socialization; and second, that in order to avert its peril we must alter our institutions—economic, political, and social. America may have started out indebted to Calvin, but its reflexive response to wickedness is now decidedly weighted toward Rousseau. Whether in domestic or foreign policy, though, the sentiment is the same: Wickedness is not indigenous, but is rather caused by an outside influence that we can, should, or should have controlled.

On first blush it might be thought that the responses that we are considering to Hegel (the Lutheran) and Calvin, respectively, might offer

[23] Jean-Jacques Rousseau, *Emile*, trans. Allan Bloom (New York: Basic Books, 1979), book I, p. 48 (emphasis added). See also book II, p. 86: "[W]hen children's wills are not spoiled by our fault, children want nothing uselessly."

[24] Rousseau's insight about the power of discipline and the malleability of the infant body are cast in a different light by Michel Foucault, *Discipline and Punish: The Birth of the Prison*, trans. Alan Sheridan (New York: Vintage, 1995). There, instead of Rousseau's claim that the body needs to be disciplined so that the soul may subsequently be free, Foucault denies that that freedom subsequently emerges at all.

[25] See Jean-Jacques Rousseau, "Discourse on the Origin and Foundations of Inequality Among Men," in *The First and Second Discourses*, ed. Victor Gourevitch (Cambridge: Cambridge University Press, 1997), part II, para. 1, p. 164: "The first man who, having enclosed a piece of ground, to whom it occurred to say *this is mine*, and found people sufficiently simply to believe him, was the true founder of civil society. How many crimes, wars, murders, how many miseries and horrors Mankind would have been spared [if this imposter had not been listened to]." (Hereafter, *Second Discourse*.)

remedies that are proportional to the illness they purport to cure. But this is not so. Luther's Christian, whom Hegel thought was the basis of modern "subjectivity," is ill with an affliction that only Christ's imputation can cure. For Calvin, this same claim obtains, though the emphasis now lies on the inscrutability of God the Father, *who may not cure that illness at all*, if He does not wish. Here, the mortal condition is far more dire than it is in Luther. Yet if we attend to "identity politics" and the literature of socialization, we find that the relationship between the two responses is reversed. "Identity politics" leaves no room for conciliation, and in its response to Hegel adopts a quasi-Calvinist notion of the "total depravity of reason." The literature of socialization, in turn, leaves no room for the intractability of all things "original," and in its response to Calvin adopts a quasi-Hegelian notion that all "differences" can be overcome.

Beyond the Reformation Categories of "Identity Politics" and Socialization

Aside from a few introductory comments, I have avoided the use of the term "mimesis" in my discussion of "identity politics" and of the idea of socialization. My intention was to return to the historical source of these tropes, with a view to illuminating their Reformation origins. Doing so, I believe, allows us to begin to clear the way for an understanding of a relationship between imitation and reason that is available in Plato's *Republic*, which long predates the tropes we have inherited from the Reformation and its outworkings. These inherited tropes are being played out, I suggest, in the debates about the tension between pluralism and "identity politics," on the one hand, and in the literature of socialization, on the other. My analysis here attempts to move beyond—or rather *behind*—that entire constellation.

Grant, then, that neither "identity politics" nor socialization is quite what I have in mind when I invoke the term "mimesis." Recall, as well, that the impetus for clearing the way for an alternative treatment of mimesis in *Plato's Fable* is the impasse to which each of these tropes has brought us: Imitation under the rubric of "identity politics" puts little stock in the arbitration of reason, since there is either no need (or no possibility) of being drawn beyond what has *already* been established; imitation under the rubric of socialization assumes that what has been already established can be *easily* altered, using "incentives" to which (calculating) reason attends.

Imitation under the rubric of mimesis—the Socratic provocation as it is set forth in the fable of the *Republic*—precedes these two understandings of the relationship between imitation and reason. It neither brings us to the impasse to which "identity politics" has surely brought us nor does it trivialize, as the literature of socialization does, the durability and depth of what in this book I will call "mortal patterns." Said otherwise, Plato's fable reveals an understanding of the relationship between imitation and reason that is not indebted to debates that developed as a consequence of the thinking of either Hegel or Calvin, but which rather turns us in another direction and, in so doing, provides us with a more profound understanding of that relationship—*and reestablishes philosophy as the preeminent task of politics.* The many pages that follow will, of course, be necessary to direct our attention toward this other understanding. For the moment, however, let me offer the following brief formulation: Mimesis, unlike "identity politics" or socialization, supposes that mortal patterns are durable and deep *and* that they can be changed only by reason—though not by reason as it is conventionally understood. To that subject, I now turn.

Reason Revisited: Plato's Critique of "Rationality"

Since the Reformation has been lurking in the background in our discussion of "identity politics" and of socialization, we might wonder whether the notion of reason with which these tropes are in tension itself emerges from Reformation categories. Notwithstanding the claim that "identity politics," socialization, and reason are purely analytical and not quasi-religious terms, might there be evidence to the contrary, which should cause us to pause?

We might ask, for example, whether the predominant idea of reason today is itself the outworking of Reformation thought, or even its latest—or last—incarnation. Religiously understood, we would note the following loose parallels: The locus for salvation is the person and not the Church ("methodological individualism"); the will that each person wills is not the will that comes to pass ("unintended consequences"), especially in communities ("collective action problem"); persons are prideful ("self-interested"); God does not reveal His essence, but rather is known through what He *shows forth* ("positivism"); reason is sufficiently corrupted, and the world sufficiently contingent, that wants shift to and fro ("preferences"); the problem of debt suffuses all aspects of life ("calculation"); and human beings have only their private conscience ("values") on which to rely in a world where God is now silent. That positivism has not, to this day, really penetrated Roman Catholic universities in America or elsewhere is suggestive that something is at work here to which we have not given sufficient attention.

But perhaps this sort of playfulness is out of place. Moreover, even if it were true that the conventional notion of reason adopted by political scientists was genetically linked with Reformation thought, why not concede, as Weber did with respect to modern-day capitalists, that we are only occasionally haunted by the religious ruminations that gave rise to the present situation?[26] We are, consequently, seldom prompted to ponder the linkage. Indeed, since Plato's *Republic* is what largely concerns us here, it seems hardly fitting to do so.

Instead of darting in and out of the shadow of the Reformation, then, let us venture on another path. Let us ask, instead, what Plato's fable might tell us about the contemporary understanding of reason? What advances, if any, have we *really* made by setting up mortals to be rational actors—rational, that is, in the way that is supposed in the sort of models set forth by political scientists?

When such models suppose that human beings are *substantively* rational in the way that economic science in the narrowest sense would predict, they do no more than echo Socrates' claim that *when the love of wealth rules*, reason (*logistikon*) "crouch[es] on the ground . . . and calculates [*logizesthai*],"[27] for the purpose of feeding a certain *narrow* set of appetites, while repressing others. Alternatively, when such models purport to become more subtle and suppose that human beings are *instrumentally* rational in ways that economic science in the narrowest sense cannot predict, they do no more than echo Socrates' claim that *when the love of equality rules* (by which he means the equality of all appetites), reason crouches down to calculate how *an enlarged* domain of appetites may be gratified. In either case—whether human beings are understood to be substantively rational with respect to the univocal scale of wealth or instrumentally rational with respect to multiple though commensurable possibilities—reason still crouches! That is, reason *calculates*; it weighs and measures.

Let us call the model that is content with the view that *substantive* ends can be rendered exclusively and exquisitely in terms of wealth the *oligarchic* model of human behavior. Let us call the model that is comfortable with the view that human beings are *instrumentally* rational toward different ends, up to the point of including all the appetites they have while they are awake,[28] the *democratic* model of human behavior.

---

[26] See Max Weber, *The Protestant Ethic and the Spirit of Capitalism*, trans. Talcott Parsons (New York: HarperCollins, 1991), part II, ch. V, p. 182: "In the field of its highest development, in the United States, the pursuit of wealth, *stripped of its religious and ethical meaning*, tends to become associated with purely mundane passions, which often actually give it the character of sport" (emphasis added).

[27] Plato, *Republic*, Book VIII, 553c–d.

[28] The distinction between appetites human beings have while they are awake and while they are asleep is as central to Plato's analysis as it is to contemporary understandings of

This is Socrates' usage in Book VIII of the *Republic*, and elsewhere, as we shall see; and it will serve us well in due course.

In either case, however, these models in no way comprehend reason *philosophically*, and in failing to do so, they suppose without question that the appetitive part of the soul rules in human affairs. *The tacit understanding in political science is that reason is a servant to human appetite; and the debate, insofar as there is one at all, is whether reason should be understood narrowly (under the oligarchic heading) or more broadly (under the democratic heading).*

Within political science proper today, there is no vantage point from which to see beyond these two alternatives of oligarchy and democracy. However diverse the *objects* of appetitive desire may be, they remain steadfastly colored by the (appetitive) principle that gave rise to them. Money, analogously, may purchase many different things, but when money is the only measure, we become suspicious that all the variety we witness falls, monotonously, under that category of "consumerism." So, too, with the multiple objects that the soul ruled by appetite wants: the appearance of their variety, fecundity, novelty, and so on, belies their singular source. While it appears that political science can account for the entire spectrum of human possibilities (in all times and in all places) under the rubric of appetitive rule, such a view is monological, since the totality of human desire is comprehended under the category of the appetites.

Honor's Place

There are, however, two alternatives to this prevalent opinion. The first of which I will briefly consider is the rule of *honor*. The rule of honor is not yet the rule of reason (in Plato's sense), which is higher still than either the rule of the appetites or of honor. But let us pause for a moment to consider honor.

In the first and second sections of conclusion, I suggest that this prejudice toward rule by the appetites is inscribed into what is called "the fable of liberalism." Political science today remains under the spell of this fable, which depicts the rejection of the honor-loving "fathers" by their wealth-loving oligarchic "sons." (This is Socrates' usage, so let us "say a prayer"[29] and follow his lead.) In so doing, the rulership of the

---

reason. For Plato, the appetites that appear in sleep are tyrannical. (See Plato, *Republic*, Book IX, 571c–d.) Here reason no longer crouches, but is narcotized and idly watches as one appetite after another overwhelms the soul. In the human sciences, this domain falls under the category of madness, the unconscious, the irrational, etc.

[29] See Plato, *Republic*, Book IV, 432c: "I am only your follower [Socrates], with sight just keen enough to see what you show me. Well, say a prayer [Glaucon] and follow me."

appetites replaces the rule of honor, and we move from what we would call the aristocratic age into the modern world.

Within political science proper there is little talk today of the rule of honor. How, after all, can honor be measured? Wealth and freedom, yes; but not honor. Dispensing with honor altogether, however, and comprehending politics under the guise of either *resources* (the oligarchic fixation) or *freedom* (the democratic fixation) leads to serious misunderstandings—and faulty predictions—about the prospects for justice, since all that would seem to be needed on this account is that everyone be provided with adequate resources or freedoms. This is fancy. Honor cares only provisionally about resources or freedom. Honor is, among other things, concerned with leaving behind the memory of one's name through glorious deeds. Above all, it means a willingness to die, which belies any calculus of preference of the sort that the oligarchic "sons" endorse. Because of this, political science will always be caught off-guard when honor makes an appearance. Political science, because it is under the spell of the fable of liberalism, will therefore never be able fully to comprehend war—and some of its practitioners are apt to conclude that the cause of war is that nations with resources and freedoms are themselves responsible for the wars that do emerge, because in having acquired resources and freedoms for themselves, they have kept them from others. This sort of idea emerges predictably out of the fable of liberalism. Whether one endorses this particular view of the political Left, and concludes that war is caused by capitalism, or adopts a free-market conservative version, and concludes that war is caused by *not enough* capitalism, the result is the same: War remains uncomprehended because honor is either ruled out entirely or erroneously subsumed under the calculus of "preferences."

The place where honor *does* appear in political science today is in the study of the history of political thought. One can hardly read that history without encountering authors who bristle at the thought that the rule of the appetites might replace the rule of honor: Aristotle, any number of Romans (above all the Romans, as Augustine points out),[30] Aquinas, Rousseau, and, in his own way, Nietzsche, to name only a few, all are dubious about the rule of the appetites. If there is a haven for

---

[30] See Augustine, *City of God*, vol. 6, book V, ch. 15, p. 277: "[The Romans] subordinated their private property to the common welfare, that is, to the republic and the public treasury. They resisted the temptation to avarice. They gave their counsel freely in the councils of state. They indulged in neither public crime nor private passion. They thought they were on the right road when they strove, by all these means, for honors, rule, and glory. Honor has come to them from almost all peoples. The rule of their laws has been imposed on many peoples. And in our day, in literature and in history, glory has been given them by almost everyone" (*CG*, pp. 204–5).

honor-loving souls, then the history of political philosophy is surely it; and this no doubt accounts for more than a little of the tension within political science departments around the country. This tension, moreover, is not simply between old guard conservatives and those whose social scientific research originates, wittingly or not, from within the fable of liberalism. Since the end of the Cold War, the Left has found solace in the writings of Arendt and Foucault, who are no less hostile than old guard conservatives, really, to the fable of liberalism.

The fugitive shadow of honor, then, appears here and there in political science. It never appears, however, *as honor itself* (since this would require action and not just idle talk *about* action), but as a *longing* for honor and a contempt for the fable of liberalism. This talk takes the form of a politicized vision of the future where *all* are emancipated from the heteronomy of wealth, provided we understand and combat the forces of "oppression," on the Left, and a melancholy, though sometimes Stoic, vision of a pristine past where *a few* lived out their lives with honor, on the Right. Meanwhile, mainline political scientists continue to work within the fable of liberalism, rightly judging that the rule of honor as it has been exposited by those who study the history of political thought (on the Left or the Right) cannot much help them. War, as I mentioned, alerts them that the fable of liberalism is blind to honor and its motivations. But if war is an *interruption* in an overall march toward peace, as the fable of liberalism suggests, then that need not disturb them in any fundamental way. Political scientists are, therefore, correct in their assessment that the rule of honor is inadequate. In the *Republic*, Socrates tells us that the oligarchic "sons" are not entirely wrong in rejecting their honor-loving "fathers."[31] Political scientists are these oligarchic "sons." There is indeed an alternative to appetitive rule, but the love of honor, which is a shadowy thing, cannot provide what is needed.

(Divine) Reason

Let us now turn to the alternative that is set forth in Plato's fable: reason, or rather, *divine* reason, as it is often called—and not unwittingly. I will make no pretense here, or anywhere else, to be able to say what divine reason *is*; but what *can* be spoken of is what it is juxtaposed *against*, and why. In Plato's fable, human beings are mimetic: They dwell in a generative world where patterns reproduce themselves in their own image—a sort of Watson and Crick genetic code writ large. These patterns, however, are defective, more or less; and so the "patterns" that the "sons"

---

[31] See Plato, *Republic*, Book VIII, 553b–c.

inherit from the "fathers" are never quite what the "sons" truly need—witness the failure of the argument about justice that Polemarchus inherits from his father, Cephalus, at the outset of the *Republic*. The problem, moreover, is that these patterns are not easily altered; and when they are, the new pattern adopted is usually more defective than the one renounced—thus Book VIII of the *Republic*. What saves the "sons" from this never-ending generative irregularity, from which issues their unhappiness, is a turning away from "mortal patterns," from the defective patterns that constitute the world of coming-into-being-and-passing-away, and a turn toward the divine pattern (*paradeigma*) that "can be found somewhere in heaven for him who wants to see."[32] The mortal alternatives are not *whether* to imitate patterns, but rather *which* patterns to imitate: mortal or divine, defective or perfect.

The "turn" (*periagōgē*), as Socrates calls it,[33] away from defective patterns involves the awakening of reason from its drunken slumber. For while it remains in a languorous state, reason cannot rule and will instead crouch down and serve one or the other of two parts of the soul, either the honor-loving or the appetitive—be it oligarchic (substantive rationality) or democratic (instrumental rationality). Yet not honor nor wealth nor freedom will save us. In Plato's fable, the oligarchic and democratic "sons" from which political science currently takes its cue are drunk, poisoned, and without an antidote to help them shake off their stupor. They seek wealth and freedom to feed their ever-expanding appetites, but know no surcease. What awakens reason *to the discovery of its own divine nature* is something itself divine: the Good, the source of all things. And since philosophy is implicated in this awakening, it can be said that philosophy is bound up with things divine.

Only by the light of the Good—a divine gift, as it were—can human beings be freed from the defective "mortal patterns" that are otherwise their lot. *This* is the meaning of the saying, "only philosophy can save us." Mimesis is the *intractable* imitative patterning for which divine reason alone is the cure, which divine reason is *not* to be confused with the inebriated reason that calculates, of which the oligarchic and democratic sons boast. Awakened reason does not boast at all, for it is not a possession but a gift. But more on this in due course.

My invocation of divine gifts will no doubt dishearten those who think I have wandered into theology. It is true that many interesting comparisons between the *Republic* and biblical theology can and will be noted in what follows. The affinities between the two are not, however, intended to specify the distance or proximity between them, which is a never-

---

[32] See Plato, *Republic*, Book IX, 592b.
[33] See Plato, *Republic*, Book VII, 518d, 518e, 521c.

ending source of debate; but rather through such affinities to indicate a larger genus within which they may both be placed, the defining characteristics of which are, first, an understanding that mortal life requires divine interruption for it to go well, and, second, an understanding that this requirement obtains because of the mimetic character of human life. This book is concerned with both moments, and invokes comparisons between Plato's fable and biblical theology for the purpose of illuminating the genus itself, within which the two species can be found. My focus here is on the mimetic aspect of human life—its durability, its near intractability—and the sort of thing that may be needed to overcome it. Whenever I invoke the term "divine gifts" in the context of the *Republic*, then, think of this locution as *a-breaking-in-from-elsewhere*, a performative *deus ex machina*, which reconciles a predicament for mortal man that would otherwise remain irreconcilable. Since Socrates almost always ends his conversation with an aporia, this is perhaps the preferred way to proceed. What cannot be forgotten, however, is that mimesis confronts mortals with a predicament that they cannot, *without philosophy*, resolve. Political science may wish to reject this sort of analysis—and it will, unless what is meant by "philosophy" is made clear. But in doing so it falls back on a notion of reason proffered by a fable of liberalism, against which imitation appears under the *utterly* intractable guise of "identity politics" or under the cheery and naïve guise of socialization. My thesis here is that the bridge across the present impasse in political science between either the substantive or instrumental model of rationality and political philosophy can be built on a more profound understanding of imitation than is available through "identity politics" or the idea of socialization. It can be built on an understanding of mimesis. *This* notion allows us to understand the mortal illness for which philosophy alone is the antidote. The fable of the *Republic* is concerned with *this* problem.

The Mortal Condition in Shadowy Times

Having now introduced the problem of imitation in mortal life, and made a few tentative comments about the "divine gift" of reason, I should make clear that the fable I am going to rehearse is a less than tidy story about the clean victory of things divine over things mortal. On the account provided here, the mortal condition of living in the shadows is one for which there is an antidote. The invocation of this medical metaphor, I note, is not an accident, since the presumption throughout Plato's fable is that human beings *are* ill or, to recur to an earlier metaphor, inebriated—in any case, poisoned. As such, they require an antidote to heal them, which the philosopher-doctor purports to provide with his noble lies, his fables. There can be no cure, however, unless the patient is first ill, and so it behooves us to consider the sort of illness that mortal man has contracted.

Since the first significant reference in the *Republic* to illness pertains to "a city in a state of fever [*phlegmainousan polin*],"[34] let us briefly focus there. The reference is to a condition in which the appetites are not moderate, but rather excessive. That Plato's fable begins in earnest on *this* foundation of "appetitive transgression," of unbounded appetites, is worth noting. Human health may entail "rendering each its due [*to ta opheilomena hekastō apodidonai dikaion esti*],"[35] but such rendering is not possible unless at the outset the mortal condition is diseased. Only from here, from appetitive transgression, can the spirited part of the soul emerge, which is not afraid of death. And only *after* the spirited part emerges can the philosophic part that *practices death rightly* see the light of day and supersede the spirited, honor-loving part.

This seemingly incongruous relationship between disease and health, between immoderation and balance, and therefore between appetitive transgression and divine reason, should not be forgotten. It is an unwarranted simplification to say that Socrates shuns illness, so that he may embrace health.[36] It would be more accurate to say that in beginning with illness, the way to health opens up before him. The sort of health he has in mind is divine, to be sure, since it is predicated on the awakening of divine reason. Health is achieved, however, by beginning with appetitive transgression, which knows nothing of the domain of which it is the necessary predicate. In ancient religious terms, Plato's fable conforms to three distinct phases of the ascent of the soul: the first involving *illness* or

---

[34] See Plato, *Republic*, Book II, 372e.

[35] See Plato, *Republic*, Book I, 331e.

[36] See Friedrich Nietzsche, *Beyond Good and Evil*, trans. Walter Kaufman (New York: Vintage, 1966), preface, p. 2: "Let us not be ungrateful to it, although it must certainly be conceded that the worst, most durable, and most dangerous of all errors so far was a dogmatist's error—namely, Plato's invention of the pure spirit and the good as such. But now that it is overcome, now that Europe is breathing freely again after this nightmare and at least can enjoy a healthier sleep, we, *whose task is wakefulness itself,* are the heirs of all that strength which has been fostered by the fight against this error. To be sure, it meant standing truth on her head and denying *perspective,* the basic condition of all life, when one spoke of spirit and the good as Plato did. Indeed, as a physician one might ask: 'How could the most beautiful growth of antiquity, Plato, contract such a disease? Did the wicked Socrates corrupt him after all? Could Socrates have been the corrupter of youth after all? And did he deserve his hemlock?'" (emphasis in original). See also Friedrich Nietzsche, *The Gay Science*, trans. Walter Kaufmann (New York: Random House, 1974), book IV, sec. 340, p. 272. Cf. Plato, *Phaedo*, trans. G.M.A. Grube, in *Plato: Complete Works* (Indianapolis: Hackett, 1997), 118a: "Crito, we owe a cock to Asclepius; make this offering to him and do not forget."

impurity (Book II, 372e), the second involving *purification* (to Book VI, 501a), and the third involving *illumination* (to Book IX, 592b). Politically, this insight raises the provocative question of whether the most defective types in Plato's fable, namely, democratic and tyrannical souls, in which appetitive transgressions abound, are evidently those most capable of being doctored to health in the highest, philosophical, sense.

Without illness, there can be no health.

Chapter 2

PLATO'S FABLE

Are [not the sophists] the most compelling educators of all, *reproducing in their own image* men and women, young and old, and succeeding to their hearts' content? . . . It would be foolish even to try [to oppose them; for there] is not, never has been, and never will be an education contrary to theirs that could produce a different kind of person and a different virtue. I speak within the human context; *where divine intervention enters, all rules are set to naught. Sure it is in the present state of society and government that if anything can be saved and turned to good you will not be off the mark by attributing it to god's providence [theou moiran].*[1]

NEAR THE BEGINNING of the *Republic*, we are told, justice entails paying what is owed[2] or, less obliquely, "rendering each [its] due." This formulation, abstruse and deficient though it might be at the outset, is deepened rather than rejected as the discussion proceeds; and at the end of Plato's luminous exposition *we*—the readers— are left with the hypothesis that only the philosopher, illuminated by the Good, can render what is due to each part of the soul, and so live well.[3] Plato's fable about the nature of justice begins and ends with a stipulation about 'rendering each its due,' about what is proper to each.

The burden of my early discussion concerns the deepening of our understanding of this formulation that justice entails "rendering each its due" as the fable of *Republic* unfolds, and how this deepening, which culminates in a discussion of the bearing of the Good on justice, directs

---

[1] Plato, *Republic*, Book VI, 492b–e (emphasis added).

[2] Plato, *Republic*, Book I, 331e. The beginning of justice is debt. On this matter Plato and Nietzsche are in accord. See Nietzsche, *Genealogy of Morals*, Second Essay, sec. 4, pp. 62–63.

[3] For the divided soul (about which more in due course), Plato's claim remains unprovable. Not having been illuminated by the Good, such a soul remains in the shadow world of the Cave (*Republic*, Book VII, 514a–517a), and so possesses no evidence of the sort that can be called knowledge. Absent such knowledge, Plato must resort to myths, salutary tales, which, at best, point to the Good. Short of being illuminated by the Good, all that mortal man has is hypothesis. See ibid., Book VI, 511b–d.

our attention not only to the divine but to the all too mortal appetites that seem to be the precondition of its disclosure.

Rendering Each Its Due

The first variant of the formula "rendering each its due" is proffered, as we know, by Cephalus,[4] a character whose name, not incidentally, derives from the Greek word for "head" (*kephalē*). As an inspection of his comments about the lures of Aphrodite intimates, he is disembodied, a mere head.

> Hush, man, most gladly have I escaped the thing you talk of, as if I had run away from a raging and savage beast of a master.[5]

And further down,

> When the fierce tensions of the passions and desires relax, [then] we are rid of many and mad masters.[6]

Exactly why Plato resorts to this observation at the outset of the *Republic*, and what its bearing might be on the question of how we may "render each its due," is not immediately obvious. Moreover, in light of his apparent derogation of the Cave world "here below"—with all of its appetitive allures and vacant pleasures—the purpose Cephalus serves in the overall trajectory of the argument is unclear. Is not Cephalus free from the charms and barren delights that ensnare all but a few in this world below? Having neither squandered his father's wealth nor aroused all his faculties in the singular service of acquiring it, is he not a moderate man? His appetites having been subordinated, does not reason rule? Is he not able to live a just life, free from transgression against the living and the dead?

> It is for this, then, that I affirm that the possession of wealth is most valuable, not it may be to every man but to the good man. Not to cheat any man intentionally or play him false, *not remaining in debt* to a god for some sacrifice or to a man for money, so to depart in fear to that other world—to this result the possession of property contributes not a little.[7]

This circumscribed understanding of justice, as I have said, is deepened rather than wholly rejected as the discussion proceeds. Cephalus' understanding, as Socrates points out, is incomplete; debts should not be

---

[4] Plato, *Republic*, Book I, 331b.
[5] Ibid., 329c. The words are Sophocles', but Cephalus cites their wisdom and applicability to himself.
[6] Ibid., 329c–d.
[7] Ibid., 331b (emphasis added).

repaid if harm results. Yet what is remarkable about the entire exchange, among other things, is less the definition of justice that Cephalus offers— important as it is for the subsequent argument—than his response to being refuted. Rather than accept the death of his argument, he bequeaths the argument to his son, Polemarchus, and goes off to "attend to the sacrifices."[8]

Socrates does not remark here about this evasion of death, yet in light of what he has said in another dialogue about the relationship of the philosopher to death,[9] it is clear that Cephalus will be unable to embark on the philosophical journey necessary to fathom justice. While Cephalus recognizes himself to be on "that threshold of old age [*gēraos oudō*]"[10] that is *literal* death, it is clear that the death that he is presently to undergo is *not* the death about which Socrates is concerned. That Cephalus acknowledges Polemarchus to be his "proper heir,"[11] when we have been informed in the opening passages of the *Republic* that Polemarchus "cannot be persuaded because he will not listen,"[12] tells us a great deal about Cephalus' own capacity for philosophy. He honors the mortal coin that repays debts, not the divine currency of reason.

The argument, however, refuses to die. Cephalus lives on in Polemarchus; and so, too, does his argument that justice is "rendering each its due" live on in Polemarchus' new defense, now modified to withstand Socrates' initial objection. Polemarchus, like his father, seeks not the truth, but rather the avoidance of "death,"[13] even to the point of

---

[8] Ibid., 331d. Here, attending to the sacrifices is a diversion from philosophy. Even though Cephalus has "more frequent sightings of an approaching end" (ibid., 330e) and purports to have adjusted his thinking to take cognizance of death (ibid., 330d–331a), his evasion of Socrates' question suggests that he has yet to accept the kind of death about which Socrates is most concerned in the *Republic*.

[9] See Plato, *Phaedo*, trans. G.M.A. Grube, in *Plato: Complete Works*, 64a. Only by facing the death of what is purportedly known can there be the knowing ignorance, if you will, that is philosophy. "The one aim of those who practice philosophy in the proper manner," Socrates says, "is to practice death and dying."

[10] Plato, *Republic*, Bk. I, 328e.

[11] Ibid., 331d.

[12] Ibid., 327c: "But could you persuade us if we don't listen?"

[13] There can be no truth without death: This is a venerable theme in the *Republic*. In Book III (405d–407e), Plato criticizes doctors who follow Herodicus because they make life the highest good, rather than the Good itself. Asclepius, the doctor who "did not think it worthwhile to treat a man incapable of living a normal life" (407e), understood that survival is not the highest good. See also Rousseau, *Emile*, Book I, p. 53: "I am not able to teach living to one who thinks of nothing but how to keep himself from dying." Hegel, too, has this motif in his own writing. The "slaughter bench" about which he writes (see G.W.F. Hegel, *Reason in History*, trans. Robert S. Hartman [Indianapolis: Bobbs-Merrill, 1953], p. 27) is made necessary because of the enduring power, yet inadequacy, of the forms that arise in history and that obstruct Spirit coming to know itself as itself. *Geist* reveals itself to itself only on the slaughter bench of history. Theologically, habit forms a world that must (and can) be annulled by dying to "the world" through the Spirit. See also Hegel, *Phenomenology*, Preface, para. 32, p. 19: "[The life of Spirit] wins its truth only when, in utter dismemberment, it finds itself."

intellectual befuddlement, which his father refused to endure.[14] Polemarchus, a good son, honors his father's argument even though it is indefensible.

The argument is saved from death, it would seem, by the distinction between what is due a friend and what is due an enemy. "Justice is the art that benefits friends and injures enemies [*dikaiosunē . . . hē tois philios te kai echthrois ōphelias te kai blabas apodidousa*],"[15] Polemarchus says. Yet without understanding what is meant by benefit and harm—without, that is, some dim understanding of the Good—the argument finally dies when it reaches the absurd proposal the justice is "useless in times of peace."[16] Without knowledge of who, in fact, is good, and illuminated only by the dim light of opinion, there can be no certainty regarding who is a friend and who is an enemy.[17] Moreover, what does it mean to "benefit" friends?[18] Justice and benefit are linked, to be sure; yet to know what benefit *is* requires illumination by the Good—something we discover later when we are told that knowledge of the Good is the precondition for justice.[19]

After Polemarchus is finally compelled to admit his ignorance, Thrasymachus demands a precise definition of justice. And when pressed to disclose his own understanding of the matter, he (Thrasymachus) offers the "realistic" appraisal that there is no justice aside from power.[20] In one

[14] Plato, *Republic*, Bk. I, 334b.

[15] Ibid., 332d.

[16] Ibid., 332e; see also 333e. In "The Music of the *Republic*," Eva T. H. Brann argues that "the *Republic* is composed on the plan of concentric rings; the themes on the diameter reappear in reverse order as if they were reflected through a central axis" (in *St. John's Review* 39, nos. 1 and 2 [1989–90]: 7). Not coincidentally, then, the question of the usefulness of justice first set forth in Book I reemerges on the opposite side of the circle, that is, in Book X. There, what is concluded is that the one who best knows is the one who uses. "The user," Plato says, "will have true knowledge" (*Republic*, Book X, 601e).

[17] Plato, *Republic*, Book I, 334e–335a.

[18] With regard to that portion of Polemarchus' argument that pertains to harming enemies, Socrates is quite clear: Justice cannot diminish the peculiar excellence of things or animals—rational or otherwise. This claim (introduced at Book I, 335b) is developed further as the *Republic* proceeds and culminates in the claim that justice befriends parts of the whole but does not produce warring divisions. Justice unifies, injustice divides. "The good," Socrates says, "cannot corrupt" (ibid., 335d). Polymarchus' definition of justice is representative of the traditional Greek popular view. See Mary Whitlock Blundell, *Helping Friends and Harming Enemies* (Cambridge: Cambridge University Press, 1991).

[19] See Plato, *Republic*, Book VI, 506a: "[A] man who does not understand how justice and honor are related to the Good won't guard them very effectively."

[20] Plato, *Republic*, Book I, 338c: "I affirm that the just is nothing else than the advantage of the stronger." Cf. Karl Marx, "The Communist Manifesto," in *The Marx-Engels Reader*, ed. Robert Tucker (New York: W. W. Norton, 1978), p. 489: "The ruling ideas of each age have ever been the ideas of the ruling class."

respect, of course, his definition accords with Socrates' later formulation that justice and power must converge for all to go well.[21] Without power there can be no justice. This is not, however, the meaning that Thrasymachus has in mind. His claim is not that justice requires a philosophical orientation toward the Good so that power can be used well, but rather that in matters of justice we need not consider the Good at all. The only world, the *real* world, is *this* world. Philosophy is the domain of dreamers. He is, by contrast, a realist, concerned not with the Good, but with getting another's goods.

Let us pause here for a moment. Notwithstanding Socrates' eventual rejection of the (misnamed) realist position, Thrasymachus' claim about what is real is nontrivial. Indeed, as Adeimantus suggests and Socrates in his own way confirms, one of the central paradoxes of the *Republic* is that "appearance [*to dokein*] is mightier than reality and hence the true lord of happiness."[22] The philosopher who *knows* rather than *opines* is under no such illusion, to be sure; it is the case, nevertheless, that in the shadowy world where vision is dim, the appearance rather than the reality of power is the first thing seen—since the reality of power would burn the eyes of those whose vision is yet dim.[23] This matter will be discussed more directly in the section "Fables, Lies, and Medicine," below.

Second, some preliminary comments must be made about the relationship between the condition of the soul—its unity or disunity—and its capacity to "see." Socrates' claim, developed as the fable proceeds,[24] is that

---

[21] Plato, *Republic*, Book V, 473c–e.

[22] Plato, *Republic*, Book II, 365c.

[23] Consider, for example, the exchange between Socrates and Adeimantus about the capacity of a city oriented by the love of wealth to make war (*Republic*, Book IV, 422a–423b). The apparent power of the city ruled by wealth masks divisions, which makes unitary action impossible. For a time it may have dominion over its neighbors, but it cannot prevail because its power is only apparent. "As long as our city is governed by the rules of wisdom and temperance we set out a little while ago, it will be the greatest of cities, not in reputation, to be sure, but in reality," Socrates says (ibid., 423a). On a related note, consider Socrates' observation that "the virtuous nature, having become educated over time, will *ultimately* be able to understand itself and vice as well" (*Republic*, Book III, 409d [emphasis added]); as well as his remark that "smart but wicked men . . . bound away at the start, but in the end are laughed to scorn and run off the field uncrowned" (*Republic*, Book X, 613b–c). Initially, vice, like power, has the advantage over virtue, but not ultimately. Augustine's view is more stark: Good will triumph at the End Time only through the judgment of God; until then, mankind is confronted by the mystery that the good suffer and the evil are rewarded. See Augustine, *City of God*, in *Writings*, vol. 6, book I, chs. 8 and 9, pp. 28–33 (*CG*, pp. 13–16).

[24] The shortest, but not most penetrating, account of this relationship is provided in Socrates' second argument for the superiority of justice (*Republic*, Book IX, 580d–583b). The soul ruled by the appetites is capable of seeing only the good of wealth; the soul ruled by the spirited element is capable of seeing only the good of honor and of wealth; the soul

the soul can see what is real only to the extent that it is unified rather than divided.[25] Only the philosopher, the person whose soul is ruled by reason—who is, therefore, one rather than many—is able to see the Good, and therefore to see what truly exists. All others are divided, and so see dimly. Their vision is darkened because appetite or spiritedness usurps the place reserved for reason, which makes unity impossible. The darkened soul is at war with itself, and so is unable to "see." But let us defer the discussion of the relationship between knowing and the divided condition of the soul until the section "The Opinings of the Divided Soul," below.

Furthermore, not only does the divided soul see dimly, but also it sees imprecisely. The divided soul possesses the faculty of opinion, not knowledge; and the domain of opinion is what comes into being and passes away.[26] Shadows in the realm that opinion grasps have no precise boundaries; certainty about when and where they begin and end is unachievable—unachievable, that is, without philosophy.[27] There is considerable irony, then, in Thrasymachus' demand that Socrates be precise.

---

ruled and unified by reason is capable of seeing the Good, as well as the partial goods of honor and wealth that divided souls mistake for the Good.

[25] This linkage between the condition of the soul and its capacity to see is corroborated in a remark made elsewhere by Socrates to Phaedrus in response to a question about the probable explanation of the death of the maiden Orithyia. In his words: "I am still unable, as the Delphic inscription orders, to know myself; and it really seems to me ridiculous to look into other things before I have understood that. This is why I do not concern myself with them. I accept what is generally believed, and, as I was just saying, I look not into them but into my own self. Am I a beast more complicated and savage than Typhon, or am I a tamer, simpler animal with a share in a divine and gentle nature?" (Plato, *Phaedrus*, trans. Alexander Nehamas and Paul Woodruff, in *Plato: Complete Works*, 229e–230a). This is not a recommendation for solipsism; rather, having linked the capacity to know with unity of the soul, Socrates recognizes that what is seen is not independent of the soul that sees. While Polanyi does not move in precisely this direction, he, too, notes that knowledge and "personal development" are linked. See Michael Polanyi, *Personal Knowledge* (Chicago: University of Chicago Press, 1958), ch. 4, p. 65: "[T]he arts of doing and knowing, the valuation and the understanding of meanings, are thus seen to be only different aspects of the act of extending our person into the subsidiary awareness of particulars which compose a whole. The inherent structure of this fundamental act of personal knowing makes us both necessarily participate in its shaping and acknowledge its results with universal intent. This is the prototype of intellectual commitment. It is the act of commitment in its full structure that saves personal knowledge from being merely subjective. Intellectual commitment is a responsible decision, in submission to the compelling claims of what in good conscience I conceive to be true." I consider the limitations of Polanyi's analysis below, in note 589. See also Plato, *Republic*, Book X, 601e.

[26] See Plato, *Republic*, Bk. VI, 509e–510a.

[27] See ibid., 504b: "[O]nly by taking [the longer way of philosophy can] we reach the most precise understanding of these matters." This longer way, we are told (ibid., 504d–505b), involves a hunt for the Good.

So now say what you think justice is. Say it at last with clarity and precision, and spare us your ponderous analogies with duty or interest or profit or advantage. They produce only nonsense, and I don't put up with nonsense.[28]

While the soul that dwells among the shadows wants certainty,[29] its efforts are forever confounded—as Socrates' rebuttal of Thrasymachus' definition of justice demonstrates. Precision of the sort that Thrasymachus demands requires that his gaze be averted from the world of becoming, something he is unable to do because, as we intimate later, his is a tyrannical soul—the sort that is most at war with itself.

The Origin of the City

At the close of Book I of the *Republic*, then, the two definitions of justice to which we have been introduced have been brought to naught: the first, set forth by Cephalus and Polemarchus, the father and son, for whom the inherited wisdom of the poets of the city provides us with all that is needed to understand justice; the second, set forth by Thrasymachus, for whom justice is power. Neither one of these can endure the light of day. The task of illuminating justice then falls to Glaucon,[30] the one for whom Socrates seems to have the highest hopes, and then Adeimantus[31]—Plato's actual brothers, as it turns out. Their speeches

---

[28] Plato, *Republic*, Book I, 336c–d. In one sense, as Socrates later admits, the kind of "definition" he himself offers is nonsense. The parable of the ship's captain, for example, suggests that those who do not know how to truly pilot their ship "would call the true captain [a stargazer, and idle talker, and useless] [*meteōroskopon te kai adoleschēn kai achrēston*]" (*Republic*, Book VI, 489a). In the Allegory of the Cave, as well, there is the acknowledgment that "someone returning from divine contemplation to the miseries of men [would appear] ridiculous [*sphodra geloios*]" (*Republic*, Book VII, 517d). In both instances, what appears to be an ill-defined and "vacuous notion" (*Republic*, Book I, 336c) to the soul mired in opinion turns out to be substantial after all.

[29] Consider, in light of this claim, a passage from the opening paragraph of Descartes' *Discourse on the Method*: "[T]he power of judging well and of distinguishing the true from the false . . . is naturally equal in all men, and consequently . . . the diversity of our opinions does not arise because some of us are more reasonable than others but solely because we direct our thoughts along different paths and do not attend to the same things" (Rene Descartes, *Discourse on the Method*, in *The Philosophical Writings of Descartes*, trans. John Cottingham, Robert Stoothoff, and Dugald Murdoch [Cambridge: Cambridge University Press, 1985], vol. I, part 1, p. 111). Descartes' epistemological speculations are imbued with democratic sensibilities—a thought not lost to Tocqueville, for whom democracy and increased brooding uncertainty go together.

[30] Plato, *Republic*, Book II, 357b–362d.

[31] Ibid., 362d–367e.

highlight the temptation of injustice; yet they do not succumb, apparently because they are illuminated by a "divine spark."[32]

It will turn out, from Book VI onward, that we will not be able to understand justice at all without reference to things divine; and so the locution "divine spark" here amounts to an intimation of things to come. But before we consider such things, let us attend to the most confusing and contradictory part of soul, and the "city" to which it corresponds, namely, the city oriented by appetitive excess.

Recall, first, Cephalus, from Book I. He was without appetites, a mere head. His understanding of justice, of "rendering each its due," was shown to be defective. Might there be some significance, we might ask, to the fact that Cephalus, the man in whom the appetites no longer rule, is dismissed from Plato's fable about justice so early on? To put the matter more succinctly, might Plato be telling us that no satisfactory understanding of justice is possible without taking full account of the appetites? This notion is confirmed, as we soon discover, in Socrates' introductory remarks about the origins of the just city, to which we turn in order that our perplexities about justice *writ large* may be illuminated.[33]

Socrates begins with a consideration of the rudiments of human life in which only the appetites play a part.

> Very well. A city—or a state—is a response to needs. No human being is self-sufficient, and all of us have many wants. . . . Come, then, let us construct a city beginning with its origins, keeping in mind that the origin of every real city is human needs [*chreia*].[34]

We know from the end of Plato's fable, of course, that Socrates finishes his account of justice with "[the city whose] pattern can be found somewhere in heaven for him who wants to see."[35] *He does not, however, begin there.* He begins with the "appetitive city." We cannot ascend to the heights, it appears, without starting from the muddled confusion of the appetites.

---

[32] See ibid., 368a: "[T]here must indeed be *some divine spark [theion peponthate]* at work in your natures [Glaucon and Adeimantus] that you should be able to make such formidable arguments on behalf of injustice and yet resist being convinced by your own reasoning" (emphasis added).

[33] See ibid., 368d: "[S]ince our wits are not always sharp, we should do well to adopt a method of examination similar to that used when people without very keen vision are required to read small letters from a distance. This method would draw their attention to the same letters writ large, and I think *they would count it a godsend [hermaion an ephanē]* if they could read the larger letters first then check the smaller letters against they to see if they correspond" (emphasis added). Because divided souls see only the shadow world of becoming, they must be treated as people "without very keen vision." The reason why the city must be invoked at all is because of the dim vision of those with whom Socrates is engaged: He sees clearly; his interlocutors cannot.

[34] Ibid., 369b–c.

[35] Plato, *Republic*, Book IX, 592b.

This is not a trivial insight. Indeed, without making too much of the connection, it is worth noting that it conforms to, and predates, the formulation provided through St. Paul, on which much later Christian theology rests:

[the first is not spiritual], but that which was natural; and afterward that which is spiritual. The first man is of the earth, earthy; the second man is of the Lord from Heaven.[36]

Augustine is equally paradigmatic,[37] as is Luther.[38] Human beings have a "Home" at which they can arrive only after being "cured" of their

[36] I Cor. 15:46–47. Man comes to Christ (spirit) through Adam (nature). See also I Cor. 15:21–22; Rom. 5:18–19. Paul Ricoeur refers to St. Paul's configuration of Adam and Christ as the Adamic Myth (see *The Symbolism of Evil* [Boston: Beacon, 1967], part II, ch. III, pp. 232–78). God (spirit) is revealed only through the brokenness of nature—a thought not lost to Hegel in his assessment of the Jews. (See Hegel, *Philosophy of History*, part III, sec. III, ch. 2, pp. 320–21: "[In the Roman world, the] higher condition, in which the soul itself feels pain and longing . . . is still absent. [What is lacking is that] outward suffering must, as already said, be merged in a sorrow of the inner man. He must feel himself as the negation of himself; he must see that his misery is the misery of his nature—that he is in himself a divided and discordant being. This state of mind, the self-chastening, this pain occasioned by our individual nothingness—the wretchedness of our isolated self, and the longing to transcend this condition—must be looked for elsewhere than in the properly Roman world. It is this which gives to the Jewish People their World-Historical importance and weight."

[37] See Augustine, *City of God*, in *Writings*, vol. 7, book XIII, ch. 23, pp. 333–34 (*CG*, pp. 536–37): "[T]he first man of the earth, earthly, became a living soul, but not life-giving spirit. That was reserved for him as a reward for obedience." See also Augustine, *Confessions*, trans. Henry Chadwick (Oxford: Oxford University Press, 1991), book I, ch. ii, p. 4: "So why do I request you to come to me when, unless you were within me, I would have no being at all." The mystery of creation, from the point of view of man the creature, is why he is not so cut off from the ground of his being that he is oblivious to it, but not so attuned to it that he doesn't stray from and forget that knowledge. Walking between *nihilo* and timelessness, man knows of his insecurity but seeks to redress it without recourse to the ground of his being out of which he arises. Through "rebirth," through an irruptive gift from above, man is liberated from the mortal necessity of transgression (sin). Faith is sin's overlayment; faith wins its victory against the backdrop of the primordiality—from man's point of view—of the intransigence of sin.

[38] For Luther, the Old Law does speak to Christians, but only insofar as it speaks beyond itself and of the spiritual realm. It is valuable only in superseding itself. The Law, like the "iron bars of ceremony" (Luther, "Freedom," in *Works*, vol. 31, p. 355) is useful only to the child. And like everything in childhood, it assists fully only when it is outgrown. Here, the adult comes to know God when he or she grows beyond the childish Law. But while the adult is the goal, the goal cannot be reached without first being a child; childhood must be passed through. Christianity is not possible without Judaism. See Luther, "Lectures on Galatians," in *Luther's Works*, ed. Helmut Lehmann (Philadelphia: Fortress, 1967), vol. 27, p. 87: "[A] Christian struggles with sin continually, and yet in his struggle he does not surrender but obtains victory." That is, only through condemnation by the (Old) Law is the victory through Christ possible. See Joshua Mitchell, *Not by Reason Alone: Religion, History, and Identity in Early Modern Political Thought* (Chicago: University of Chicago Press, 1993), ch. 1, pp. 9–45.

illness. Transposed back into Plato's idiom, the city set up in the heavens is discovered only by first dwelling in the appetitive city.[39] Cephalus, the man without appetites, cannot accompany us on this journey, and so is dismissed shortly after being introduced.

Let us look more closely at this city Socrates founds in order to hunt for justice after our initial understanding proved to be of little worth. I have said that Socrates begins with the appetitive city. This description, however, is not quite accurate. Socrates *does* establish a city based on rudimentary human needs. This *moderate* city of the appetites, however, does not illuminate justice. Justice is nowhere to be found in this pseudo-harmonious city that knows nothing of excess and disease. The moderate city, the healthy city that does not yet really need doctors,[40] does not lead us to our quarry.[41]

> [The citizens of our city will] make bread, wine, clothes, shoes, and houses. . . . They will grind meal from barley and flour from wheat; then they knead and bake cakes and loaves of fine quality and serve them on mats of reeds or on clean leaves. When they eat, they will recline on beds fashioned of yew and myrtle, they and their children feasting together and drinking wine. All will wear garlands, singing hymns to the gods and enjoying one another's company.[42]

---

[39] Theologically, Adam and Eve must fall into errancy and concealment from God before a mode of atonement becomes necessary, and then finally appears. To put it otherwise, the City of God, as Augustine's *Confessions* attests, is revealed only on that sorrowful journey through the deceptive brilliance of Rome. See Augustine, *Confessions*, book V, ch. viii, p. 81: "[You] put before me the attractions of Rome to draw me there, using people who love a life of death. . . . To correct my steps you secretly made use of their and my perversity."

[40] Plato, *Republic*, Book II, 373c.

[41] There are numerous references to "hunters" (*thēreutai*) in the *Republic*, the first of which appears at Book I, 373b, just after the city with immoderate appetites is established. This is no mere coincidence. The soul ruled by the appetitive excess "hunts," but will not find what it really wants until it looks elsewhere than in the world of transient things. The hunt, however, is not unidirectional; that is, the hunt by mortal effort alone cannot secure the quarry. In addition, the quarry (the Good) seeks the hunter. Theologically, Pelagianism does not bring us to God. See Sayyed Hossein Nasr, *Knowledge and the Sacred* (New York: Crossroad, 1981), ch. 1, p. 35: "[C]ertain Muslims have called Plato a prophet and he . . . must be considered [a] metaphysician and seer like the rsis of India rather than as [a] profane philosopher. [His] doctrine is based on the Intellect which illuminates rather than simple ratiocination. With him knowledge is still impregnated with its sacred character."

[42] Plato, *Republic*, Book II, 372a–b. Since Cephalus wears a garland (Book I, 328c), we may assume that the depiction here is of Cephalus' house. Beyond that, we have here what might be called primitive communism: Alienation is absent, scarcity provisionally overcome, and conviviality possible. As with Marx, happiness in this state is only apparent. Unlike Marx, however, Socrates does not posit a final reconciliation *in time*. Rather, there is a perennial tension between the unchanging world "above" and the world of coming-into-being-and-passing-away.

Glaucon, wise despite himself, is unsatisfied. Socrates has provided no "relish [*aneu opsou*] for the feast,"[43] nothing that obtrudes on the boredom of a life without novel pleasures. This insistence on Glaucon's part is quite revealing in light of Socrates' later characterization of the true lover of knowledge, who loves all wisdom and not just fragments of it."[44] Glaucon, it turns out, is a lover of the multiplicity of particulars, of fragments; and therefore searches this way and that. In love and in all other pursuits, he "employ[s] any pretense and any fair word rather than risk losing a single one of the young flowers."[45] The soul that does not know where gratification can be truly found will always search restlessly for pleasures that, *by contrast*, seem to promise fulfillment.[46] This is the reason why Glaucon is unsatisfied with the city that Socrates sets forth.[47] Glaucon, as we know, refers to it as a "city of pigs [*huōn polin*]."[48] A city set up for human beings, he opines, would offer novel gratifications. Does not Socrates' moderate city confer tedium rather than happiness? he wonders.[49]

The austere "city of pigs," let us note, is still under the shadow of Cephalus. That is, like Cephalus, the appetites in this city evince no impropriety; they do not overstep the bounds of moderation. Both Cephalus and the "city of pigs" seem just, but this appearance is due not to the fact that the appetites there are *governed*, but rather because the full range of appetitive desire[50] has either withered (in Cephalus' case) or is nascent (in the "city of pigs"). In either case, the appetites are not truly present at hand.

[43] Plato, *Republic*, Book II, 372c.

[44] Plato, *Republic*, Book V, 475b.

[45] Ibid., 475a.

[46] I am refering here to the third argument for the superiority of justice that Socrates offers, an argument based on the relativity of pleasure and pain. See Plato, *Republic*, Book XI, 583b–587a.

[47] See Augustine, *Confessions*, book III, ch. i, p. 35: "The emptier [one] is [of the food that does not perish,] the more unappetizing such food [becomes]."

[48] Plato, *Republic*, Book II, 372d.

[49] Socrates points out Glaucon's mistake not long after he makes it, though Glaucon seems oblivious to his error. "[In the luxurious city] we shall also require swineherds. There was no need for them in our original city, for there were no pigs there" (*Republic*, Book II, 373c).

[50] The suggestion in the *Republic*, Book VIII, 555b–562a, is that once the appetitive part of the soul rules, the range of desire will forever increase. In more contemporary terms, once a society becomes oriented by consumerism (where all the appetites we have while we are awake are encouraged), it will not be able to be transformed into a culture of savers without the antidote that philosophy offers. Notwithstanding the need for savings in a society oriented by wealth, savings rates will continually diminish. Moreover, no institutional measures can correct the problem; the crisis resides in the soul, which must be "turned" in order to cure the ailment.

The rejection of the "city of pigs" turns out to be crucial to the entire project of discovering justice. Indeed, Socrates readily accedes to Glaucon's rather unknowing provocation that their investigation of the just city must turn to the luxurious city.

> Your suggestion is probably a good one because it is in the luxurious city that we are more likely to discover the roots of justice and injustice.[51]

This is an extraordinary admission. Socrates has conceded that justice will be found in "a city in a state of fever,"[52] in a city where "painting and embroidery, and gold and ivory will be sought after as ornamentation."[53] The sick city, the city where appearance prevails over substance, is the city where justice will be (ultimately) found. Here, ornamentation, appearance, art, material superfluity, imitation—the entire constellation of vice against which Rousseau railed[54]—is the condition under which justice may be revealed. Heidegger noted that the concealment and revelation of Being are constituents of the ontic structure of Dasein.[55] Socrates has a kindred insight: The revelation of justice involves an

---

[51] Plato, *Republic*, Book II, 372e.

[52] Ibid.

[53] Ibid., 373a.

[54] See Jean-Jacques Rousseau, "Whether the Restoration of the Sciences and Arts Has Contributed to the Purification of Morals," in *The First and Second Discourses*, ed. Victor Gourevitch (Cambridge: Cambridge University Press, 1997), part I, para. 10, p. 7: "How sweet it would be to live among us if the outward countenance were always the image of the heart's disposition; if decency were virtue; if our maxims were our rules; if genuine philosophy were inseparable from the title of philosopher! . . . [The good man] despises all those vile ornaments which would hinder his use of his strength, and most of which were invented only to conceal some deformity" (hereafter, *First Discourse*). The complexities surrounding his remarks about Famed Societies aside (ibid., part II, paras. 55–61, pp. 24–28), Rousseau decries our defection, if you will, from that original ignorance in which nature placed us. He longs for authenticity amid the concealment of human beings to themselves and to each other, yet finds no way out of the difficulty he reveals. Socrates has no such illusions about this situation: If reality is disclosed only through the city where ornamentation and appearance prevails, then reality and appearance are necessarily coincident. Said otherwise, there can be no depth without surfaces. Rousseau misapprehends this relationship and wallows in a metaphysics of disenchantment. Kant seems to have understood the paradox that Rousseau did not: "Without those in themselves unamiable characteristics of unsociability from whence opposition springs . . . all talents would remain hidden, unborn in an Arcadian shepherd's life, with all its concord, contentment, and mutual affection" (Immanuel Kant, "Idea for a Universal History from a Cosmopolitan Point of View," in *On History*, ed. Lewis White Beck [New York: Macmillan, 1963], Fourth Thesis, p. 15. Finally, consider Nietzsche on this matter: "[L]et nobody doubt that whoever stands that much in *need* of the cult of surfaces must at some time have reached *beneath* them with disastrous results" (*Beyond Good and Evil*, part III, sec. 59, p. 71).

[55] Martin Heidegger, *Being and Time*, trans. John Macquarrie and Edward Robinson (New York: Harper and Row, 1962), division I, ch. 5, para. 38, pp. 219–224 *passim*.

initial veiling, or concealment. Justice is revealed, it seems, only in the city that ornaments and imitates.

This veiling, I suggest, is coincident with the transgressive nature of the appetitive part of the soul.[56] By this I mean that unless the appetites overstep the bounds of moderation, justice cannot be revealed. Unless the argument moves out from under the shadow of Cephalus, the hunt cannot go forward. *There can be no justice without transgression.* It is no accident, in other words, that the search for justice must pass through the sick city, the city in need of doctors, before the standard of human health can be located.

> Then we must further enlarge our city. The well-founded city we started with will no longer be big enough. It must be extended and filled up with superfluities.[57]

And further on,

> [In our new city] the territory which was at one time sufficient to feed the city will no longer be adequate. [Under these conditions] we shall covet our neighbor's land in order to expand our pasture and tillage. And if our neighbor has also disregarded the limits set by necessity and has given himself over to the unlimited acquisition of wealth, he in turn will covet what belongs to us.[58]

The hunt for justice, as I have said, is possible only when the appetites become truly what they are, *viz.*, unlimited.[59] And unlimited appetite, Socrates immediately points out, is the occasion for the prospect of war—something impossible under the shadow and impotence of Cephalus.

The emergence of a second part of the "city," namely, the guardians,[60] requires that unlimited appetite make its appearance in a finite world. *And since it is from the guardians that the philosopher later emerges,*

---

[56] See Plato, *Republic*, Book X, 611d–612a: "[Like the sea god Glaucus, the soul] has suffered dismemberment of some parts of his body, while others have been worn down by waves. At the same time, such things as shells and seaweed and rocks have grown upon him, so that he appears more like a beast than what nature first intended him to be. . . . We must see how it looks with those rocks and barnacles scraped off which have accumulated during the course of its earthly feasting." Initially, the soul is concealed by virtue of its "earthly feasting." Philosophy uncovers its true nature.

[57] Plato, *Republic*, Book II, 373b.

[58] Ibid., 373d.

[59] See Plato, *Republic*, Book IV, 442a: "Then, when reason and spirit have been trained to understand their proper functions, they must aid each other to govern the appetites that constitute in each of us *the largest and most insatiable part* of our nature" (*ho dē pleiston tēs psuchēs en hekastō esti kai chrēmatōn phusei aplēstotaton*) (emphasis added).

[60] See Plato, *Republic*, Book II, 374a: "[S]o our city must be enlarged once more [because of the possibility of war], this time by nothing less that a whole army." Cf. Plato, *Phaedo*, 66c: "Only the body and its desires cause war, civil discord, and battles."

from this we may conclude that justice—and therefore unity[61]—is a genuine possibility only when occasioned by appetitive transgression and the perennial possibility of war. The 'rendering each its due' that constitutes the true happiness of the philosopher always-already entails appetitive transgression[62] and war. War is, as it were, antecedent to the very possibility of justice. As a being constituted with the possibility of "rendering each its due," strife (*eris*) is inscribed into our very constitution.[63] Transgression (or strife) does not constitute the essence of the human condition; it is, nevertheless, a necessary condition for the disclosure of the homeland of the soul: the Good. This claim will become more credible after the all the parts of the "city" (and soul) have made their appearance, and the basis of their friendly relations established. Therefore, I defer further consideration of the matter, and rest here with the understanding that the ascent to justice begins with appetitive transgression and the prospect for war.

Fables, Lies, and Medicine

How shall we manage [the upbringing and education of the guardians]? Is this question not germane to the principle objective of our study, namely,

---

[61] Recall that only the philosopher can see the so-called goods of the Cave for what they are: idols over which those who are ruled by the appetites—those who do not render each its due—fight and die. See Plato, *Republic*, Book VII, 520c. See also *Republic*, Book I, 351d: "[I]njustice generates hatred, quarrels, and factions. Only justice can create unity and love [*homonoian kai philian*]."

[62] See also Plato, *Symposium*, trans. Alexander Nehamas and Paul Woodruff, in *Plato: Complete Works*, 210a–211d. Diotima there tells Socrates of the ascension to the love of Beauty itself from the love of the bodily beauty. Love of Beauty itself is made possible only by ascension through earthly feasting, which is the occasion for strife.

[63] Cf. Martin Heidegger, *An Introduction to Metaphysics*, trans. Ralph Manheim (New Haven: Yale University Press, 1959), ch. 2, p. 62: "[T]he polemos [about which Heraclitus thinks] is a conflict that prevailed prior to everything divine and human, not a war in the human sense. This conflict, as Heraclitus thought it, first caused the realm of being to separate into opposites; it first gave rise to position and order and rank. . . . Not only does conflict as such give rise to [*ent-stehen lassen*] the essent; it also preserves the essent in its permanence [*Standigkeit*]." See also J. Glenn Gray, *The Warriors: Reflections on Men in Battle* (New York: Harper & Row, 1970), p. 242: "[A]ny study of war must strive to deal with gods and devils in the form of man. It is recorded in the Holy Scriptures that there was once war in heaven, and the nether regions are still supposed to be the scene of incessant strife. Interpreted symbolically, this must mean that the final secrets of why men fight must be sought beyond the human, in the nature of being itself." Gray, a student of Heidegger's, writes eloquently of his years as an intelligence officer in World War II. War, he concludes, reveals certain truths about men that peace obscures. Though he does not celebrate this strife, he recognizes that peace is fragile and is not long endured. Cf. Eph. 6:11–17.

the origin and role of justice and injustice in the city [*dikaiosunēn te kai adikian tina tropon en polei gignetai*]?[64]

"Could we find tools that would teach their own use," Socrates says, "we should have discovered something truly beyond price."[65] The early education in the *Republic*, however, involves tools that have "costs" of the sort that teaching the young entails. In due course we will see that this costly upbringing points beyond itself and that it is the precondition for the emergence of the third component of the "city," the part that rules—namely, divine reason. The education unto reason, it turns out, is not, strictly speaking, a mortal affair, which raises a host of questions that must be deferred. So let us turn to the education of the spirited part of the soul, to music (*mousikē*) and to gymnastics (*gumnastikē*)—those two gifts of the gods[66] on which mortals must rely to fortify the soul against the allures of pleasure and the fear of death.[67]

The education of the guardians begins, Socrates says, with the "telling of tales and recounting of fables [*hōsper en muthō muthologountes*]."[68] Why this is so requires our consideration here. To do so—and in order to understand the quandary with which Socrates is confronted—it is necessary to raise an issue that was broached in Book II of the *Republic* (in the speeches by Glaucon and Adeimantus) that plagues Socrates throughout: how to convey the nature of what is real to a soul immersed in the domain of seeming. Thrasymachus' speech in Book I, in praise of injustice, had left Glaucon and Adeimantus dazed and unsure about what justice was and why it was worth living in accordance with; and so, in Book II, they request of Socrates that he illuminate the advantage of justice in and of itself, without respect to appearances. The advantage of *seeming* to be just without being so cannot constitute an adequate defense. Justice itself is demanded, not its semblance. Glaucon asks for what justice *is*, not for what it *shows*.

I have already briefly commented about the relationship between the unity of the soul and its capacity to see. If Glaucon's soul is divided, then the burden of his appeal cannot be discharged by Socrates—not, that is, in any way that Glaucon could understand,[69] because the divided soul cannot see beyond appearances. It is taken in by coatings and glitter, and

[64] Plato, *Republic*, Bk. II, 376c–d.

[65] Ibid., 374d.

[66] Plato, *Republic*, Book III, 411e.

[67] Ibid., 413d–414b.

[68] Plato, *Republic*, Book II, 376d.

[69] See Plato, *Republic*, Book VI, 506d: "I fear [Glaucon] that my powers may not be able to reach as far [as to be able to show you the Good]; I fear that my zeal might only make me ludicrous. No, my comrades, let us set aside for a time the nature of the good

cannot break through the surface of things—hence the appeal of tyranny.[70] Whatever words Socrates offers must take cognizance of this limitation.[71]

While Glaucon sets up the problem, to which there is no obvious answer, Adeimantus highlights it. The poets, he says, promise rewards of the sort that could be appealing only to the soul preoccupied in the frenzy of appetitive transgression. If "the fairest reward of virtue and the just life is [to be] an eternal drunk,"[72] to dwell amid poisons forever,[73] then only the soul for whom that prospect is attractive will love justice. Since we learn in the course of the *Republic* that the just soul finds true happiness through the rule of reason rather than in the rule of the appetites,[74] the incentive to be just offered by the poets turns out to appeal only to the soul who dwells, so to speak, on the surface of things.

The promise of appetitive feasting as the reward for a just life, then, only further abets the rule of the appetites. The ruling principle of the soul remains undisturbed. Yet nothing less than a disruption of the sovereignty of the appetites must occur if justice is to prevail and the true object of human knowledge be revealed.

> The way each of us learns compares with what happens to the eye; it cannot be turned away from darkness to face the light without turning the whole body. So it is with our capacity to know; together with the entire soul one must turn away from the world of transient things [*ek tou gigno-*

---

itself. At the present moment I believe that it is too great a task to attain what it appears to be in my thoughts. However, I am willing to speak of what is most nearly like the good." Socrates can offer only the "interest" on the "principal" to Glaucon and the others with divided souls (ibid., 507a). This notion authorizes my consideration of the *Republic* as a fable, since fables are not themselves the truth but are an earnest of the truth.

[70] See Plato, *Republic*, Book IX, 577a: "[T]he only proper judge of men is one who is able to penetrate into the inmost soul and temper of other men. He will not be like a child, dazzled by the pomp of the court which tyrants contrive to deceive outsiders. [The philosopher] will see through it all." Tyranny has an appealing surface.

[71] See also Plato, *Phaedrus*, 276e–277a: "The dialectician chooses a proper soul and plants and sows within it discourse accompanied by knowledge—discourse capable of helping itself as well as the man who planted it, which is not barren but produces a seed from which more discourse grows in the character of others. Such discourse makes the seed forever immortal and renders the man who has it as happy as any human being can be."

[72] Plato, *Republic*, Book II, 363d.

[73] Cf. Augustine, *Confessions*, book II, ch. ii, p. 37: "[This] unhappy sheep wandering from your flock and impatient of your protection was infected by a disgusting sore. . . . [I longed for sufferings that] scratched me on the surface, [that] produced inflamed spots, pus, and repulsive sores. That was my kind of life. Surely, my God, it was no real life at all." For Augustine, life without God carries with it the disposition to seek poisons that yield muted suffering. The soul lost to God finds solace in dwelling in its poisons, and only through the grace of God does it relinquishes them.

[74] See especially Plato, *Republic*, Book IX, 580d–583b.

menou periakteon einai] toward the world of perpetual being, until finally one learns to endure the sight of its most radiant manifestation. This is what we call goodness [*tagathon*].[75]

Without turning away from the rule of the appetites, there can be no justice; yet without *already being* just, the capacity of the soul to see the advantage of justice over the life of the "eternal drunk" cannot yet exist. This is, again, an apparently intractable problem.[76]

How, then, must Socrates (the one who knows) speak to Glaucon (the one who opines)? To put it otherwise, how may words be used to draw the soul upward and away from the earthly feasting toward which it is inclined, when the soul in such a condition is genuinely incapable of listening?[77]

A clue to answering this question is to be found in Socrates' discussion of God, lies (*pseudesthai*), and medicine.[78] "Intrinsically and beautiful, a

---

[75] Plato, *Republic*, Book VII, 518c–d.

[76] See Jacques Derrida, "Plato's Pharmacy," in *Dissemination*, trans. Barbara Johnson (Chicago: University of Chicago Press, 1981), pp. 62–171. Derrida's exposition reveals the interpenetration of poisons and antidotes, which interpretation precludes an easy withdrawal from the tainted world and into the purity of the philosophical domain. "The pharmakon," Derrida says, "which is older than either of the opposites [of poison and antidote], is 'caught' by philosophy, by 'Platonism' which is constituted by this apprehension, as a mixture of two pure, heterogeneous terms. And one could follow the word pharmakon as a guiding thread within the whole Platonic problematic of the mixture" (ibid., part II, sec. 6, p. 128). On Derrida's view this establishes an intractable dilemma, from which there is no escape. Consider Augustine on this matter of poisons as well. So powerful is the propensity of man to turn from God, and to glory in the City of Man, that God had to take mortal form. Had God taken merely human form, he could not have averted man's destruction; had God remained God and not taken human form, he could not have mediated between God and man (*City of God*, vol. 7, book IX, ch. 15, pp. 99–101 [CG, pp. 359–61]). He must have taken on the poison of mortal life, in order to provide the antidote to the sin that characterizes it. See St. Augustine, *The Trinity*, trans. Edmund Hill (New York: New City Press, 1991), book IV, ch. 4, sec. 24, p. 169: "[H]ealth is the opposite pole from sickness, but the cure should be half-way between the two, and unless it has some affinity with sickness it will not lead to health." Also see ibid., book VIII, ch. 3, sec. 7, p. 247: "[T]his indeed it is useful for us to believe and to hold firm and unshaken in our hearts, that the humility thanks to which God was born of a woman, and led through such abuse at the hands of mortal men to his death, is a medicine to heal the tumor of our pride and a high sacrament to break the chains of our sin." Christ is the antidote to man's poison; He takes on mortal form with divine immunity. In this light, consider the verses added by the early Church fathers to the Gospel of Mark (Mk. 16:8–20), notably 16:18 ("They shall take up serpents; and if they drink any deadly thing, it shall not hurt them; they shall lay hands on the sick, and they shall recover"). Mortal poisons receive their antidote through the resurrected Christ.

[77] The saying of Polemarchus in the Pireaus, "How can you persuade us if we will not listen?" (Plato, *Republic*, Book I, 327b), takes on a deeper meaning in light of the state of affairs we encounter here.

[78] Plato, *Republic*, Book II, 381e–382e.

god abides simply and forever in his own form," Socrates says.[79] More-over, "a god would [not] lie in word or deed [nor would he] seek to vic-timize us with illusions."[80] Men, however, do not share these attributes. To come right to the point: Men lie.[81] That is, where a god has perspicu-ity with respect to who or what he is, men do not. There is, with men, a disjunction between what is uttered in word and what is harbored in the recesses of their soul. A god does not harbor the truth from himself; men do. A god knows who or what He is; men, in their divided condition, have no knowledge at all. They are plagued by

> the lie that finds lodging in the inmost part of [their] souls [which] remains there to deceive them about all the things most important to their lives.[82]

I will not enter into the debate about whether a god could lie, except to suggest that the matter could be decided only *after* the nature and magni-tude of human self-deception is disclosed—the knowledge of which can be had only on illumination by the Good.[83] Rather, I wish to turn to an examination of the distinction, crucial to the success of the undertaking of the *Republic*, between lies of words and lies harbored in men's souls.

> The lie of words [*pseudos en tois logois*] [contrary to the lie harbored in the soul] does no more than imitate what the [deeper] lie does to the soul. It bears only a shadowy resemblance to the [lie in the soul] and is not alto-gether false.[84]

The more repugnant lie here is not the lie of words, but rather the lie that is harbored in the soul. Lies of words are imitations, shadows, re-semblances; lies in the soul, in contrast, have every appearance of being indelible.[85] Indeed, only through the philosophical practice of death can they be relinquished. This understanding, to be sure, is incongruous with the more conventional liberal view about lies of words and lies in the

---

[79] Ibid., 381c.

[80] Ibid., 381e.

[81] Especially Cretians. See Titus 1:10–12.

[82] Plato, *Republic*, Book II, 382a. See also Augustine, *Confessions*, book V, ch. iii, p. 75: "About the creation [people] say many things that are true; but the truth, the artificer of creation, [those with darkened hearts] do not seek in a devout spirit and so they fail to find him. . . . They change your truth into a lie and serve the creation rather than the Creator."

[83] Cf. Rene Descartes, *Meditations on First Philosophy*, in *Philosophical Writings*, vol. II, "Fourth Meditation," pp. 37–43. In Plato's fable, it would be impossible for the di-vided soul to establish that God does not lie. Only the soul that is one, not many—the soul that is not deceived by "lies harbored in the soul"—can make this determination.

[84] Plato, *Republic*, Book II, 382b–c.

[85] Early education is important because "whatever [young] minds absorb is likely to become fixed and unalterable [*duseknipta te kai ametastata*]" (ibid., 378d–e). Imitation of the right patterns, therefore, is crucial for the formation of the character. Yet Socrates,

soul—a view that would have it that to be truthful is to say true words.[86] The possibility Socrates entertains, *viz.*, that lies of words may serve to dislodge the more egregious lies that are harbored in the soul, is rejected by liberal thought. Yet such lies, Socrates says, "[might] be helpful as a sort of medicine [*hōs pharmakon*]."[87]

This allusion to medicine warrants further attention. First, we have already discovered that doctors are needed only after the moderate city has been set aside, and the luxurious city invoked. Most of the doctors in that latter city, it turns out, are concerned with extending life; for them, life is the highest good. The luxurious city evinces "variety [*poikilia*],"[88] which is both the consequence and cause of disease (*noson*). The antidotes most doctors administer, however, produce only "lingering death [*macron . . . ton thanaton hautō poiēsas*]."[89] This, at least, was the medicine Herodicus dispenses as a cure.

---

perhaps unlike Aristotle, does not think that mimesis alone can orient the soul toward the Good. (See, e.g., *Republic*, Book VII, 538c–539d, where the "right" habits that early education have instantiated are superseded through the practice of dialectic.) Consider also Thomas Hobbes, *Leviathan*, ed. Edwin Curley (Indianapolis: Hackett, 1994), part I, ch. xii, para. 21, p. 61, where custom is rejected as a basis for political order. While Hobbes rejects custom, however, he locates sovereignty not in divine reason, but rather in the *person* of the Leviathan.

[86] See Hobbes, *Leviathan*, part I, ch. iv, para. 11, p. 18: "[F]or true and false are attributes of speech, not of things. And where speech is not, there is neither truth nor falsehood." Mill's view, despite its obvious divergences, is more akin to Hobbes than to Socrates.' See J. S. Mill, "On Liberty," in *On Liberty and Other Essays*, ed. John Gray (Oxford: Oxford University Press, 1991), sec. I, p. 15: "[L]iberty, as a principle, has no application to any state of things anterior to the time when mankind have become capable of being improved by free and equal discussion." For Mill, human progress becomes possible only when social and political conditions that allow for differences of opinion are present. True-sayings cease to be true in the absence of an opposing opinion (see ibid., sec. 2, pp. 40–51). Notwithstanding Mill's admiration of Socrates (ibid., p. 29), he seems unable to comprehend the place of "lies of words" in Plato's fable. Moreover, he seems unable to account for what might be called the fortification of truth that death may accomplish. Contrast Mill's remarks about the Christian martyrs (ibid., sec. II, pp. 32–34), for example, with what Augustine says about them (*City of God*, in *Writings*, vol. 8, book XXII, ch. 10, pp. 452–53 [*CG*, pp. 1048–49]).

[87] Plato, *Republic*, Book II, 382c. Cf. *Republic*, Book I, 331d: "Then we must say that telling the truth and repaying one's debts cannot serve as an adequate definition of justice." This is the first, though still veiled, allusion in the *Republic* to the need for lies of a certain sort. Within Augustine's writings, there is a historical twist to this claim about the veiling of truth, which should not be overlooked. Because Augustine understood the Trinity of Father, Son, and Holy Spirit in terms of *being, knowing*, and *joy* (*City of God*, vol. 7, book XI, ch. 26, pp. 228–29 [*CG*, pp. 459–60]), the Incarnation of the Son was the occasion for the revelation of the truth. Prior to the advent of Christ the truth *had* to be veiled. Cf. Mark 15:38.

[88] Plato, *Republic*, Book III, 404e.

[89] Ibid., 406b. Cf. Augustine, *City of God*, in *Writings*, vol. 8, book XXII, ch. 22, p. 474 (*CG*, p. 1065): "[T]his present life of ours (if a state full of so much grievous misery can be

Thus his struggle against death left him no time for the business of life. The reward for his skill was that he managed to prolong such a life until old age.[90]

Living the life that only keeps death at bay, the life for which survival is the highest good,[91] patients in the "city in fever" seek antidotes for diseases that arise from their immoderation—antidotes, moreover, that allow them to continue living an immoderate life. Seeking life, they find only lingering death. The cure they ingest evinces a naïveté about health, which, like justice, is to be valued both for itself and for its effects.[92]

Second, there are other kinds of antidotes available, from other kinds of doctors and for other kinds of patients. Asclepius, whom Socrates calls "a real politician [*politikon*],"[93] administers antidotes that "preclude perpetual illness and constant doctoring."[94] These bring health or bring death, but in any case *not* the veneration of a life that is neither alive nor dead.[95] Higher than life is the Good, the giver of life.[96] The doctor who has not grasped this is an idolater. Herodicus is to Aaron at the

---

called life)," Augustine says, "can only be relieved through the gift of Jesus Christ." No mortal medicine can affect a cure for the lingering death that was occasioned by the first sin.

[90] Plato, *Republic*, Book III, 406b.

[91] See Karl Marx's letter to Friedrich Engels of August 2, 1862, in *Marx-Engels Correspondence* (Moscow: Progress, 1955), p. 120: "[I]t is remarkable how Darwin recognizes among beasts and plants his English society." Elsewhere he comments: "[T]he nature which comes to be in human history—the genesis of human society—is man's real nature; hence nature as it comes to be through industry, even though in an estranged form, is true anthropological nature" ("Private Property and Communism" [from Economic and Philosophic Manuscripts of 1844], in *The Marx-Engels Reader*, p. 90 [emphasis added]). For Nietzsche's judgment on the social applications of Darwinian biology, see *Genealogy*, Second Essay, sec. 12, pp. 78–79. Where Marx locates the origin of the idea that survival is the highest good in economics, and Nietzsche finds it in the psyche of the wounded man, Socrates detects it in the soul where the appetites prevail, but without satisfaction. In one respect he agrees with both Marx and Nietzsche: Only the sick soul holds survival to be the highest good. For a more recent, scientific exposition, see Richard Dawkins, *The Selfish Gene* (New York: Oxford University Press, 1976).

[92] See Plato, *Republic*, Book II, 357c, where justice is akin to sight, knowledge, and health. The true philosopher, the one who sees and knows, is also the best doctor for the soul. Cf. Nietzsche, *Genealogy*, First Essay, sec. 6, p. 32: "[M]ankind itself is still ill with the effects of this priestly naïveté in medicine." For Nietzsche, the inoculations of Plato, the cures of the doctor who is oriented by the Good, fail to restore health.

[93] Plato, *Republic*, Book III, 407e.

[94] Ibid., 406c.

[95] See Plato, *Gorgias*, trans. Donald J. Zeyl, in *Plato: Complete Works*, 492e. "[With respect to the soul that nourishes the appetitive part of the soul in every way] I shouldn't be surprised that Euripides' lines are true when he says, 'But who knows whether being alive is being dead. And being dead is being alive.' Perhaps in reality we're dead."

[96] See Plato, *Republic*, Book VI, 509b: "[Like the sun, the Good] confers visibility on all that can be seen but is equally the source of generation, nurture, and growth [*tēn genesin kai auxēn kai trophēn*] in all things."

foot of Mount Sinai as Asclepius is to Moses.[97] The true doctor looks to the Good. The antidote he administers, moreover, must be appropriate for the patient in his charge and must address the real illness: the lies harbored in the soul. This antidote is medicinal in a deeper sense than is mere medicine, which can, at best, treat only the symptoms, the manifestations, of a soul in distress.[98]

The antidote administered, to return to the question of lies, is words of a certain sort: words that poison the hearer, which cause him to approach death, yet at the same time draw him onward beyond death toward a life that can scarcely be comprehended—and so must be alluded to, if at all, by lies of a certain sort. The "untruth" of the words administered poison the deeper lie harbored in the soul, so that the soul may truly live.

Let us be wary, however, of administering such poisons ourselves, for in the wrong hands they do not bring health. Doctors are entitled to use lies because they know the standard of human health that is justice; that is their warrant for administering deceptions that cure. The mortal sickness of "lingering death" is pregnancy in the hands of such doctors. What they bring forth—but do not cause—is new life.[99] In the hands of the those who have no such gifts, the result is stillbirth. Doctor-philosophers and sophists alike use lies of words.[100] The poison in such lies can be an antidote to a mortal disease, but only in the hands of true doctors.

---

[97] Exodus 32:4. When Moses withdraws to Sinai, the people, under the temporary leadership of Aaron, fashion a molten calf. Long accustomed to servitude, in their "illness" they misapprehend to whom their allegiance is owed, and worship an image.

[98] On this reading, the current medical crisis cannot be solved by either nationalized health care, or more efficient private management. It is neither a political nor economic problem, but rather one of preventative care, in the broadest sense. In a culture dedicated to "consumption" the constrains on the appetites are loosened, and this is bound to have deleterious effects upon "health." In the luxurious city, Plato says, "disease and licentiousness . . . will give rise to increased numbers and hospitals and courts of law" (*Republic*, Book III, 405a). The cost of orienting a culture toward consumption is illness. See also Rousseau, *Second Discourse*, part I, para. 9, pp. 137–38: "[E]xcesses of every kind, the immoderate transports of all the passions, the fatigues and exhaustion of the mind, the innumerable sorrows and pains that are experienced in every station of life and the constantly gnaw away at men's soul's; such are the fatal proofs that most of our ills are of our own making, and that we would have avoided almost all of them if we had retained the simple, uniform and solitary way of life prescribed to us by Nature."

[99] See Plato, *Theaetetus*, trans. M. J. Levett, in *Plato: Complete Works*, 149c–d: "And this too is natural, isn't it?—or perhaps necessary? I mean that it is the midwives who have the power to bring on the pains, and also, if they think fit, to relieve them; they do this by the use of simple drugs, and by singing incantation. In difficult cases, too, they can bring about the birth; or, if they consider it advisable, they can promote miscarriage." See also ibid., 151b: "[A]t times, Theaetetus, I come across people who do not seem to me somehow to be pregnant. Then I realize that they have no need of me."

[100] See Plato, *Sophist*, trans. Nicholas P. White, in *Plato: Complete Works*, 223b: "So according to our account now, Theaetetus, [the Sophist's] sort of expertise belongs to

Who is it, however, that is entitled to use such lies? We said before that the gods have no use for lies [*pseudos*]. If that is right, and if it is also right that lies are useful to men only as a kind of medicine or remedy, then only doctors should be permitted to use them. Laypersons [*idiōtais*] have no business lying.[101]

The endorsement of lies of words by Socrates, then, is a highly circumspect one. Only a few are really capable of inoculating with lies of words.[102] The rest, who live with their poisons in the state of "lingering death," should not attempt to use such poisons medicinally. Only the few who are healthy, the true doctors, can treat illness.[103]

Let us return to the disease for which lies of words are an antidote in the right hands. Recall that the soul who opines that injustice is profitable— think here of Thrasymachus—is the soul taken in by the appearances of power. This opinion, the so-called realist opinion, is predicated on the view that appearance is all that matters. On such a view, the Good is "abstract," while appearance—all that shows itself to the divided soul— is "concrete." The burden of Socrates' discussion is to demonstrate that

---

appropriation, taking possession, hunting, animal-hunting, hunting on land, human hunting, hunting by persuasion, hunting privately, and money-earning. It's the hunting of rich prominent young men. And according to the way our account has turned out, it's what should be called the expertise of the sophist." Here, too, there is the hunt; yet because the sophist hunts men, the lies of words they administer do not bring health. The soul that hunts men has only a "semblance of education." True doctors help direct the hunt for the Good.

[101] Plato, *Republic*, Book III, 389b.

[102] In this respect, the formidable difference between Socrates and liberal thought is attenuated. While Socrates, unlike liberal thought, lays open the possibility of using lies of words, because these poisons in the hands of the poisoned cannot cure, they are best laid aside for all but the philosopher-king. "Lay persons," recall, are not to lie (*Republic*, Book III, 389b). Yet given that the unlikelihood that a philosopher-king will rule, the use of lies of words as an antidote to the lies harbored in the soul is all but foreclosed. While the result (without a philosopher-king) may be the same, however, Socrates at least comprehends the problem that does not much occupy liberal thought, *viz.*, that lies harbored in the soul are a profound problem, which cannot much be attenuated by "free and open discussion" (Mill, "On Liberty," sec. I, p. 15).

[103] See Plato, *Republic*, Book III, 408c–e. When Glaucon asks Socrates whether the best doctor knows illness because of his long experience with it, Socrates responds that "the doctor's mind [*psuchē*] [must] be kept free from evils; a diseased mind is not competent to cure anything" (ibid., 408e). The condition of the doctor's body—whether or not it has been poisoned by disease—has no bearing on whether his soul can rightly use poisons to cure others. If his soul is healthy, then the antidotes he administers will bring health. Because the true basis of health is not bodily, the bodily health or disease of the doctor cannot be used as a standard by which he, as a doctor, is evaluated. See also Augustine, *Confessions*, book II, ch. vii, p. 33: "[T]he one [Christ] who delivered me from the great sickness of my sins . . . has himself not been a victim of the same great sickness."

the opposite relation, in fact, obtains: The Good alone is concrete.[104] All else is abstract, intangible, disembodied.[105]

The disease, then, for which Socrates must provide an antidote, is the inability to see what is really Real. This inability, as I have indicated on several occasions, is attributed to the condition in which the divided—that is, diseased—soul finds itself. Socrates must, consequently, use lies of words to draw the divided soul toward health, toward the Good, so that it will be able to see the appearances of power for what they are: mere shadows.

The fable of the *Republic* is just such a antidote; it is a lie (*pseudos*), which in the hands of the true doctor can dislodge the deeper lie lodged in the soul of its readers. The medicine administered allows such souls to intimate, but not yet see clearly, the advantage of being unified rather than divided, of being just rather than unjust—the definitive confirmation of which can really be revealed only when the soul is unified. Like all medicines, this one is a *supplement* for health, but is not itself health. It works only if it "takes."[106]

Consider, now, a smaller fable within the larger fabulous tale: the Myth of the Metals.

---

[104] See Nasr, *Knowledge and the Sacred*, ch. 4, p. 134: "[The Supreme Substance] is the Origin but also the End, the alpha and the omega. It is Emptiness if the world is envisioned as fullness and Fullness if the relative is perceived in the light of its ontological poverty and essential nothingness." See also Augustine, *Confessions*, book III, ch. v, p. 41: "Food pictured in dreams is extremely like food received in the waking state; yet sleepers receive no nourishment, they are simply sleeping." Those who sleep—the ones who dwell amid abstractions and shadows—seek nourishment that does not fortify.

[105] Theologically, only God is able to say, "I AM THAT I AM" (Exodus 3:14); all other beings *are* only inasmuch as they participate in God. The source of all beings is that which Is. See Augustine, *Confessions*, book I, ch. ii, p. 4: "Without you, whatever exists would not exist."

[106] A few comments about the difference between Plato and Aristotle on this matter of supplements and poisons are warranted here. Aristotle does seem to understand that at their best, arguments are supplements that "take" only in souls that are "generous minded" and "gently born" (*Nicomachean Ethics*, book X, ch. 9, 1179b4–10). Elsewhere, in his treatment of tragedy, the medical model he invokes pertains not to supplements but to purgatives. This is a somewhat different medical model of how the problem of poisons in the soul should be treated. The "catharsis" (see *Poetics*, trans. I. Bywater, in *Complete Works*, ch. 6, 1449b28) that tragedy produces when, in public performances, pity and fear are treated well *purges the excess* of passion that is present in the audience. Plato rejected tragedy, in part, because he thought that periodically purging the poison in no way solved the problem—and may in fact exacerbate it, since it appeals to that part of the soul that ought not to rule (see *Republic*, Book X, 606a *passim*). Aristotle might have responded by saying that this catharsis actually educates the passions and, through regular attendance, brings them under the purview of reason. Where Plato offers "stories and fables," told to a few away from public places, Aristotle requires tragedy as a public event.

All right, I shall speak, even though I hardly know where to find the words or the audacity to utter them. I shall try to persuade first the rulers, then the soldiers, and then the rest of the people that all the training and education they have received from us are actually products of their own imaginations, just the way it is in a dream. In reality, they were the whole time deep within the earth being given form and feature, and the same with their weapons and all other accouterments. When the process was complete, all were delivered up to the surface by their mother earth, whence it comes that they care for their land as if it were their mother and nurse and feel bound to defend it from any attack. Likewise do they regard their fellow citizens as brothers born of the same soil.

No wonder you hesitated so long before telling your lie.

Yes, I had good reason, didn't I? But hear the rest of the tale. We shall tell them that although they are all brothers, *god differentiated those qualified to rule by mixing in gold at their birth.* Hence they are most honored. The auxiliaries he compounded with silver, and the craftsmen and farmers with iron and brass. So endowed each will usually beget his own kind.[107]

Let us disregard for the time being the explicit claim that rightful boundaries are drawn by divine assistance, and instead continue attending to the question of why fables are necessary, and for whom. To begin with, the emergence from dreaming to wakefulness spoken of by Socrates here is not trivial. Indeed, the central allegory of the *Republic*, the allegory of the Cave, conveys this very notion.[108] Consider, also, the final sentence of the *Republic*, which reads:

So shall we fare well here and during that thousand-year journey [*en tē chilietei poreia*] whose story I have now told you.[109]

This reference to the "thousand-year journey" is no mere piece of hyperbole. Socrates has spoken about it several pages earlier, within the confines of the Myth of Er:

Those whose journey took them beneath the earth for a thousand years wept and lamented as they recalled the burdens of their manifold sufferings. Those from above [*ek tou ouranou*] tried to describe the inconceivable beauty they saw and experienced in heaven.[110]

---

[107] Plato, *Republic*, Book III, 414d–415a (emphasis added).

[108] See Plato, *Republic*, Book VII, 520c–d: "Together and wide awake [upon returning to the cave], you and we will govern our city, far differently from most cities today whose inhabitants are ruled darkly as in a dream by men who will fight with each other over shadows and use faction in order to rule."

[109] Plato, *Republic*, Book X, 621d.

[110] Ibid., 614e–615a.

The thousand-year journey refers to the journey through suffering that seems to be life, but which in fact is only the "lingering death" that constitutes life lived in the underworld amid appetitive transgression.[111] Socrates' task is to bring souls up from their "thousand year journey" so that they might choose a (true) life that is free from the sorrows that the unjust soul unremittingly suffers.[112] His task is to lead souls from the dreamy world of appetitive transgression toward justice, toward an ordering of the soul wherein rightful boundaries are honored. Only then can the Good be seen—and, paradoxically, only by seeing the Good can rightful boundaries be honored.

All of these tales—the Myth of the Metals, the Allegory of the Cave, the myth of Er—pertain, then, to emerging from a dream world. Yet what are we to make of the idioms of "mother earth" and "father God," to recast the terms only somewhat, in this first noble lie told to our guardians? Where the myth of Er is largely about death and the afterlife, and the Allegory of the Cave is about life in its middle years, the Myth of the Metals is a tale about children. In a double sense, it is appropriate that Socrates starts with the Myth of the Metals: It is a tale *about* children conveyed in a manner appropriate *for* children—that is, it is offered in the picture-thinking idiom appropriate to children. The philosopher, on the other hand, is the adult who requires no images at all.

> [I]n the highest subdivision [of knowledge] the soul makes no use of images. It also begins with assumptions and hypotheses but rises to a level where it relies exclusively on forms, a level of intellection that is free from all hypothetical thinking.[113]

"Children" need images and surfaces, as points of reference. For them, consequently, Socrates must invoke images, picture thinking,[114] in order to draw their souls upward on their journey. Such images, moreover,

---

[111] Cf. Augustine, *Confessions*, book I, ch. xxviii, p. 20: "To live [in the world] in lustful passions is to live in darkness and be far from [God's] face."

[112] See Brann, "The Music of the *Republic*," p. 12: "This then is the setting of the *Republic*: Hades with its tales and a deliverer willing to go down and able to come up—a most appropriate setting, for down there, so it is said, justice is close at hand" (*Republic*, Book I, 330d; Book X, 614c; *Apology* 41a). This thought accords with the claim made earlier that justice comes into view not in the healthy city, but rather in the unhealthy city that has "frequent sightings of an approaching end" (Book I, 330e), for which doctors are needed.

[113] Plato, *Republic*, Book VI, 510b.

[114] I have already invoked this notion from Hegel (*Phenomenology*, para. 765, p. 463), in the Introduction (note 12). Both Plato and Hegel ascend through picture thinking to unmediated knowledge, the difference being that Hegel does so through a dialectic involving successive incarnations *in* time, while Plato does so through a dialectic involving an ascent to the timeless.

must be crafted to the specific requirements of the souls of those to whom he speaks,[115] if his medicine is to be effective. Like the poets,[116] Socrates must rely on images. Unlike the poets, however, Socrates intends by his conveyances, his lies of words, to help assist his interlocutors on their journey from appearance to reality, from the darkened Cave to the divine light of the Good. Poets cannot be allowed to educate guardians, he says, unless their intention is to help the young to become "godlike, insofar as that is possible for men [*anthrōpō*]."[117] Only doctor-poets in the philosophical sense we have been considering can do this; the rest begin and end with appearances.

In the Myth of the Metals, the good doctor-poet Socrates conveys something about justice to dreamy children; he intimates to those who yet slumber what being awake might be like. Justice—this wakefulness that eludes them—involves "rendering each its due," and therefore entails both unity (signified by mother earth) and differentiation (signified by a god). Each part works for the good of the whole, "loves its mother," so to speak, but remains what it is, unalloyed with the other parts, by virtue of a different kind of metal—divine gold—to which Socrates' words introduce us here.

In light of the conversation that follows Socrates' myth, however, we may safely conclude that the poison he has administered with his noble lie has not dislodged the lies harbored in the souls of his interlocutors. Nor could it. He has offered an image intimating that the rightful divisions involved in "rendering each its due" are possible only with divine assistance. Yet the interlocutors are unable to see this because they dwell in the twilight world that knows nothing of the divine light that makes justice possible.[118] While they have listened to the tale, they do not as yet have any understanding of what they have just heard. Perhaps, like hem-

---

[115] Throughout the *Republic*, Socrates tries to ascertain what kind of souls his interlocutors have. When Glaucon says, early in the dialogue, that he understands "money and honors as inducements to enter public life" (*Republic*, Book I, 347a), but not penalties, he reveals to Socrates that his soul is oligarchic, or perhaps timocratic, but not yet aristocratic. Socrates must understand his character before he can administer any medicine. See also Plato, *Laws*, trans. Trevor J. Saunders, in *Plato: Complete Works*, Book I, 650b: "So this insight into the nature and disposition of a man's soul [that drinking parties reveal] will rank as one of the most useful aids available to the art which is concerned to foster a good character—the art of statesmanship, I take it?" Properly run drinking parties, says the Athenian stranger, help to reveal to the statesman the hidden character of his citizens.

[116] See Plato, *Republic*, Book X, 601b–c: "Are not [the poets] words like faces that were young but never beautiful and from which youth is not departed? . . . Consider still another proposition: The imitator, the one who creates illusions, does not understand reality [*tou men ontos*] but only what reality appears to be" (*tou de phainomenou*).

[117] Plato, *Republic*, Book II, 383c.

[118] See Plato, *Republic*, Book VII, 518c–d.

lock, it takes some time for Socrates' medicine to take effect. Still, the interlocutors continue with their hunt for justice, though without any clear understanding of why boundaries must be granted their due. Still in the city of appetitive transgression, in the city that has emerged from the lowest element of the soul, Socrates' interlocutors cannot understand why the masters of this metallic city that he has just described should "get no advantage from it."[119] To this darkened city, which would "mix" metals and which cannot as yet "render each its due," we turn next.

Fool's Gold

In sum [Adeimantus interposed, the citizens of your city] possess what you would deny to your governors. They have stores of gold and silver and an abundance of everything coveted by those who expect to live the good life. Your rulers, on the other hand, seem to be mere mercenaries hired by the city to do nothing but *sit still* [*kathēsthai*] and stand guard.[120]

The interlocutors who have just been told of the city that has emerged "as if from a dream" in the Myth of the Metals do not yet know why— or how—each must be "rendered its due." Notwithstanding his ostensible defense of justice against the onslaught of Thrasymachus earlier, by his perplexity here Adeimantus reveals that he, too, believes that rulership involves "advantage" of the sort Socrates wishes to repudiate. Where Thrasymachus wished for power, Adeimantus wishes for wealth; whereas Thrasymachus has a tyrannical soul, Adeimantus has an oligarchic soul. Neither is oriented by the Good, and so each lacks real understanding. They differ in degree, not in kind. Neither finds "advantage" in the Good.

What Adeimantus does not recognize is the need to distinguish between rulership and wealth. Rulers, he opines, ought to be able to possess wealth—by which he means what I will hereafter call "mortal gold." Not having awakened the god-like element of reason,[121] Adeimantus is like a dreaming child ruled still by his appetites,[122] a child who cannot as yet comprehend why the rulers of the city should be "de-

---

[119] Plato, *Republic*, Book IV, 419a.

[120] Ibid., 419e–420a (emphasis added). Adeimantus here suggests, in effect, that the justice made possible by the guardians is useless. From the vantage point of those who dwell in the city of appetitive transgression, justice will inevitably appear useless—as the allegory of the Cave suggests (see Plato, *Republic*, Book VII, 517a). Consider also the parable of the pilot (*Republic*, Book VI, 488a–489c).

[121] See Plato, *Republic*, Book VII, 518d–e: "Wisdom [*phronēsai*], then, seems to be of an order different from those other things that are called the virtues of the soul."

[122] Plato, *Republic*, Book VII, 519a–b. Socrates suggests here that pleasures of the appetites are "attached to us at birth like leaden weights."

prived" of earthly "treasures." We will discover later that only from the vantage of awakened reason *could* he see that Socrates' injunction against mixing things mortal and divine is no deprivation at all. Gold in the soul—"divine gold"—is treasure enough for the those who are illuminated by it.

> Will anyone believe that he could profit by taking gold unjustly after considering [that] the moment he takes the gold, he will have enslaved the best part of himself to the worst? . . . [And in that] there could be not profit for him no matter how much he pocketed.[123]

There is, to be sure, profit in gold. The question confronting Adeimantus, however, is *which* gold really yields profit and strength: the seemingly abstract and intangible gold loved by the just soul, which cannot be possessed, or the apparently concrete and tangible gold that is loved and possessed by the oligarchic soul?

The question is brought to the fore in the discussion of how a city may be strong without the love of wealth—that prerequisite for generating a credible military threat. Can there be strength, in a word, without putting mortal gold first?

We should recall, here, that the need for a credible military threat emerges in the first place in the city of appetitive transgression. In such a city, Adeimantus now argues, mortal gold should rule, and the city be safeguarded with the armaments it can buy. Can strength be based, however, on the "earthly feasting"[124] of the appetites?[125] Or is real strength made possible by virtue of something more divine? The Myth of the Metals has already provided an answer of sorts. Yet Socrates does not return to the formulation offered there. Instead, he charts a new heading, with a view to the question of the relationship between strength and unity. Here begins Socrates' extended discussion of the divisions within the city and the soul, which culminates in the claim that the unity that "renders each its due" is made possible only through divine illumination.

What, then, is the problem with wealth, with mortal gold? Why is it not the true source of strength? More to the point: "How will the city

---

[123] Plato, *Republic*, Book IX, 589d–e.

[124] Plato, *Republic*, Book X, 612a.

[125] In this respect, Plato and Aristotle are in agreement, against the reading of Adam Smith by the Chicago School. For Aristotle, the having-in-common evinced by political friendship is the basis of unity among many (Aristotle, *Ethics*, book VIII, ch. 9, 1159b29–32). In contrast to the quasi-friendships based on pleasure and use (which, contra Adam Smith [*Wealth of Nations* (Chicago: University of Chicago Press, 1976), book I, ch. 2, p. 18], can never be the basis for an enduring society [Aristotle, *Ethics*, book IX, ch. 9, 1169a9]), the true friend loves what is most noble in himself. On this basis he can love others.

make war without having wealth, especially if it must fight a city with plenty in the treasury?"[126] Socrates' answer is that the kind of strength wealth exhibits is only apparent. While oligarchy is *not yet* tyranny (about which more in due course), it evinces the same defect, *viz.*, its apparent strength is belied by its *open* internal divisions. (Honor-loving timocracy has its divisions too, as we shall see, but they are concealed.) Like tyranny, the surface of oligarchy conveys strength; its interior, however, is bedeviled by strife. And the weakness of its strength, if you will, lies in the fact that it is at war with itself. The oligarchic city is able to generate the appearance of power, but at the cost of internal division,[127] which eventually becomes debilitating unless reason comes to the rescue.

Internal contradictions, however, are not the concern of the soul bedazzled by the splendor of surfaces and appearances. The warfare that arises from appetitive transgression seems to require precisely the front, the face, the show of power that mortal gold produces—whose cost, again, is internal division. The city ruled by wisdom, Socrates says, "will be the greatest city, not in reputation, to be sure, but in reality [*hōs alēthōs megistē*]."[128] Yet to prevail in a world of war, reputation, not reality, rules. Without mortal gold and the armaments it produces, there can be no triumph in war. We are back, again, with Adeimantus' wary claim that "appearance is mightier than reality and hence the true lord of happiness."[129] Familiar only with appetitive transgression that gives rise to war, we are, by this incapacity to distinguish between mortal and divine gold, condemned to war *ad infinitum*. From war and the death that it brings, there is no escape; the world of appearances thrusts war upon us.

> Like cattle [such souls] graze, fatten, and copulate. Greed drives them to kick and butt one another with horns and hoofs of iron. Because they are insatiable, they slay one another. And they are insatiable because they neglect to seek real refreshment for that part of the soul that is real and pure.[130]

Let us not be too quick, however, to bemoan the deadly consequences of living in this world of appearances. What haunts the appetitive soul, of course, is the specter of death. Yet Socrates seems rather to welcome

[126] Plato, *Republic*, Book IV, 422a.

[127] See Plato, *Republic*, Book VIII, 551d: "[S]uch a city should of necessity be not one, but two, a city of the rich and a city of the poor, dwelling together, and always plotting against one another." The latter portions of Rousseau's *Second Discourse* convey the same thought, *viz.*, that when the love of wealth comes to rule, there will eventually be only two classes.

[128] Plato, *Republic*, Book IV, 423a.

[129] Plato, *Republic*, Book II, 365c.

[130] Plato, *Republic*, Book IX, 586b.

this new possibility to which the appetitive soul that misunderstands reality gives rise; for lurking within this emergent prospect of death is philosophy, which also practices death, though in a different way than does the warrior who defends the city of appetitive transgression. Only through philosophy, it will turn out, can the "real refreshment" about which Socrates speaks be located. The appetitive transgression of the post-Cephaletic world to which we have been brought confronts us with a death that payment of the sort by which Cephalus ordered his life cannot redress or appease. We are in the territory of war, which issues from unbounded desire and yields only mimetic violence[131]—unless philosophy comes to the rescue.

Notwithstanding that philosophy would "be the least change that would transform bad government into good government [*politeias*],"[132] the soul that is only familiar with surfaces and appearances does not want to be shown this truth.[133] It purports to be content with "the way things are," in spite of its trepidation about death. Unilluminated by the true Light, the darkness of war perennially overshadows the appetitive soul that is enchained in the Cave. Death lurks in this place[134] that knows nothing yet of the philosophical practice of death toward which warfare points.

And without the further articulation of this warfaring type, the dying

---

[131] See Rene Girard, *Violence and the Sacred*, trans. Patrick Gregory (Baltimore: Johns Hopkins University Press, 1977), p. 144: "Nothing, perhaps, could be more banal than the role of violence in awakening desire. Our modern terms for this phenomenon are sadism or masochism. . . . We [moderns] believe that the normal form of desire is nonviolent and that this nonviolent form is characteristic of the generality of mankind. . . . [T]his hopeful belief [however] is clearly without foundation." Girard observes that violence must be circumvented through ritual violence. These observations comport with those offered by Socrates: Violence is rooted in desire and is mimetic. The antidote Socrates offers, which restores the community to health, is not the ritual violence of sacrifice, but rather the rule by those philosophical souls who have *sacrificed themselves*, so to speak, in the practice of death. Consistent with Girard's analysis of the linkage between desire and sadism and masochism is Socrates' remark about souls ruled by the appetites: "So they must live with the facades and illusions of true pleasure: Their pleasures must be *mixed* with pain" (*Republic*, Book IX, 586b [emphasis added]). I treat this matter more fully below in the section on "Sadomasochism." The importance of sacrifice was not lost to Paul, for whom earthly blood could atone for the sins of a particular people, but heavenly blood alone could atone for the universal sin of all in Adam. See Heb. 9:13–14 ("For if the blood of bulls and of goats, and the ashes of an heifer sprinkling the unclean, sanctifies to the purifying of the flesh: How much more shall the blood of Christ, who through the eternal Spirit offered himself without spot to God, purge your conscience from dead works to serve the living God?").

[132] Plato, *Republic*, Book V, 473b.

[133] See Plato, *Republic*, Book IV, 426a: "But [the] most charming characteristic [of the errant soul] is this: the one who tells them the truth will be deemed their worst enemy."

[134] See Eva Brann, "The Music of the *Republic*," p. 9: "A strange light is thrown on [the opening scenes of the *Republic*—the Pireaus, the withdrawal to Cephalus' house] by an

that is done does not bring death of the sort that is needed. Without further differentiation, there is only a "sickness unto death"[135] that takes the form of the never-ending oligarchic hope of forestalling death, but which is perennially dashed by the war that is coeval with the rule of the appetites. This intractable dilemma, as I have indicated, is a consequence of the love of mortal gold that yields brilliant but transitory strength at the cost of real durability.[136] Wanting gold of the sort that the ruling element should shun, oligarchy is unable to "render each its due." Out of appetitive rule comes war—which points beyond itself to philosophy, to be sure, but which itself offers no assurance that philosophy will emerge. For philosophy to emerge, "education" will be necessary. Through education we find a way out of the intractable problem set up by the confusion over which sort of gold will rule in our souls.[137]

Noble Education—and Beyond

Let us continue to consider things mortal and divine, but this time by attending to the preliminary education Socrates sets forth, and the ques-

---

ancient source that reports that [Cephalus] was over thirty years dead at the dramatic date of the dialogue, namely between 411 and 405 B.C.; his son has only a few more years to live before his death at the hands of the Thirty Tyrants. [From this we must conclude that] we are in the city of shades, in the house of Pluto" (emphasis in original).

[135] See Søren Kierkegaard, *The Sickness unto Death*, trans. and ed. Howard V. Hong and Adna H. Hong (Princeton: Princeton University Press, 1980), part I, A, p. 18: "[T]he torment of despair is precisely this inability to die. Thus it has more in common with the situation of a mortally ill person when he lies struggling with death and yet cannot die. Thus to be sick unto death is to be unable to die, yet not as if there were hope for life; no, the hopelessness is that there is not even the ultimate hope, death." The "lingering death" about which Socrates speaks is akin to this dying-that-cannot-die, but not equivalent. Despair arises from sin, not ignorance, Kierkegaard says (ibid., part II, A, pp. 87–96); with all things Socratic, he warns, "men have come to feel an urge to go further" (p. 86). (For corroboration, see Augustine, *Confessions*, book VII, ch. xxi, pp. 130–31.) For Kierkegaard, the antidote for despair is the Christ who proclaims that "[Lazarus]' sickness is not unto death" (John 11:4), even while he dies (John 11:14). Beyond the death that can, through Christ, be died, is life. Philosophy, however, offers a different resolution to this dilemma.

[136] Rousseau phrases the problem of modernity, if you will, in the same language. See Rousseau, *First Discourse*, part II, para. 43, p. 19: "What, then, precisely is at issue in this question of luxury? To know what matters most to Empires, to be brilliant and short-lived, or virtuous or long-lasting. I say brilliant, but by what luster? A taste to ostentation is scarcely ever combined in one soul with a taste for the honest. No, minds debased by a host of futile cares cannot possibly ever rise to anything great; and even if they had the requisite strength, they would lack the courage." Strength is the outward show of power; courage entails the application of that power toward wise ends.

[137] See also Zephaniah 1:17: "Neither their silver nor their gold shall be able to deliver them on the day of the wrath of the lord." Cf. Matt. 25:14–15, 19–29.

tions it raises. In the *Republic*, education is not introduced until the honor-loving and war-practicing part of the soul makes its appearance. The appetites, it seems, cannot be educated. They remain what they are, avaricious and inattentive, except when prodded by shame or governed by reason. Because of this, the preliminary education of the honor-loving part of the soul is concerned with developing the *habits* that provide the soul with an instrument to ward off the "lawlessness and license [*para-nomia*]"[138] to which the appetites are prone. Education unto habit trains the honor-loving part of the soul. Education makes it *noble*.

Construed under the guise of habituation, the education about which Socrates speaks here is akin to the education about which Aristotle writes in the *Nicomachean Ethics*.[139] Noble patterns must be given so that noble natures are produced. Imitation (*mimēsis*) of a certain sort is necessary—especially in the realm of music and poetry,[140] those "arts that imitate."[141] When the patterns given to the young by the city are taken up and reproduced within their souls, lawlessness is averted from within, so to speak, and the laws of the city are not burdened with a task they cannot by themselves accomplish.[142]

> There is no need, said Adeimantus, to impose laws about these matters on good men. They will find out soon enough for themselves what kinds of administrative regulations are necessary. Yes, my friend, if only god helps them to preserve the laws we have already given them. It's true. *Without god's help they will go on making and mending both their laws and their lives in search of perfection.* You make them sound like sick men who will not leave off their intemperate habits. What a charming life they have: always doctoring themselves with the results that their ailments multiply and worsen. Then if anyone comes along peddling some nostrum, they are convinced it will cure them.[143]

---

[138] Plato, *Republic*, Book IV, 424d.

[139] See Aristotle, Nicomachean *Ethics*, book II, 1103a34–b6, cited in Introduction, note 19.

[140] Plato, *Republic*, Book IV, 424c–d.

[141] Plato, *Republic*, Book X, 601d.

[142] See Judge Learned Hand, *The Spirit of Liberty*, ed. Irving Dillard (New York: Alfred A. Knopf, 1960), pp. 189–90: "I often wonder whether we do not rest our hopes too much on constitutions, upon laws and upon courts. These are false hopes; believe me, these are false hopes. Liberty lies in the hearts of men and women; when it dies there, no constitution, no law, no court can save it; no constitutions, no law, no court can even do much to help it. While it lies there it needs no constitution, no law, no court to save it." Consider also Socrates' discussion of the just man in the *Republic*, at Book VIII, 549d: "He will not fight for money in private lawsuits nor brawl about it in public assembly" because he knows that law, which purports to distinguish between "mine" and "thine," offers no remedy for a soul that is disordered.

[143] Plato, *Republic*, Book IV, 425e–426a (emphasis added).

Nobly educated men, it would seem, know how to "render each its due," and so do not need law to make distinctions between "mine and thine."[144] Without such an education, laws will be enacted that constantly adjust the boundaries between "mine and thine." Yet these alone can never bring the soul unto health.[145] Legal adjustments alone are like bad doctoring: The poisons they administer to sick souls only make "ailments multiply and worsen." Law can have a sort of medicinal power,[146] to be sure, but only in souls that are *already* well formed. The burden of education, it seems, is habituation unto noble patterns.

What is remarkable about Socrates' lengthy discussion of this education— let us call it "mortal education"—is that its guiding thought, that noble patterns produce noble men, is adopted by his interlocutors without question. Indeed, the chilling project of censorship in the *Republic* is predicated on this assumption that education is about the bequeathing of patterns to children, which they then take in upon themselves as their own. Souls ruled by the love of honor may believe this, but there is reason to suspect that here, amid all this talk of the censorship of bad patterns, Socrates is attempting to alert his interlocutors that mortal education does not quite capture what he has in mind when he speaks of education.

---

[144] Worth pondering are the many legal metaphors that are found at the outset of the *Republic*, Book V (450d–451b). The discussion about the distinction between men and women that follows (451c–457b) seems to have the same intention as does the law, *viz.*, to make distinctions. Socrates there suggests that the confusion over the relationship between the sexes stems from not knowing the relevant distinctions: "They imagine they are reasoning together when, in fact, they are only picking quarrels. This happens because they are unable to define the issues being considered nor are they able to analyze it into its logical components. So instead of engaging in dialectic, they merely engage in debate" (454a). Dialectic relies on the standard of reason, which is Greek (452c–d), not the barbarian standard that forever draws its lines of distinction in the wrong place—and so laughs at women who exercise naked (457a). "[A]ny man who laughs at [the standard provided by reason]," he says, "does not know what he ridicules nor where his laughter leads" (457b). Prior to Book V, law is understood as a noble pattern given to the children *by the city*; in Book V we begin to move to the higher standard of reason itself.

[145] See Plato, *Republic*, Book IV, 426e: "[Those] who go on making and amending laws. . . . don't see that they are simply cutting of the Hydra's heads." See also *Republic*, Book IX, 588c. Cf. Tocqueville, *Democracy in America*, vol. I, part II, ch. 8, p. 270: "There is hardly a political question in the United States which does not sooner or later become a judicial one." Note, however, that Tocqueville did not think that this development was necessarily a bad one, since the involvement of citizens in the jury system served the purpose of drawing them out of their narrow, isolated worlds.

[146] See Plato, *Republic*, Book V, 459c–d: "[T]he rulers will probably have to resort to frequent doses of lies and mystifications [*tō pseudei kai tē apatē*] for the benefit of their subjects."

If education is mimetic, for example, what are we to make of the reference in the passage recently cited to the need for god's help? A god's intervention, as Augustine later reminds us,[147] is made necessary precisely because mimesis—the entire imitative complex of habit—is *not* enough to assure human health. Socrates is not compelled, as Augustine is, to attribute the defect of mimesis to sin.[148] There is, nevertheless, a profound insufficiency about habit, and in this respect, perhaps, he departs significantly from Aristotle.

Much of what follows in the two subsequent sections below is an attempt to specify the distance between mortal education and the sort of education that is considered later in the *Republic*, which involves a mysterious "turn" that no merely mortal education can accomplish. By way of preparation, let me provide some preliminary evidence that this first, mortal education points beyond itself.

Consider a passage from the Allegory of the Cave, in which Socrates contrasts those professors who claim that

> they can *transplant* [entithenai] the power of knowledge into a soul that has none, as if they were engrafting vision into blind eyes,[149]

with an alternative:

> this power is already in the soul of each. The way each of us learns compares with what happens to the eye: it cannot be turned away from darkness to face the light without turning the whole body. So it is with our capacity to know; together with the entire soul one must turn away from the world of transient things toward the world of perpetual being.[150]

This "world of perpetual being [*to on*]," Socrates says elsewhere, is illuminated by the Good, which offers the light by which reason receives vision.[151] True education involves this mysterious illumination, that third

---

[147] See Augustine, *Confessions*, book VII, ch. v, pp. 140–41: "The consequence of [sin] is passion. By servitude to passion, habit is formed, and habit to which there is no resistance becomes necessity.... The law of sin is the violence of habit by which even the unwilling mind is dragged down and held.... 'Wretched man that I was, who would deliver me from this body of death other than your grace through Jesus Christ our Lord' (Rom. 7:24–25)." Worth pondering, as well, are Heidegger's near-final words: "[O]nly a God can save us" (Martin Heidegger, "Nur Ein Gott Kann Uns Retten," in *Der Speigel* 30, no. 23 [May 31, 1976]: 209).

[148] See Plato, *Republic*, Book X, 602d.

[149] Plato, *Republic*, Book VII, 518b–c (emphasis added). See also Plato, *Protagoras*, trans. Stanley Lombardo and Karen Bell, in *Plato: Complete Works*, 320d–329d, where Protagoras argues that education involves teaching and that he is worth the fee that he charges (ibid., 328b).

[150] Plato, *Republic*, Book VII, 518c. Cf. Plato, *Protagoras*, 319b: "The truth is, Protagoras, I have never thought that this could be taught."

[151] Plato, *Republic*, Book VI, 507e–509a.

thing that stands between the knower and the known, and which gives the gift of light.

> When the soul beholds the realm illuminated by the splendor of truth and reality, it knows and understands and so appears to possess reason. But when it turns its gaze to that region where darkness and light intermingle, to the transient world [*to gignomenon te kai apollumenon*] where all things are either quickening or dying, reason's edge is blunted.[152]

The illumination that the Good gives is not to be confused with mortal education, which habituates unto noble patterns. Wisdom, Socrates says, "[cannot] be cultivated by exercise and habit, [for] the ability to think is more divine [*mallon theioterou*]."[153] Mortal education produces nobility; philosophic education is something grander still.

The interlocutors, of course, seem quite content to rest with this mortal education, which apparently stands in no need of the divine. Yet Socrates indicates that even with respect to mortal education, there are divine causes involved:

> It seems to me that some god [*tina theon*] conveyed to men the two arts of music and gymnastics, one to instruct a man in his quest for knowledge and the one to tutor his high spirits. These arts pertain to the categories of body and soul only indirectly; they have to do first of all with philosophy and spirit and with the ebb and flow of tension and relaxation that brings about their harmonious adjustment.[154]

Even the education unto music and gymnastics, then, whose purpose it is to form character in a certain way through habituation unto right patterns, is a gift of the gods. Mortal education is not so mortal after all. Even in this education that is but an overture to justice, we are being guided by things divine, as Socrates later seems to suggest:

> Then [we must conclude that] justice is nothing else than the power that brings forth well-governed men and well-governed cities. [Finished, then, and brought to completion is our dream.] We have made real what we only surmised at the outset of our inquiry when we suspected that *some divine power [theon tina]* was drawing our attention to a basic pattern of justice.[155]

In the early stages of education, when immersed in the darkness of appetitive transgression, when still far from the illuminating homeland of the soul "[whose] prototype can be found somewhere in heaven for him

---

152 Ibid., 508d.
153 Plato, *Republic*, Book VII, 518d–e.
154 Plato, *Republic*, Book III, 411e (emphasis added).
155 Plato, *Republic*, Book IV, 443b–c (emphasis added).

who wants to see,"[156] the mortal education that draws the soul on toward things divine *appears* not to be a gift. Until we are more fully drawn upward toward the light, the dimness of our vision precludes us from seeing that the Good lights our way *even in the darkness of (early) mimetic education*. In darkness, we are unable to recognize the gifts that descend from above. In that sleepy, poisoned, and drunken condition[157] in which the prisoners find themselves, *could* Socrates really do anything else other than cautiously intimate what the nature of real education is: a divine rather than mortal pattern that is a gift from above? Only eyes habituated to the light of the Good could see the truth of the matter. His interlocutors, however, are still nearly blind.

From the City to the Soul

Having assayed the rough feature of the terrain ahead, let us resume the quest for justice in the city of appetitive transgression that has been founded, which is now ruled by guardians nobly educated. Next, Socrates says,

> [we] must find something that will illuminate the city. The light must be clear and strong so that we may discover where justice and injustice are located. We must be able to see what is the difference between them.[158]

Light, the very watchword for knowledge in the *Republic*, is now needed to illuminate—and then set aside—wisdom, courage, and temperance.[159] These, it turns out, are not our quarry, notwithstanding that justice is "the ultimate cause and condition of their existence."[160] We are, however, close to catching our prey.

> The fourth and final quarry is justice. But here we must take care that it does not elude us. We must be like hunters who surround a thicket to make sure that the quarry doesn't escape. Justice is somewhere hereabouts. Look sharp, and call me if you see it first.
>
> I wish I could. But I am only your follower, with sight just keen enough to see what you show me.
>
> *Well, say a prayer and follow me.*

---

[156] Plato, *Republic*, Book IX, 592b.

[157] Recall Plato, *Republic*, Book IV, 426b: "They do not want to hear that nothing can help them—nor drugs, nor surgery, nor amulets, nor incantations, nor anything else—until they give up idling, gluttony, wenching, and drunkenness."

[158] Plato, *Republic*, Book IV, 427d (emphasis added).

[159] Ibid., 427e–432a.

[160] Ibid., 433b–c.

Show me the way.

[It seems an inaccessible and dark place.] We will have a hard time flushing out the quarry. Still we must push on. . . . There, I see something Glaucon![161]

What Socrates sees, as I have just said, is that justice is the "cause and condition" of wisdom, courage, and temperance. Justice, moreover, "sustains and perfects" them.[162] Whatever Socrates wishes to convey by this formulation seems lost on Glaucon, at least for the moment. His vision is yet too dim to see. Nevertheless, the city that has been founded has served its purpose: to cast light enough, not that we may "look in the distance" at the city, but rather that we may see "what [is] already in [our] grasp."[163] Might justice truly be seen, Socrates asks shortly afterward with apparent innocence, not in the city, but rather in the soul?

> Now that we have wisdom, courage, temperance, and justice fairly before us, it would be hard to decide which of the four virtues effectually contributes most to the excellence of the city. Is it the harmony existing between rulers and subjects? Or is it the soldier's fidelity to what he has learned about real and fictitious dangers? Or is wisdom and watchfulness in the rulers? *Or finally, is it the virtue that is found in everyone*—children, women, slaves and freemen, craftsmen, rulers, and subjects—which leads them each to do his own work and not to interfere with others?[164]

Glaucon listens to Socrates' intimation, but seems neither to want to move in this direction nor to be able to see clearly at what Socrates is pointing. His vision is still set on things far away, on the "city," rather than on what is close at hand, *viz.*, his own soul—the grounds for an adequate treatment of which have now been provided through Socrates' discussion of the more brightly illuminated city and its parts. Glaucon accedes to Socrates' shift in focus from the city to the soul without really understanding its significance, as any number of his subsequent remarks betray.[165] Here and elsewhere, the scandalous complicity of Socrates' interlocutors in

---

[161] Ibid., 432b–d (emphasis added).

[162] Ibid., 433c.

[163] Ibid., 432e.

[164] Ibid., 433c–d (emphasis added). See also *Republic*, Book IX, 591c, where Socrates reproaches the laboring man "only if the best in him is so weak that he cannot govern the beasts within himself."

[165] Plato, *Republic*, Book V, 450b–c. The opening remarks of Book V, for example, are more clearly a commentary on Adeimantus, Polemarchus, and Thrasymachus than on Glaucon; yet Glaucon, too, does seem to understand that at the conclusion of Book IV, *the city is no longer the object of our quest*. Their collective inability to see what Socrates is showing them close at hand, moreover, is significant in light of the first two of the "three waves" in Book V (451c–473b). Any interpretation of what is said there must take cognizance of this

the *Republic* is belied by subtle yet pervasive, though not wholly debilitating, misunderstandings that go unmentioned.

Let us reiterate where we really are: Having now found the light that may guide the discussion toward an understanding of the soul, *the larger city may now be set aside.*

> We used the city as our larger measure. We founded the best city we could because we were confident that in a good city we would find justice. Now let us apply our findings to the individual.[166]

While the final, breathtaking, pronouncement about where this new path leads comes much later,[167] should we have eyes that can see, the light that guides the discussion now is cast in a new direction, toward the soul itself.

> But the early model was analogy, not reality. The reality is that justice is not a matter of external behavior, but the way a man privately and truly governs his inner self [*peri heauton kai ta heautou*].[168]

A discussion of the ironic "minor question [*phaulon skemma*]"[169] of whether the soul has the same divisions that were discovered during the hunt for justice in the city cannot detain us here.[170] The argument in its defense is less my concern than is the significance of the change of focus from the city to the soul, from politics of the seemingly more overt sort

---

misunderstanding on their part and be attentive to the fact that Socrates must labor in order to advance the quest toward the Good *through* that very misunderstanding.

[166] Plato, *Republic*, Book IV, 434e.

[167] See Plato, *Republic*, Book IX, 592a–b: "I understand [said Glaucon]. You mean [the just man] would only take part in the politics of the city we have founded and built with our words. For I don't believe it can be found anywhere on earth. It makes no difference whether such a city now exists or ever will [said Socrates]. But perhaps its prototype can be found somewhere in heaven for him who wants to see. Seeing it, he will declare himself its citizen. The politics of this city would be his politics and none other."

[168] Plato, *Republic*, Book IV, 443c–d.

[169] Ibid., 435c.

[170] See ibid., 435e: "Indeed, it is obvious that the individual transmits [its own divisions] to the city." Eric Voegelin is, I think, largely right when he says: "[For Plato, a] political society in existence will have to be an ordered cosmion, but not at the price of man; it should be not only a microcosmos, but also a macroanthropos" (*The New Science of Politics* [Chicago: University of Chicago Press, 1952], ch. II, sec. 4, p. 61). Moreover, he recognizes that the philosopher forms the true type, by which all other corrupt types are measured (p. 63). Voegelin's emphasis on the experience of the philosopher, however, subtly shifts attention away from the Good that illuminates to the philosopher for whom "[t]he truth of the soul [is] achieved through it loving orientation toward the sophon" (p. 63). The focus on experience and its articulations, in a word, supposes not that the Good gives itself to the philosopher, but rather that the hunt for the Good can be comprehended

to the politics of the soul, which comes into view only when our capacity to see is made more acute. The source of this light is my concern here, for only by such light can we truly understand the nature and prerequisite of justice in the fullest sense.

The Philosopher

[We have now reached] the point where we may see truth clearly with our own eyes. We are close to proving our conclusions, and this is no time to slow up.

Certainly not.

Come up here, Glaucon, and observe all the forms of evil—or, at least, the forms worth considering.[171]

So ends Book IV. Socrates implores Glaucon to "come up" to where he may see clearly—a conspicuous allusion to the world beyond the Cave, where the Good may be finally seen illuminating all that is and all that becomes. The "forms [of evil] worth considering," we learn in the course of Book VIII, are the corruptions of timocracy, oligarchy, democracy, and tyranny (a treatment of which will be provided in the section "The Decline toward Tyranny," below). That discussion, however, is deferred, and for reasons that by now should be apparent: Without illumination from the Good, the respect in which they *are* corruptions cannot be seen. A human being, Socrates says, looks like one rather than many "to anyone who looks only at the surface and is not able to see beneath [*ta entos*]."[172] Disabling divisions, of which abject injustice is the supreme example, are visible only to the philosopher who is illuminated by the Good; the rest are charmed by surface appearances. The vantage reached by Socrates is too high, and too bright, for his interlocutors to bear.

The hunt continues, then, for the Good, whose light illuminates the pattern with which we must conform if we wish to "render each its due."[173] Now, however, the hunt recommences at lower elevation.

---

through the significations that the experience of the philosopher articulates. If the Good gives itself—as a gift—then the *Republic* cannot be understood to articulate a macroanthropos, as Voegelin suggests. Through the gift alone is the true type, the philosopher, possible.

[171] Plato, *Republic*, Book IV, 445b–c (emphasis added).

[172] Plato, *Republic*, Book IX, 588e.

[173] Earlier I considered Socrates' intimation that education is habituation unto patterns whose origins are divine. In Book V, as a prolegomenon to his discussion of the philosopher, Socrates again reminds Glaucon about patterns that must be followed: "[In our discussion]

The first "two waves" of Book V, seemingly concerned with the respects in which men and women are the same and different, and with the meaning of having-in-common, I shall pass over with little comment, except to note the enormity of Socrates' task in light of Glaucon's failure (along with that of the others) to be brought up to the place where the Good can be seen and the corruptions of city and soul adequately understood. He must therefore draw his interlocutors *beyond* their misunderstanding while remaining *within* their misunderstanding.[174] The "two waves" are about more than they seem.[175]

The more urgent matter to consider is the 'third wave,' that almost impossible-possibility of philosophic rule:

> Unless philosophers become kings in our cities, or unless those who now are kings and rulers become true philosophers, so that political power and

---

we were looking for ideals and patterns of instruction. We wanted to bring them into focus as models so that we might judge our own happiness or unhappiness according to the standards they set and according to the degree we reflect them" (Plato, *Republic*, Book V, 472c). In Book VI, in the preamble to Socrates' discussion of the Good, he also speaks of patterns: "Is there any discernible difference between those who lack knowledge of the true essence of things and those who are physically blind? I mean those whose souls are void of any clear pattern?" (*Republic*, Book VI, 484c). Socrates' final observation about patterns occurs, of course, at Book IX, 592a–b, when he alludes to "the divine pattern set up in the heavens."

[174] Perhaps the most prominent instance of this general formula is Glaucon's misunderstanding of the justice of the first city that Socrates invokes (Plato, *Republic*, Book II, 372b–e). Had he been content with Socrates' initial account, the ascent toward justice would have been halted.

[175] A few comments about the "first wave" have been made already at note 144 above. The "second wave," like the first, ends with allusions to the difference between Greek and barbarian. (The conclusion of the "first wave," recall, is that dialectic must rely on the standard of reason, which is Greek [Book V, 452c–d], and not the barbarian standard that forever draws its lines of distinction in the wrong place. Only through reason can lines be drawn in the right place.) The "second wave" ends [ibid., 469b–471b] with the claim that relations between Greek and Greek ought to be termed faction rather than war (ibid., 470b). "War [*polemos*]," Socrates says, "is the proper name for enmity and hatred" (ibid., 470c). And since "Greek" is synonymous with "reason," we may conclude that war is caused when reason does not rule. "The city being founded," Socrates says, "will be a Greek city, will it not?" (ibid., 470e). The first "two waves" speak to the need for reason to rule, in imagery appropriate to those who do not yet see. Something must be said, as well, about that portion of the "second wave" that suggests that children should not know their parents—that they should be, in effect, orphans (ibid., 461d). At this place the suggestion seems almost bizarre; yet later, when Socrates speaks about the dialectic (Book VII, 537c–540a), he says that its practitioner discovers that "he is not the child of those who call themselves his parents" (ibid., 538a). The practice of dialectic reveals that parents do not, in the truest sense, beget their children; parents are not the final generative source to which the child is beholden. The dialectic leads children "to turn upward the vision of their souls and fix their gaze on that which sheds light on all" (ibid., 540a). They discover then that the Good is the real source of their generation.

philosophic intelligence converge, and unless those lesser natures who run after one without the other are excluded from governing, I believe there can be no end to troubles, my dear Glaucon, in our cities or for all mankind.[176]

To begin with, Socrates' suggestion that this will be opposed by "those who are not common"[177] is ironic. Such self-professed uncommon men nevertheless suffer from dim vision; they are adept only at identifying the passing shadows—as we learn later from the Allegory of the Cave.[178] Like their counterparts from the Cave, they "will snatch the first handy tool [and] rush at you full tilt, fully prepared to do dreadful deeds,"[179] if they are told that philosophy, not their sophisticated opinions, is what is most needed.

The problem, however, is not merely their dim vision, but also the likelihood that their sort of education will prevail. Darkness begets darkness; it constitutes a world in its own image. The dim prospect that a philosopher can come into being at all in the city is the most striking feature of Socrates' first extended discussion of philosophy.

To be sure, this nearly impossible-possibility seems to warrant the view that the citadel of philosophy must be protected from trespass by the vulgar multitude[180] or from violation by the sophisticated few.[181] Without further qualification, however, this insight remains incomplete, not to say self-congratulatory. Above all, it does not comprehend the problem of misunderstanding, as I have called it, with which the philosopher is faced, and tends to adopt a posture of nobility whose roots are more to be found in Nietzsche's contempt for the Last Man[182] than in

[176] Plato, *Republic*, Book V, 473c–d. Socrates' claim here was anticipated in his earlier discussion with Thrasymachus (Book I, 351b–352a).

[177] Plato, *Republic*, Book V, 473e. Sterling and Scott have "[the] leading men of learning," which is hardly literal, but captures Socrates' dubiety about the professed "uncommon man." I rely on Sterling and Scott's rendition hereafter.

[178] See Plato, *Republic*, Book VII, 516c: "Suppose prizes were offered for the one quickest to identify the shadows as they go by and best able to remember the sequence and configurations in which they appear. All these skills, in turn, would enhance the ability to guess what would come next. . . . Do you think [one illuminated by the Good] would covet such rewards?"

[179] Plato, *Republic*, Book V, 474a. Cf. *Republic*, Book VII, 517a: "Further, if anyone tried to release the prisoners and lead them up and they could get their hands on him and kill him, would they not kill him?"

[180] See Plato, *Republic*, Book VI, 489b: "It follows that philosophy—the love of wisdom—is impossible for the multitude."

[181] Consider here the suitor (ibid., 495b–496a) who would wish to marry philosophy, but who is unworthy.

[182] See Friedrich Nietzsche, *Thus Spoke Zarathustra*, trans. Walter Kaufman (New York: Penguin, 1968), Prologue, sec. 5, p. 17: "Behold, I show you the last man. 'What is love?

Socrates' gentle and forgiving urgency. *The truth protects itself*; it needs no assistance from the noble soul. Enlightened, philosophical knowledge does not yield contempt for others—no matter how "dim" the others may be; for the light that lights reason's way is not man's to possess. A condescending establishment of distance between the noble few and the multitude, the self-satisfaction in virtue of one's own pretended nobility, is not warranted.[183] Let us concede that "[the philosophers'] greater knowledge is itself the warrant of their excellence."[184] Nevertheless, true nobility is granted as a gift, not possessed as a mark of distinction. Socrates had already made this clear in Book II, much earlier.

> If there is a convincing rebuttal to these arguments [defending injustice], it could come only from a man with enough trust in the superiority of justice to be gentle with the unjust. He will not be angry, for he knows that a man can lead a just life only if [*by his divine nature he is unable to endure injustice*]. Or else, a person is won to justice through the attainment of wisdom. No others are willingly just.[185]

In his account of philosophy Socrates is concerned not with how to elevate nobility above the lower defective types, but rather with whether the sort of education offered by the sophists, which purports to *pass on* wisdom, will prevail. In this regard, not only the so-called uncommon man, but also the multitude, the "chief sophist [*megistous sophistas*],"[186] oppose him. Crediting themselves with the capacity to educate, their conjoined influence is confined to the conveyance of images. The pattern they seek to establish in the souls of the young bears only a shadowy resemblance to the pattern that must be set up in the philosopher's soul—yet they claim that the patterns they impute are all that is needed.

These professed educators, however, do not educate. Rather, they opine, in that domain "whose light is less than knowledge but brighter

---

What is creation? What is longing? What is a star?' thus asks the last man, and he blinks. The earth has become small, and on it hops the last man, who makes everything small."

[183] The typology of Book VIII suggests that notwithstanding its superiority over the oligarchic and democratic type to which Nietzsche is so averse, the timocratic, honor-loving, noble man is not the highest type. Higher than honor is reason, which achieves its power to rule only when illuminated by the light of the Good. Absent such rule, neither honor nor wealth can find their rightful place. Without the Good, honor is not honorable (the timocratic failing), wealth is not profitable (the oligarchic failing), and freedom is not liberating (the democratic failure).

[184] Plato, *Republic*, Book VI, 484d.

[185] Plato, *Republic*, Book II, 366c–d (emphasis added). Sterling and Scott have the somewhat cumbersome "if the divine in human nature has consecrated in him a hatred of injustice."

[186] Plato, *Republic*, Book VI, 492b.

than ignorance."[187] Bereft of the light that the Good gives, they wander amid the shadows and proudly adjudicate over the domain of things that are shifting and relative, over things that never unequivocally *are* what a faulty power of discernment makes them out to be. So situated in the realm of opinion (*doxa*),[188] they proclaim that truth is *relative*. And so they should, since without the true measure, without the divine pattern, any claim to the contrary would be pretense or fancy. Without the divine measure, the dye taken in by the soul,[189] the pattern to which it conforms mimetically, will never bear anything more than a shadowy resemblance to the real measure.

> If a man doesn't know how to measure and is told by a crowd equally ignorant that he is six feet tall, how can you expect him not to believe it?[190]

Opinion can reproduce itself, but it cannot produce knowledge any more than vice can generate virtue.[191] All that is good is dependent on the Good alone.[192]

The amazing fact about the early education, we are now able to understand, is that despite Socrates' steadfast insistence that evil patterns be censored and that children be exposed only to good patterns, this noble aspiration cannot solve the problem for which education is needed. Only the Good gives the right pattern.[193] Mortal education, the education of both the public and private sophist, "[reproduces] in [its] own image men and women, young and old."[194]

---

[187] Plato, *Republic*, Book V, 478c.

[188] See Plato, *Republic*, Book VI, 508d: "[In the region] where darkness and light intermingle . . . the soul becomes mired in opinion; and since opinion shifts from one direction to another, it appears that reason has vanished."

[189] Plato, *Republic*, Book IV, 429e–430b.

[190] Ibid., 426e.

[191] See Plato, *Republic*, Book III, 409d: "For vice will never understand virtue nor, for that matter, will it understand itself. But virtuous nature, having become educated over time, will ultimately be able to understand itself and vice as well."

[192] See ibid., 379c: "The good we receive we must attribute to God alone; for the causes of evil we must look elsewhere." See also *Republic*, Book X, 617e: "The gods will not choose a spirit to guide you; you shall choose that spirit yourself. He whose lot bids him choose first must, like all souls, select a life to which he will be bound by necessity. Yet virtue is not bound by any master, so that each will possess as much virtue or as little as he does honor her. The blame belongs to him that chooses. God is blameless [*anaitios*]."

[193] See Plato, *Republic*, Book VII, 540a: "[A]nd when they have beheld the Good itself they shall use it as a pattern for the right ordering of the state and the citizens throughout the remainder of their lives."

[194] Plato, *Republic*, Book VI, 492b. See also Calvin, *Institutes*, vol. I, book I, ch. VI, sec. 3, p. 73: "For errors can never be uprooted from human hearts until true knowledge of God is planted therein." In a subsequent passage he says that only God can plant such true knowledge (see ibid., ch. VII, sec. 4, p. 80: "[U]ntil [God] illuminates their minds, they ever

There is, then, a need for something more than mere mortal education if there is to be philosophical knowledge.[195] The patterns established by mortal education—no matter how "good"—are still only a facsimile of what is needed. Transposed, for a moment, into a comparable theological idiom, it may be said that: "God himself is [alone] the sole and proper witness of himself."[196] Transposed back into Plato's fable: the Good *gives itself* as the only adequate measure *of* itself.[197]

At this point in our ascent, where our eyes are unable as yet to endure the brightness of the Good,[198] Socrates instead directs our attention to the slightly less brilliant but still unchanging world that is begotten and illuminated by the Good,[199] for the purpose of disclosing something about the task of philosophy, and its impossibility by mortal means.

> Need I remind you—or do you remember—that we said if a man loves something, he ought to love all of it? It will not do for him to say that some of it he likes and some not. . . . As a lover you should know how everyone in the flower of youth somehow stirs and arouses emotion in the lover's breast, and all appear desirable and worthy of his attentions. Is that not how you respond to the fair? . . . In short, you will employ any pretense and any fair word rather than risk losing a single one of the young flowers.[200]

The illustration Socrates gives seems innocuous enough. Leaving aside for a time the uncanny resemblance of this passage to a later one wherein Socrates describes the tyrant,[201] what is being suggested here is that the philosopher is illuminated by the reality of Beauty and not charmed by its

---

waver among many doubts"). This knowledge is akin to the unmediated knowledge about which Socrates speaks (*Republic*, Book V, 476d).

[195] It is worth noting here that in the Myth of Er, at the end of the *Republic*, the first (dead) man that is forced to chose a life into which he will be subsequently born chooses the life of tyranny, because in his former life he had practiced "virtue by habit, without philosophy" (*Republic*, Book X, 619c–d).

[196] See Calvin, *Institutes*, vol. I, part I, ch. XI, sec. 1, p. 100.

[197] In Christianity, the symbol of the virgin birth conveys a kindred insight: God the Son comes *into* the world, but is not *from* the world. In the terms of Plato's fable, the divine "pattern" could not have come into the world if it relied only on mortal genesis, for such genesis can only reproduce its own "impurity." See Isaiah 7:14; Matt. 1:23. See also Job 25:4 ("Who, born of a woman, would be pure?").

[198] Recall that prior to being illuminated by the Good, the released prisoner can endure only the sight of the Forms, which owe their existence to the Good. See Plato, *Republic*, Book VII, 516a–b.

[199] Plato, *Republic*, Book VI, 509b.

[200] Plato, *Republic*, Book V, 474d–475a.

[201] Plato, *Republic*, Book IX, 574b–c.

partial manifestations. These latter come into being and pass away. To truly love the whole is not to love the many different and partial instantiations that are beautiful, but rather to love Beauty itself.[202] The "whole" pertains to unity, not multiplicity. Those who behold only multiplicity, he says, "wander about inspecting swarms of irrelevancies."[203]

The mortal dilemma, however, is that these irrelevancies do not appear to be irrelevant to the soul lost in the domain of images and opinion. The irrelevancies appear to be useful; and, as a corollary, what turns out to be truly useful appears to be useless.[204] To illuminate the situation, as we might expect, Socrates recurs to a parable.

> Let us imagine, then, a set of events happening aboard many ships or even only one ship. Imagine first the captain. He is taller and stronger than any of the crew. At the same time, he is a little deaf and somewhat shortsighted. Further his navigational skills are about on par with his hearing and his vision. The sailors are quarreling with each other about who should take the helm. . . . Then, after fettering the worthy shipmaster and putting him into a stupor with narcotic or drink, they take command of the ship. Feasting and drinking, they consume the ship's stores and make a voyage of it as might be expected from such a crew. Further, they will use such terms as master mariner, navigator, and pilot to flatter the man who has the most cunning in persuading or forcing the captain to turn over control of the ship. The man who is innocent of such skills they will call useless. . . . With such activities going on would it surprise you if the sailors running the ship would call the true captain [a stargazer, and idle talker, and useless]?[205]

[202] The first instance of misunderstanding this distinction is evinced by Thrasymachus, early in the *Republic*. "Those who are unjust," he says, "will get it all, and the just will get nothing" (Book I, 343e). "Getting it all," he opines, pertains to the world of things. Sterling and Scott perhaps stretch the meaning here, since the Greek word, *pleonexia*, refers to moral vice or overreaching. Nevertheless, the magnitude of the overreaching in the case of tyrant seems to justify the use of the term "getting it all."

[203] Plato, *Republic*, Book VI, 484b. Literally, "many and of all sorts of kinds of things" (*pollois kai patoiōs*). Translating this as "swarms of irrelevancies" seems justified not only by the narrative context, but also by virtue of standing throughout Plato's fable of the objects that inhabit the world of coming-into-being-and-passing-away.

[204] A new light is now cast on Socrates' earlier remark: "Could we find tools that would teach their own use, we should have discovered something truly beyond price" (*Republic*, Book II, 374d). Philosophical knowledge, it turns out, cannot be taught, and does "teach its own use." That is, philosophical knowledge confirms itself. This kind of knowledge, Socrates points out—in a manner consistent with his rejection of earthly gold—is "truly beyond price." Cf. Ralph Waldo Emerson, "Self Reliance," in *Essays and Lectures* (New York: Library of America, 1983), pp. 278–79: "[O]f the adopted talent of another, you have only an extemporaneous, half possession. That which each can do best, none but his Maker can teach him."

[205] Plato, *Republic*, Book VI, 488a–e.

The philosopher (captain), in "being somewhat short-sighted [*horōnta hōsautōs brachu*]," sees differently from the rest and has a different understanding of what is useful. What is useful differs in accordance with the extent to which vision—and, hence, knowledge—is truly present. The sailors who understand usefulness in the wrong way, and who are not oriented by "the pattern set up in the heavens,"[206] will seek to poison the ship captain, to make him, as Adeimantus says, "an eternal drunk."[207] Those who already slumber wish to narcotize the wakeful one, to transport his soul to "Hades," where the soul languishes eternally in stupor.[208] The drunken man sees little that is useful in what the sober man knows and does, and so puts sobriety to sleep. The antithesis of the philosopher, he is content with the mortal patterns he inherits or with none at all, and has no wish to discover the divine pattern that is the corrective. He wants to possess honor, things, freedom, or power; finds talk of the unchanging world useless; and is satisfied remaining a stupefied sailor on a ship destined to founder. From this drunken, mortal, point of view, which is self-satisfied, philosophy is impossible. Philosophy is useless, mortally speaking.

So let us concede in earnest that what is necessary for philosophy to see the light of day is more than mortal education can provide.[209] What, then, are we to make of the following remark?

> But if sowing, planting, and germination [of philosophy] take place in the wrong environment, the contrary outcome must be anticipated—*unless some god comes to the rescue [ean mē tis autē boēthēsas theōn tuchē]*.[210]

And let us also consider this:

---

[206] Plato, *Republic*, Book IX, 592b.

[207] Plato, *Republic*, Book II, 363d.

[208] Several remarks by Socrates suggest that the awakening of the soul from its drunken slumber is an upward ascent from Hades. The man who is drunk, it seems, "has no idea where he is" (*Republic*, Book III, 403e); the Myth of the Metals suggests that "all the training and education [the guardians] received from us was actually products of their own imagination, just the way it is with a dream. In reality, they were the whole time deep within the earth being given form and feature" (ibid., 413d); and when Socrates introduces the dialectic, he asks, "Should we then proceed to consider how such men might be produced and led upward to the light in the same way that some men are said to have ascended from Hades to the halls of the gods?" (*Republic*, Book VII, 521c).

[209] See Ralph Waldo Emerson, "An Address to the Senior Class in Divinity College," in *Selected Essays*, pp. 88–89: "Let me admonish you, first of all, to go alone; to refuse the good models, even those which are sacred in the imaginations of men, and dare to love God without mediator or veil. . . . *Imitation cannot go above its model*. The imitator dooms himself to hopeless mediocrity" (emphasis added).

[210] Plato, *Republic*, Book VI, 492a (emphasis added).

Sure it is in the present state of society and government that if anything can be saved and turned to the good *you will not be off the mark by attributing it to god's providence.*[211]

Adeimantus, unfortunately, does not seem to understand the import of what Socrates has just said, as his subsequent question clearly indicates.

I would like to know [Socrates] *which* of our current governments you think are suitable to philosophy.[212]

Like his brother Glaucon, who sees only the multiplicity of things, Adeimantus wonders *which* "mortal city," to coin a phrase, can best nurture the divine in man. What mortal measure, Adeimantus wonders, can be used. Socrates answers:

Not a single one of today's cities could accommodate the philosophical na- ture. This is precisely why such a nature is perverted and distorted: just as foreign seed sown in alien soil tends to lose its identity and yield place to the native growth, so the philosophic nature does not preserve its own qual- ity but degenerates into a deviant type.[213]

No mortal thing can fully accommodate what is divine; its brilliance cannot be borne by impure eyes.[214] Said otherwise, nature cannot com- prehend spirit.[215] Those enchained in the Cave below cannot comprehend the light that illuminates both the Real World and the translucent events that materialize where they dwell. It is rather the other way around: Only those who have been illuminated by the light of the Good can see what is Real and what is illusory. Only by the light of the Good does the

---

[211] Ibid., 492e–493a (emphasis added).

[212] Ibid., VI, 497a.

[213] Ibid., VI, 497b (emphasis added).

[214] See Exod. 19:21 ("And the Lord said to Moses, Go down, charge the people, lest they break through unto the Lord to gaze, and many of them perish"); Job 14:4 ("Who can bring a clean thing out of an unclean? Not one").

[215] See John 3:6 ("That which is born of the flesh is flesh; and that which is born of the Spirit is spirit"). See Romans 8:5 ("For they that are after the flesh do mind the things of the flesh; but they that are after the Spirit the things of the Spirit"); 1 Cor. 3:18 ("If any man among you seemeth to be wise in this world, let him become a fool, that he may be wise"). See Martin Luther, "The Freedom of a Christian," in *Luther's Works*, vol. 31, p. 363, where "nature of itself cannot drive out [faith] or even recognize it." See Calvin, *Institutes*, vol. I, ch. VII, sec. 5, p. 81: "[O]nly those to whom it is given can comprehend the mysteries of God." See Hegel, "The Spirit of Christianity and Its Fate," in *Early Theo- logical Writings*, sec. iv, p. 255: "[O]nly spirit grasps and comprehends spirit." See also Matt. 9:17; Mark 2:22, on the impossibility of putting new wine in old bottles; and 1 Cor. 2:11 ("For what man knoweth the things of man, save the spirit of man which is in him? Even so the things of God knoweth no man, but the Spirit of God").

Cave reveal itself to be the kind of thing that it is. Only the divine measure will do; all others are no standard at all.

The philosopher cannot come into being, then, by mortal effort alone. The education given to the sons by the fathers, the mortal education that Socrates so vigorously defends early on in the *Republic*, will not produce the philosopher.

> [T]here will never be a perfect state or perfect man unless some chance obliges the uncorrupted remnant of philosophers now termed useless to take over governance of the state—whether they wished it or not—and constrains the citizens to obey them. Alternatively, *by some divine inspiration [ek tinos theias epipnoias]*, an authentic passion for true philosophy must be instilled into the sons of men now holding power and sovereignty or into the fathers themselves.[216]

Only those who already possess the pattern, or those who will someday receive it, can be philosophers. The fathers, it turns out, cannot educate their sons—as we learn again and again, with painful consequences, in Book VIII. The philosopher stands in reverence of the true source of his generation, which is not his mortal father.[217] His home and hearth is the Good. By that other fire which warms the inhabitants of the (Cave) world, he finds little comfort.

The Hunt for the Good

> [W]ho could acquiesce in the decrees of his ancestors, or enactments of the people, as to receive without hesitation a god humanly taught him? Each man will stand upon his own judgment rather than subject himself to another's decision. Therefore, since either the custom of the city or the agreement of tradition is too weak and frail a bond of piety to follow in worshipping God, *it remains for God himself to give witness of himself from heaven.*[218]

Those who would form the perfect city, Socrates now proclaims, "[must] take the record of the city and its citizens and wipe it clean [*katharan poiēseian*]."[219] The previous city, which emerged from appeti-

---

[216] Plato, *Republic*, Book VI, 499b–c (emphasis added).

[217] See Emerson, "An Address," in *Selected Essays*, p. 79: "[The truth] cannot be received at second hand. Truly speaking, it is not instruction, but provocation, that I can receive from another soul."

[218] Calvin, *Institutes*, vol. I, ch. V, sec. 13, p. 68 (emphasis added).

[219] Plato, *Republic*, Book VI, 501a.

tive transgression, which is built on filial piety and which concludes with guardians who have "surmounted challenges posed by pleasure and pain,"[220] is not yet the just city, the city capable of "rendering each its due." "The subject of the rulers needs to be reexamined," Socrates says, "from the very beginning."[221] The hunt is not over; the quarry is still at large, and cannot be cornered by those who adhere to (mortal) standards that are only approximate. The guardians were warned at the close of Book III, let us recall, that because

> they have already in their souls [gold and silver] in divine measure from the gods . . . they should [not] profane *the divine gift* by exposing it to the contamination that comes with coveting mortal currencies.[222]

Might we now understand this to mean that mortal standards are not pure enough to bring the hunt to a successful conclusion? Like the soul mired in the domain of relative pleasures and pains in Book IX,[223] we have up until now been without the true standard; and without it, the distance we have traveled is of little consolation. *Our trip has been useless.* We have not yet found a way to "render each its due."[224] There is yet a chasm to be traversed, one that cannot be leapt by mortal means. The exchange between Socrates and Adeimantus discloses Adeimantus' continued obliviousness to the problem:

> The result [of our approach thus far], I think, was a deficiency in precision; but if you were content, that is for you to say.
>
> Well [Adiemantus said], I found it satisfying in good measure, and I think the others did too.
>
> No, my friend, in such matters any measure that falls short of reality is no measure at all. Nothing that is imperfect is the measure of anything, even though some people sometimes think that enough has been done and that no further inquiry is needed.[225]

---

[220] Ibid., 503a; see also 503d–504a.

[221] Ibid., 502e.

[222] Plato, *Republic*, Book III, 416e–417a (emphasis added).

[223] Plato, *Republic*, Book IX, 583b–586c.

[224] Recall that the unjust city was plagued with lawsuits (*Republic*, Book III, 405a) and that in the best city, it was purported, "indictments and lawsuits vanish" (*Republic*, Book V, 464d). The best *mortal* city, however, turns out to be no more capable of granting each its due than the unjust city. The best city by mortal measure is still only mortal, as it were. In that light, the austere and rigorous city that Socrates defends in the first two waves of Book V (457d–472a), *before* the city they have been founding was "wiped clean," should be read ironically, since it will turn out that a city worthy of that name is possible only through an orientation to the Divine pattern to which Socrates now directs our attention.

[225] Plato, *Republic*, Book VI, 504b–c.

As it turns out, of course, a great deal of further inquiry is needed. The "good measure" with which Adeimantus is satisfied turns out to be no measure at all. Without the vision to see it, however, the extent to which there is a chasm between the true and defective measures remains unknown.[226] The long hunt brings the hunters to a precipice, albeit one unknown to them,[227] whose breadth can perhaps be intimated by a new lie of words (the Allegory of the Cave) that conveys, without fully disclosing, the relationship between true and approximate standards in terms of distance and position—considerations of which every hunter must be cognizant.

Let us restate what is by now becoming conspicuous, even if we cannot fully understand it: The approximate standards with which Adeimantus purports to find satisfaction are not the measure of the Good, but rather the other way around. From within the Cave only approximations eventuate. Approximations are blind to the light of day (*hēlios*).[228] In Socrates' words, again, "in such matters any measure that falls short of reality is no measure at all."[229] Herein lies the root cause of the misunderstandings throughout Plato's fable. Without the luminous light of the Good, which gives the true standard, what the unturned soul most needs goes unnoticed. The unturned soul does not recognize that there is a chasm between where it now stands and the journey's end, nor can it understand that the "distance" is too great for Socrates to take it there. The more sophisticated will believe that they can get there by "polishing [their] own intellect."[230] The less sophisticated believe that they can get there by pursuing pleasure.[231] The Good, however, does not

---

[226] The theological analogue to this in Christianity is sin. Sin, *hamartia*, means "missing the mark." Sin is the false measure on which man relies, which turns out to be no measure at all, whose root is the curvature of the will back in on itself. Sin is "original" in the sense that is logically and chronologically prior to the coming into being of the consciousness *that* wills; it is a corruption the extent of which—and this is the fundamental point—cannot be known until *after* the purification made possible through Christ and the Holy Spirit. Purification reveals an anterior corruption heretofore unknown, but nonetheless resident. The idea of original sin is, therefore, thinkable only within the context of a claim that the Divine measure reveals itself, Incarnate, to man.

[227] Cf. Nietzsche, *Thus Spoke Zarathustra*, part II, sec. 21, p. 142: "Not the height but the precipice is terrible."

[228] See Plato, *Republic*, Book VII, 515c: "By every measure, then, reality for the prisoners would be nothing but shadows cast by artifacts."

[229] Plato, *Republic*, Book VI, 504c.

[230] Ibid., 500d. Literally, "and not only to mold himself" (*kai mē monon heauton plattein*). Sterling and Scott are perhaps a bit too poetic here. Cf. Nietzsche, *Thus Spoke Zarathustra*, part II, sec. 20, pp. 138–39, on "inverse cripples."

[231] Plato, *Republic*, Book VI, 505b.

fall under the auspice of sensualists and logic-choppers more intent upon argumentation than dialectic.[232]

A clue to how the Good comes to be known is provided in the Allegory of the Cave, at the place where Socrates describes how the prisoner is freed from his chains. We are told at the outset that the prisoners "have seen [nothing] of themselves or of one another."[233] In addition, little doubt is left regarding the prisoners' ability to talk to and understand one another.[234] Because they are all shackled and can look only forward,[235] the prisoner's liberation must therefore be attributed to someone or something other than his fellow prisoners.

The passive constructions Socrates uses to describe the horrifying ascent—he "is freed [lutheiē]"; "let him be compelled [anagkazoito] to look directly into the light"; "let him be dragged [helkoi] by force up through the rough and steep incline of the cave's passageway"[236]—suggests that the cause of the philosopher's liberation is an overpowering presence that intrudes into the Cave out of sight of the other prisoners, perhaps an irruption of light into the darkness of a beneficent sort.

It would be a mistake to conclude that another philosopher is a *cause* of the liberation of the prisoner. However important dialogue surely is for the ascent of the soul, Socrates is under no illusion that the philosopher can break through to give the prisoner knowledge. *Not listening*, moreover, is a defining feature of the soul who finds philosophy useless; Polemarchus led us to this conclusion at the outset,[237] and now Socrates' description of the prisoners corroborates it. To this let us add that even if the philosopher *could* talk to the prisoners without being misunderstood, their hostility toward the philosopher who would liberate them should not be underestimated.

> Further, if anyone tried to release the prisoners and lead them up and they could get their hands on him and kill him, would they not kill him?[238]

---

[232] See Plato, *Republic*, Book VII, 539d: "[A philosopher] will prefer to follow the example of someone who wants to use dialectic in the service of truth and not play games of contradiction."

[233] Ibid., 515b.

[234] See ibid., 515b: "*If, then*, they could talk to one another, don't you think they would impute reality to those passing shadows?" (emphasis added). The conditional form of the sentence suggests the impossibility of genuine communication.

[235] Ibid., 514b.

[236] Ibid., 515c–e.

[237] Plato, *Republic*, Book I, 327c.

[238] Plato, *Republic*, Book VII, 517a. See also *Republic*, Book VI, 488a: "Nothing in all of nature can be found to match the cruelty with which society treats its best men."

That Socrates says nothing about the source of the prisoner's liberation is itself ground enough to think that the cause of the prisoner's turn toward the Good is the Good itself, which breaks in "suddenly [*exaiphnēs*]"[239] as an irruption from beyond the Cave. Would not fidelity to the unspeakability of the Good require that the mystery of its agency remain unannounced? Might liberation be brought about by the unmediated light that burns away the illusions of reality while it shows itself to be that which "makes things real [but] is not in itself being"?[240] Several references to the light that penetrates the Cave raise the specter of this possibility.[241]

To this silence let us add the following consideration. Why, we may ask, does Socrates implore Glaucon to "be still" after Socrates has suggested that the Good, in its eternal abundance, gives the light that illuminates knowledge and truth? At that place in the discussion, Glaucon tries, somewhat pathetically, to define the Good in terms of pleasure. The Good is beyond imagination, he admits; *but he does not cease to fill the silence by trying to name it*.[242] Might it be that here, at this place, hunters can no longer search over familiar territory, but rather must *receive* a gift that is unfamiliar, luminous, awesome? The quarry now *gives itself*—to those who in stillness have been "turned," to those who do not try to comprehend what has irrupted in terms of the paltry resources that are ready-at-hand inside the Cave.[243] Without this irruption, the hunt for the Good would end only in one or another part of the Cave. The hunters' search would be futile *without a countervailing movement of the Good toward the hunters*.

Bearing in mind this chasm that mortals cannot surmount, for which Socrates' words must be reckoned as signs that point to what must mysteriously appear before us rather than be negotiated with mortal resources, let us imaginatively attend to what Socrates says about the Good.

The scandalous argument—or, rather, provocation—that Socrates

[239] Plato, *Republic*, Book VII, 515c.

[240] Plato, *Republic*, Book VI, 509b.

[241] Plato, *Republic*, Book VII, 514a, 515c, 515e, 516a.

[242] Plato, *Republic*, Book VI, 509a. Cf. Ps. 46:10 ("Be still and know that I am God"). See also Martin Buber, *I and Thou*, trans. Ronald Gregor Smith (New York: Charles Scribner's Sons, 1958), Part Two, pp. 39–40: "Only silence before the *Thou*—silence of *all* tongues, silent patience in the undivided word that precedes the formal and vocal response—leaves the *Thou* free. . . . Every response binds up the *Thou* in the world of *It*. That is the melancholy of man, and his greatness."

[243] Here Plato predates Levinas, for whom there is the possibility of "a signification without a context" (Emmanuel Levinas, *Totality and Infinity*, trans. Alphonso Lingis [Pittsburgh: Duquesne University Press, 1969], Preface, p. 23).

provides is vaguely familiar to almost every sophomore philosophy student, and treated with incredulity by the most sophisticated scholars.[244]

> If we pursue the comparison [between the sun and the Good], the objects of knowledge are not only made manifest by the presence of goodness [*tou agathou*]. Goodness makes them real. Still goodness is not itself being. It transcends being, exceeding all else in dignity and power.[245]

Like the sun, the Good is the source of generation for all that is Real.[246] What is Real is revealed to the faculty of reason, which is to be distinguished from the faculty of opining, whose objects are those dim things that come into being and pass away in the Cave. Knowledge pertains to an unchanging world "above," of which opinion knows nothing.

The brief deposition Socrates offers has a certain measure of elegance about it, to be sure; its plausibility, however, is a matter about which we can have little to say. All our talk is but a further contribution to the echoes in the Cave.[247] In a word, we who dwell in the Cave, who search for sustenance within its domain, who have not been turned toward the Good, are incapable of corroborating Socrates' claim.

I do not say this lightly or with the intention of deflecting legitimate objections, should they exist. Fidelity to the entirety of his account, however, requires more than an earnest effort on our part to extract a "Doctrine of the Forms" from what he says about the likeness of the sun to the Good, and to the world it begets.[248] In Socrates' preamble we are, after all, given a warning, which ought to be heeded.

> I wish I could pay the full account today, so that you could receive the principal now and not just the interest. But accept the interest, in any case, together with the child of the good. However, take care that I don't falsely reckon the interest and unwittingly deceive you.[249]

The interest on the principal can—and *will*—deceive while we remain in the Cave. His "Doctrine" is foolishness without the corroboration that only knowledge of the Good can give.

---

[244] See Leo Strauss, *The City and Man* (Chicago: Rand McNally, 1963), ch. II, pp. 118–21. See also Thomas Pangle's Introduction to Leo Strauss, *Studies in Platonic Political Philosophy*, ed. Thomas Pangle (Chicago: University of Chicago Press, 1983), pp. 2–5. In his words: "[Strauss] is extremely skeptical about whether Plato seriously meant the explicit teaching about the ideas he has Socrates present to the young boys there" (p. 3).

[245] Plato, *Republic*, Book VI, 509b.

[246] See ibid., 508d.

[247] See ibid., 492b–c.

[248] Ibid., 507b–509d.

[249] Ibid., 507a.

Consider, for example, *when* we are told about the Good in the Allegory of the Cave.

> It is at this stage [meta taut'][after having one's eyes burned, and gradually becoming habituated to the light] that he would be able to conclude that the sun is the cause of the seasons and of the year's turning, that it governs the entire visible world and is in some sense also the cause of all visible things.[250]

Only *after* the ascent is made can we corroborate Socrates' assertion that the Good generates the "Forms" and all that passes in and out of existence.[251] To put the matter somewhat contentiously, his metaphysical claims are confirmable only by the aristocratic soul, not by the "pygmies" [anthrōpiskoi] who now court philosophy[252] nor by the multitude that finds it useless.[253] We the readers, along with Glaucon and the rest, have been brought to an impasse. Our hunt has been stopped short. Glaucon opines that "we are in sight of the goal."[254] Socrates, however, knows better. "I believe that it is too great a task to attain what [the Good] appears to be in my thoughts," he says.[255] The trail has gone cold for those without the requisite vision.

The fable of the *Republic* does not stop here, though. We must ask, therefore, what course is left open to Socrates now that his words have brought him up short? His interlocutors have not been "turned," and so know nothing of the mystery of the Good. Sleepy, inebriated, enshackled by their chains, Socrates steps back across the barrier that separates the world of True Light from the world of passing things[256] in order, this time, to show his interlocutors that *all paths, save the one to the Good,*

---

[250] Plato, *Republic*, Book VII, 516b–c (emphasis added).

[251] Aristotle seems not to have taken this aspect of Plato's claim seriously and sought to evaluate it without the caution I have noted in mind. After taking Plato at his word, so to speak, he suggests that the doctrine is incoherent. (See Aristotle, *Metaphysics*, trans. W. D. Ross, in *Complete Works*, book VII, ch. 14, 1039b17–19: "If, then, these consequences are impossible, clearly there are not Forms of sensible things in the sense in which some maintain their existence.")

[252] Plato, *Republic*, Book VI, 495b–496a.

[253] Ibid., 489b: "the best philosophers are of no use to the multitude." See also 494a.

[254] Ibid., 506d.

[255] Ibid., 506e.

[256] See Buber, *I and Thou*, Part Two, p. 57: "The dogma of [temporal processes] is the abdication of man before the exuberant world of *It*. He [who invokes this dogma] misuses the name of destiny: destiny is not a dome pressed tightly down on the world of men; no one meets it but he who went out from freedom. But the dogma of [temporal process] leaves no room for freedom, none for its most real revelation of all, whose calm strength changes the face of the earth: *turning*" (emphasis added).

lead toward the splendor of the tyrant's palace, that empty and impoverished place that masquerades as fullness to souls that cannot see. Herein lays the subject of Book VIII, that celebrated descent that, at the end, discloses the condition under which the divided soul *may* come to know where sustenance *cannot* be found.[257] For concealed underneath the frantic, appetitive, and insatiable exterior of the tyrant lies the solitary poverty of an exhausted soul that, in its hidden futility, is *perhaps* finally disposed to heed Socrates' injunction to "be still." Illumination by the Good requires a "turn" that the interlocutors cannot make; short of that, Socrates seeks to convince them that the alternative to such a leap is faltering in one way or another.

The Decline toward Tyranny

The decline of the ideal city, we are informed, occurs because, among other things, the sons are "unworthy [*anaxioi*] of their fathers."[258] To make sense of this claim, let us consider first some remarks in the *Republic* made by Socrates about fathers.

On numerous occasions in the *Republic*, Socrates has said that the citizens of our just city must honor their fathers; indeed, that Polemarchus honors his father (Cephalus) as his "proper heir"[259] by carrying forward the argument right at the outset of the *Republic* suggests the importance of this theme.

Consider, as well, Socrates' concern that stories about the gods not contain any reference to battles between fathers and sons, for fear that such behavior will be imitated by mortals.

---

[257] Cf. John Calvin, "Commentary on the Epistle of Paul the Apostle to the Romans," in *Calvin's New Testament Commentaries*, ed. David W. Torrance and Thomas F. Torrance (Grand Rapids, Mich.: William B. Eerdmans, 1995), p. 148: "When man is left to his own nature, he is completely borne away by his lust without resistance. Although the ungodly are tormented by the stings of conscience, and cannot take such delight in their vices without having some taste of bitterness, yet we cannot deduce from this either that they hate evil or love good. The Lord permits them to endure such torments, in order to reveal his judgment of them in some way, but not to move them either with a love of righteousness or with a hatred of sin." Plato's tyrant would here correspond to Calvin's sinful man: Each is in bondage; each finds pleasure tainted; each is haunted by the inadequacy of the resources at hand; each requires something more than mortal means can provide.

[258] Plato, *Republic*, Book VIII, 546d. See also Plato, *Laches*, trans. Rosamond Kent Sprague, in *Plato: Complete Works*, 179c–e: "[E]ach of us has a great many fine things to say to the young men about his own father, things they achieved both in war and in peace in the management of the affairs both of their allies and of the city here. But neither of us has a word to say about his own accomplishments." Among other things, *Laches* is about how the sons are unworthy of the fathers, and how that may be remedied.

[259] Plato, *Republic*, Book I, 331d.

Nor should the child be taught to believe that in abandoning all restraint in order to punish the misdeeds of his father he will only be following the example of the first and greatest gods.[260]

Other passages, as well, confirm this thought: "the young [should observe] a respectful silence in the presence of their elders,"[261] he says. And elsewhere: "Would [our citizen] fail to honor his parents or neglect divine service?"[262]

Nevertheless, as with so much that Socrates says, there are countervailing intimations that our initial conclusions must be superseded if we are to attain knowledge. To begin with, there is the glaring embarrassment that Polemarchus—who clearly would wish to be worthy of his father—has been abandoned without the resources to honor what his father has bequeathed to him in the way of an understanding of justice; or rather, what his father has bequeathed him is itself inadequate.

Adeimantus, in his own way, confirms this by his thinly veiled suggestion (when speaking of the difficulty of making the case for the superiority of justice) that the "fathers" have not done well by the sons.

You know well how fathers lecture their sons (and guardians their charges) about a man's obligation and also how they use words that compliment not justice but the good repute that comes with it.[263]

And a little further along,

No one has ever provided proof that [justice] is the greatest of goods and [injustice] the greatest of evils. *Why do all of you not do this from the beginning and convince us from our youth up?*[264]

A curious light is thrown on Socrates' remark about the inappropriateness of the sons imitating the crimes said to have been perpetrated by the gods against their fathers by the observation that follows immediately below it:

Even were these stories true, they ought not to be told indiscriminately to young and thoughtless persons. It would be best if they could be buried in

---

[260] Plato, *Republic*, Book II, 378b. See also Plato, *Euthyphro*, trans. G.M.A. Grube, in *Plato: Complete Works*, 5e–6a. Euthypro there claims that he is justified in taking his father to task because Zeus did the same.

[261] Plato, *Republic*, Book IV, 425b.

[262] Ibid., 443a. See also *Republic*, Book X, 615c: "Er told of still greater rewards and punishments for piety and impiety toward the gods and toward one's parents."

[263] Plato, *Republic*, Book II, 363a. An interesting parallel is found in the Calvin's reflections about iconography. The sons of the Church turned to images, he says, when the reality of God was lost to them. See Calvin, *Institutes*, vol. I, part I, ch. XI, sec. 7, p. 107.

[264] Plato, *Republic*, Book II, 366e–367a (emphasis added).

silence. If they absolutely must be retold, it should only be to a chosen few under conditions of total secrecy.[265]

Even if the sons have good cause to doubt their fathers, it seems, such knowledge is dangerous to all but a very few.

Socrates' comment is not, I think, simply a passing provocation. The danger of the sons doubting their fathers is, after all, revisited in Book VII, at the place where Socrates speaks of the liberating power of the dialectic. Those who wrongly practice it, he says, react in unbecoming ways to the discovery that they are orphans; their discovery that they are "homeless" leads them to reject the fathers they have heretofore honored.

> [The situation of the man who currently practices the dialectic] resembles that of an adopted son raised in a great and numerous family with abundant wealth, all of which has attracted a horde of flatters. On reaching manhood he becomes aware that he is not the flesh and blood of his adopted parents and that he will be unable to locate his real parents. Can you imagine the difference in his feelings toward his adopted family and toward those flatterers before and after he learns the truth about his adoption?[266]

Importantly, Socrates does not deny that the practice of the dialectic leads the sons to realize that they are, in fact, orphans; his point here is rather that on discovering that the father is not the true father, the soul may consequently abandon itself to the rule of the appetites.

Finally, as if there weren't already some doubt about the capacity of the fathers to guide their sons, there is the final thought of Book VII:

> [Those who would produce good rulers] will take over the children, taking care that they are far removed from the dispositions and habits [*tropois kai nomois*] of their parents.[267]

Let us accept, then, that the fathers may be unable to convey the reality of justice to the sons, and so leave them without the knowledge they truly need. The sons themselves further compound the problem. The fathers may be unable to convey to the sons the substance of justice, but it is no less true that the sons could not receive it even if the fathers did possess the knowledge that they needed. Socrates remarks, for example, that although Asclepius knew the right use of medicine,[268] it was the "sons of Asclepius"[269] (of which Herodicus is one) who invented linger-

---

[265] Ibid., 378a.
[266] Plato, *Republic*, Book VII, 538a.
[267] Ibid., 541a.
[268] He was, as we discovered earlier, a "real politician" (Plato, *Republic*, Book III, 407e).
[269] Ibid., 405d.

ing death. The good doctor, it seems, is unable to pass on his knowledge to his son.

Both of these aspects—the fathers being unworthy of the sons, and the sons being unworthy of the fathers—are evident in Book VIII, and this because the Good alone, and not the fathers, can give what is needed. Mortal fathers are not the generative source that the philosopher must honor.[270] In Book VIII, the good (aristocratic) father cannot guide his son because the latter cannot see the divine pattern by which the father is oriented.[271] At every latter stage of the development that Socrates traces there, the well-meaning son does not imitate his corrupted father because he (the son) opines that his father's measure falls short of the mark.[272] The son must reject the father, though not in the manner that the son opines he must, as we shall see.

The decline in Book VIII serves to illustrate two points, which incidentally occur side by side in the Gospel of Luke:

> For nothing is secret, that shall not be made manifest; neither anything hid, that shall not be made manifest. Take heed therefore how ye hear: for whosoever hath, to him shall be given; and whosoever hath not, from him shall be taken even that which he seemeth to have.[273]

First, the stability of each kind of corruption—timocracy, oligarchy, and democracy—is only apparent. Unable to render each its due, to

---

[270] Cf. Tocqueville, *Democracy in America*, vol. I, part I, ch. 2, pp. 40–41: "In 1628 a charter . . . was granted by Charles I to the emigrants who were going to found the colony of Massachusetts. . . . The new settlers, without denying the supremacy of the homeland, did not derive thence the source of their powers. . . . [Rather] they enacted laws as if they were dependent on God alone." See also ibid., part II, ch. 9, p. 279: "[The Americans'] fathers gave them a love of equality and liberty, but it was God who, by handing a limitless continent over to them, gave them the means of long remaining equal and free." See also Gen. 12:1–2, where Abram is instructed to leave his father's house by God the father. Abram goes without a murmur. More chilling, but no less revealing of the source of all fecundity, is the story of the binding of Isaac (Gen. 22:1–18).

[271] See Plato, *Republic*, Book VIII, 550a: "[The timocratic son of the aristocratic father] learns that men who mind their own business are called fools and held in low repute."

[272] See also Calvin, *Institutes*, Book II, ch. VIII, sec.18, p. 384: "[God's jealousy] will extend to the children, the grandchildren, and the great-grandchildren, who obviously will become *imitators* of their father's impiety" (emphasis added). Here, Calvin reads in the Old Testament claim that the sins of the fathers are visited upon the sons for three or four generations (Exodus 34:7; Num. 14:18), a confirmation of the magnitude of the degeneration to which human life is subject once the Divine pattern, if you will, is depicted as a graven image—an image that, on Calvin's account, is generated out of human imagination (see ibid., sec.17, pp. 383–84).

[273] Luke 8:17,18.

draw the boundaries in the right place, what is harbored in each of those types is eventually revealed,[274] until at last the secret of all corrupt types emerges: "tyranny indeed, *openly avowed* [*homologoumenē*]."[275] Philosophy is the only real type, Socrates says; all others conceal tyranny. Socrates and Thrasymachus are the two great alternatives.

Second, what each corrupt type *has*, properly speaking, is only the shadow of what is Real. The defective father seeks to retain his own measure, yet the son intimates that, in fact, the father's measure is no measure at all. Because the son does not know where to look for the measure, however, when he (rightly) betrays his father, his measure turns out to be even less robust than was his father's. Those who appear to possess a robust shadow of the true measure have that taken away. "Bereft of the best guardian," Socrates says, "[a man's] virtue will not remain unsullied and pure."[276]

These ideas are confirmed throughout Book VIII. In rejecting the measure of the father, the son searches for a different measure to fill the void in his soul that his father's measure could not fill. Not knowing that only the Good can fill this void,[277] however, his search brings him only greater emptiness. Appearances notwithstanding, without the antidote for his disease, the son's disrespect for his (mortal, drunken, and slumbering) father concludes, as it did with Ham, in his becoming an unfree servant.[278]

Timocracy

The defection from justice, which gives rise to all that follows, occurs because rightful boundaries are not drawn, because "each is not granted its due."

> Those who are appointed rulers from this generation, in turn, will hardly show much aptitude when it comes to distinguishing Hesiod's race—or discriminating between gold, silver, bronze, and iron of our race. The resulting intermixture of silver and iron and gold with bronze will spawn chaos, inequality, and disharmony.[279]

---

[274] The inner truth of the love of public honor is private greed (Book VIII, 549e–551a); the inner truth of the love of wealth is poverty (ibid., 555b); the inner truth of the love of freedom is servitude (ibid., 564a).

[275] Ibid., 569b (emphasis added).

[276] Ibid., 549b.

[277] See Plato, *Republic*, Book IX, 585b–d.

[278] Gen. 9:25.

[279] Plato, *Republic*, Book VIII, 546e–547a. See also 550b: "Subject to two contradictory influences [the son] chooses the intermediate ground."

We would do well to recall the situation at the outset of Book IV,[280] where a faction of rulers failed to understand that once mortal gold is coveted by the ruling element, there can be no justice. Here in Book VIII, this ruling faction that secretly covets mortal gold cannot be drawn back to justice by entreaties from the other ruling faction, which appears to be *visibly* poorer but, in fact, possesses the true measure.[281] The visibly richer faction has already renounced reason, whose currency is invisible and divine. Consequently, no mortal thing could convince it to return. Like the prisoners enthralled and enchained in the Cave, this faction has no knowledge of truly "higher things"[282] and so, like Polemarchus, "will not listen."[283]

The compromise reached between the two factions by "mixing"— there is no philosophical clarity here that divine gold cannot be mixed with lesser metals—dethrones reason but does not yet enthrone the appetites. This type bears a shadowy resemblance to the true type, and so evinces aspects of aristocracy even while it portends the reign of the appetites under oligarchy.

For our purpose, the shadowy resemblance within timocracy worth considering is the relationship of the timocrat to death. Let us recall that once we entered the post-Cephaletic city, war appeared, and with it the practice of death, literally understood. This sort of death subsequently turned out to be a shadowy imitation of the practice of death that philosophy involves. The death that is died through philosophy betokens Eternity, while the death died in battle only *defers* death insofar as those caught up in the generative cycle of life and death remember those heroic deeds done on behalf of the city and pass such memories on to the next generation. The philosopher understands that the leverage against death that such remembrance occasions is, against the standard of Eternity, short-lived. Dialectic, not remembrance, is what is needed.

> [Only through the dialectic are men] produced and led upward to the light in the same way that some men are said to have ascended from Hades to the halls of the gods.[284]

To be sure, death is ever-present in the timocratic regime; but the dying that is done involves practicing death in a mistaken way. To such souls Socrates might say, "let the dead bury their dead."[285] Not knowing the

---

[280] Plato, *Republic*, Book IV, 419d.
[281] Plato, *Republic*, Book VIII, 547b.
[282] Plato, *Republic*, Book VII, 529a–c.
[283] Plato, *Republic*, Book I, 327c.
[284] Plato, *Republic*, Book VII, 521c.
[285] Matt. 8:22.

true standard, the soul that honors honor lives a life of lingering death, and then dies. While the honor-loving soul "has a passion . . . for the hunt,"[286] it never truly lives.

The distinction being made here can be further illuminated by considering which sort of death dislodges the hypotheses concerning how to live well that stand in the way of unmediated knowledge. The timocratic regime, we are told, "covets honor and insists on victory."[287] Honor and victory, of course, already suppose standards of excellence; standards that, unlike what is revealed through dialectic, offer the black and white of victory and defeat, of a "child's game of flipping shells."[288] Under timocracy, there is an aversion to disrupting the hypothesis laid down concerning how to live well. Absent the proper education, which would illuminate the manner of moving beyond those hypotheses to unmediated knowledge, the timocratic soul is transfixed in the world of coming-into-being-and-passing-away. Warriors are not philosophers: The former die without ascending to the unmediated knowledge that liberates; the latter are freed from the chains of lingering death and, so, truly live. Warriors take for granted some extant and unexamined standard and evaluate themselves on its basis. They are, in effect, sportsmen, who "operate with the kind of assumptions that lead to conclusions and not to first principles."[289] Here is *the competitive regime*, which, unable or unwilling to be turned toward the burning light of the Good, hungers for victory but knows nothing of the true victory that exceeds Olympian honors.[290] Although the lesser victory that competitiveness announces is everywhere present, the timocratic sons of aristocratic fathers find no real sustenance.

Not knowing the true standard, the divine gold that glistens in the abode of reason, this soul searches for a surrogate whose radiance its weak eyes can endure. The divine eye of reason not having been opened, so to speak, the mortal eye that knows only earthly feasting demands that its vision rule. The eye is rightly drawn to gold that glistens, but without the requisite vision, which the aristocratic fathers cannot convey to their timocratic sons, the sons can see only mortal gold. The competitive regime, the regime that practices death wrongly, is secretly drawn to that mortal gold it mistakenly deems to have an unsurpassable luster. Absent divine reason, there is no bulwark against the dominion of

---

[286] Plato, *Republic*, Book VIII, 549a.

[287] Ibid., 545a.

[288] Plato, *Republic*, Book VII, 521c.

[289] Plato, *Republic*, Book VI, 510b.

[290] See Plato, *Republic*, Book V, 466a: "They will live a life happier than the most blessed lives of the Olympic victors."

the appetites. Within a timocratic regime, reason is a tool of "equivo-cators [who are neither] simple [nor] straightforward."[291] So ruled in darkness, mortal currency gives the appearance of possessing unrivaled luster.

As I have said, the timocratic sons do not—indeed, cannot—adopt the divine pattern that illuminates the souls of their aristocratic fathers. Whereas the aristocratic fathers "render each its due," their offspring secretly nourish their appetites and run away from the prospect of any constraint being placed on them "like boys [run] from a father."[292] Reason should rule; in timocracy, it has lost its sway. Boundaries are drawn, to be sure; yet they are drawn in the wrong place. The sons "build walls around their houses,"[293] but these lines of demarcation no longer serve the whole, which only reason can grasp. By the lines they draw, they purport to "provide for themselves,"[294] yet the sons only be-come impoverished by their demarcations—even while they attempt to "prove [themselves] to be more of a man than [their] father[s]."[295] For-going the divine gold that dwells in the house of reason, they hoard a shadowy imitation of it in their own homes.[296] They show themselves to be spirited and manly; yet they conceal the secret dominion of their appetites.

Oligarchy

Whereas death is practiced, albeit wrongly, under timocracy, under oli-garchy (and in each successive type where appetite, too, rules), death is altogether shunned. Like the spirited part of the soul, the appetitive part can have no right relationship to death; unlike the spirited part, the ap-petitive part flees from death. Ironically, however, in oligarchy death obtrudes in a way that it does not in aristocracy and timocracy. Rather than being welcomed, as it was earlier, it now brings terror. Extensive ef-forts, therefore, are directed at keeping it at bay.[297] Cephalus provided the first confirmation of this disposition in the opening passages of Book I.

---

[291] Plato, *Republic*, Book VIII, 547e.

[292] Ibid., 548b.

[293] Ibid., 548a.

[294] Ibid., 548b.

[295] Ibid., 549e–550a.

[296] Cf. Plato, *Republic*, Book III, 417a–b: "This way of life [we have sketched in which guardians covet only the gold in their souls] will make them saviors of the state and of themselves. But if they begin to acquire houses, lands, and money, they will become house-holders and farmers instead of guardians."

[297] Cf. Rousseau, *Emile*, Book IV, p. 282: "[T]he more [man] wants to flee [death], the more he senses it."

There, recall, he opines that the right use of wealth is to ward off fears of the afterworld.[298] Not being able or willing to practice death rightly, he is haunted by it. I consider this shortly. Before that, however, there is the small matter of the appearance in oligarchy of divisions and confusions about boundaries that will become only more acute as the decline toward tyranny occurs, and for that reason, a few comments are warranted here.

In oligarchy, we learn, wealth is honored and virtue dishonored.[299] Where in timocracy the pertinent boundary, the boundary that proved to be a fault line, was between public virtue and private vice, in oligarchy new distinctions are drawn; now that wealth is honored, the pertinent demarcation is between those who unabashedly possess it and those who are without it. Here are the rich and the poor.[300] The honor-loving soul understands the world in terms of virtue and vice; the money-loving soul understands the world in terms of wealth and poverty.[301]

> And so the lovers of victory and honor finally become lovers of money and profit. The rich receive praise and respect and public office; the poor are despised.[302]

There is a curious development here that should not be overlooked. On the one hand, as I have just said, the oligarchic regime firmly marks

---

[298] Plato, *Republic*, Book I, 330d.

[299] Plato, *Republic*, Book VIII, 550e.

[300] Under oligarchy there will always be those who are destitute. Because the appetites are infinite, the rule by the appetites will always create a condition of scarcity. In a finite world, infinite appetites will never be fully gratified. There will not be enough for all when oligarchy rules. The secret that the oligarch harbors—that all their desires wish to be gratified—leads to a scarcity of which the poor are the victims. At first, perhaps, the wealthy will invest their mortal currency; eventually, however, they spend their money on items that will gratify the appetites that they try to suppress. Rousseau's observations in his *First Discourse* corroborate this claim (part I, para. 9, p. 6), as do Tocqueville's subsequent remarks: "[What men in democracies] most desire is power. . . . As a result, very vulgar tastes often go with their enjoyment of extraordinary prosperity, and it would seem that their only object in raising to supreme power was to gratify trivial and coarse appetites more easily" (Tocqueville, *Democracy in America*, vol. II, part III, ch. 19, p. 631). Consider also Marshall Sahlins, *Stone Age Economics* (Chicago: Aldine-Atherton, 1972), ch. 1, p. 4: "[T]he market-industrial system *institutes* scarcity, in a manner completely unparalleled and to a degree nowhere else approximated. Where production and distribution are arranged through the behavior of prices, and all livelihoods depend upon getting and spending, insufficiency of material means becomes the explicit, calculable starting point of all economic activity" (emphasis added). Scarcity, for Sahlins, is not an objective condition, but rather a relationship that supposes infinite desire in a finite world.

[301] See Rousseau, *First Discourse*, part II, para. 41, p. 18: "[W]hat will become of virtue when one has to get rich at all costs? The ancient politicians forever spoke of morals and of virtue, ours speak only of commerce and of money."

[302] Plato, *Republic*, Book VIII, 551a.

the boundary between wealth and poverty. On the other hand, under oligarchy we find the beginnings of a concerted effort to obliterate boundaries as well—an effort that seems to be endemic to the appetitive part of the soul in general.

> [There is] the tendency among citizens of [an oligarchy] to be busybodies [to *polupragmonein*], each wanting to be a farmer, moneymaker, and soldier all in one.[303]

Not understanding how or where to "render each its due," oligarchy, like each succeeding type, both draws boundaries firmly and seeks to obliterate them altogether. This twin movement will be considered more thoroughly below, in the context of the democratic regime. Here I note only that *if* justice and the lines of demarcation that it entails are inscribed always already into human life, then such demarcations can never be eradicated from the mortal enterprise: The soul that in one place tries to eradicate them elsewhere fortifies them in the wrong place. This pattern of eradication and fortification is present in each of the corrupt types and grows more acute as tyranny is approached. In oligarchy we see the first instance of the acuity of the problem—hence the extensive need for lawyers and courts of law concerned with establishing "mine" and "thine."

The manner of enforcing the distinctions that oligarchy sets forth, "by force of arms [or by] intimidation,"[304] suggests that this is the first defective type that begins to show signs of fragmentation. Notwithstanding its proximity to timocracy, oligarchy more fully reveals a problem that was only lurking under timocracy: here each "part" is no longer a part of the whole. Socrates characterizes this as "the greatest of all evils."[305] A polity worthy of the name "renders each its due" in accordance with "the pattern set up in the heavens."[306] Yet no such rendering is possible without a whole within which the parts may be ordered. Without such parts, there can be transient relations based on moneyed transactions. There can be an economy, but not, properly speaking, a polity.[307]

Under oligarchy, the real power of justice to draw together and sepa-

---

[303] Ibid., 551e–552a. Timocracy evinced this trait, to be sure, but to a lesser extent. See 550a.

[304] Ibid., 551b.

[305] Ibid., 552a.

[306] Plato, *Republic*, Book IX, 592b.

[307] Cf. Tocqueville, *Democracy in America*, vol. II, part II, ch. 20, p. 557: "To be exact, although there are rich men, [they] have neither corporate spirit nor objects in common, neither common traditions nor hopes. There are limbs, but no body." Both Plato and Tocqueville understood what Marx did not, *viz.*, that no strong basis of unity can exist between those who love wealth.

rate is supplanted by the lesser power of money,[308] which draws together and separates in distorted fashion. In oligarchy, justice involves "rendering each its due" with money, which is to say that justice is understood as paying debts with what Socrates long ago suggested was fool's gold. Each therefore cannot be truly rendered its due in oligarchy, and this is because money's luster bears only a slight resemblance to the divine gold of reason.[309] It is interest on the principle.[310] Said otherwise, if the value of wealth is being able to pay one's debts, as Cephalus suggested in Book I,[311] then oligarchy reveals itself to be poor indeed. Knowing neither the nature of real wealth nor of "rendering each its due," oligarchy always runs a deficit. It spends more than its feeble resources are able to generate. All of Midas's gold would not be enough to sustain it.[312] A "city" of consumers[313] cannot really be held together, no matter how much money it has at its disposal.

Besides paying debts, we know that the love of wealth is directed toward averting death. Adeimantus, for example, indicates at the outset of Book IV that wealth may be directed toward fending off foreign threats.[314] Wealth is useful because it insulates the city and the soul from death. Doctors of a certain sort, too, do this, as Socrates' discussion of gymnastics in Book III discloses.[315] In both instances, however, in keeping death at bay from without and from within, the wealth that oligarchy amasses

---

[308] Cf. Karl Marx, "Economic and Philosophical Manuscripts of 1844," *The Marx-Engels Reader*, p. 103: "That which is for me through the medium of *money*—that for which I can pay (i.e., which money can buy)—that am *I*, the possessor of money. The extent of money is the extent of my power. . . . I am bad, dishonest, unscrupulous, stupid; but money is honored, and therefore so is its possessor" (emphasis in original). Rousseau anticipates Marx's thought in *Emile*, Book III, p. 202: "[I]f [a man] has the misfortune of being raised in Paris and of being rich, he is lost. So long as there are skillful artists there, he will have all their talents; but far away from them he will no longer have any." Marx's dialectic, which supposes that history is driven forward by economic forces, is only a partial account of the dynamics at work. An oligarchic soul sees the oligarchic principle everywhere and everywhen. Deeper than the love of wealth, however, is the love of power—which is revealed, perhaps, only after the love of wealth dominates a period of human history. The love of wealth conceals deeper motives.

[309] Plato, *Republic*, Book III, 416e.

[310] See Plato, *Republic*, Book VI, 507a.

[311] Plato, *Republic*, Book I, 331b.

[312] See Plato, *Republic*, Book III, 408b: "[The true doctor would believe that] the art of medicine ought not to be squandered on [a man for whom life is the highest good,] and that he should not receive treatment even if he were richer than Midas." The soul ruled by the appetites cannot be saved.

[313] Plato, *Republic*, Book VIII, 552b. See also Hannah Arendt's critique in *The Human Condition* (Chicago: University of Chicago Press, 1958), ch., III, sec.17, pp. 126–35.

[314] Plato, *Republic*, Book IV, 422a.

[315] Plato, *Republic*, Book III, 406b.

turns out to be inadequate to pay the cost of fending off death. That the love of wealth is ultimately unable to ward off the death that comes from foreign invasion is an observation confirmed by too many authors throughout history to warrant detailed attention here.[316] More interesting for our purposes is the thought that wealth can, through the exchange of mortal coin, *purchase* the health its possessors lack from doctors who are heirs of Herodicus.

Herodicus, recall, held that life was the highest good, and so invented "lingering death,"[317] that condition of Cave dwellers who subsist by the dim light that is between the darkness of death and the luminescence of life outside the Cave. The expense of maintaining a life that requires costly operations and lengthy procedures, however, soon becomes unsustainable, as our own medical predicament is beginning to suggest.

Consider Socrates' alternative:

> When a carpenter falls ill, he expects his doctor to give him a medication that will [soon make him well]. Should the doctor prescribe instead a prolonged course of treatment . . . the carpenter will make haste to say that he has no time to be sick and that life without work and preoccupied with illness isn't worth living. Then he will bid farewell to such a doctor and resume his customary way of life, attending to his business—or, if his body cannot take the strain, he dies and is thus freed from his troubles.[318]

This seems overly harsh, to be sure; yet the alternative, if viewed from the vantage point from which the philosopher beholds true health, is more deadly than Socrates' portrayal of the good life that does not shun death. Higher than "lingering death" is living well; the former supposes life to be the highest good, the latter that the Good is higher still. A man who is oriented and sustained by the Good practices death and so lives fully while dwelling in the world of coming-into-being-and-passing-away. The alternative is the life that perennially practices death, on the one hand, or the "lingering death" that purports to keep death at bay,

---

[316] See Augustine, *City of God*, in *Writings*, vol. 6, book I, ch. 30, p. 67 (*CG*, p. 42): "[The great Scipio] refused to consent to the destruction of Carthage, then challenging Rome's bid for power. He stood out against Cato, who was all for it. For, Scipio feared complacent security as the enemy of feeble spirits, and believed that a vigilant fear would be a better, and a badly needed, teacher for the Romans." See also Rousseau, *First Discourse*, part II, para. 47, p. 20: "While the conveniences of life increase, the arts improve, and luxury spreads; true courage is enervated [and] the military virtues vanish"; and ibid., para. 48, p. 21: "The Romans admitted that military virtue died out among them in proportion as they began to be knowledgeable about paintings, etchings, goldsmiths' vessels, and to cultivate the fine arts." Plato addresses this matter in the *Republic* at Book IV, 421e–423b; Book VIII, 551d–e; 556c–e.

[317] Plato, *Republic*, Book III, 406b.

[318] Ibid., 406d–e.

on the other. In both cases, death cannot be avoided.[319] Asclepius knows this, Herodicus does not.

Let us now draw together a composite picture of oligarchy from the aspects that have been recently discussed—and this, in order to expose the powerlessness of oligarchy, notwithstanding its appearance. While the gold that oligarchy amasses conveys the appearance of power, for those who are not "dazzled [and who] can see through it all [*hikanōs diora*],"[320] the picture is otherwise: Oligarchy subtends citizenship with consumerism; it is rendered impotent by intractable divisions between rich and poor and by the escalating costs for the services of lawyers (who futilely attempt to draw lines of distinction because the soul cannot) and of doctors (who engender lingering death). No matter how much "wealth" is amassed in the coffers of the few, the "costs" associated with these problems eventually impoverish the whole. The true oligarch, Socrates says, "fights with only a small part of his resources, he is usually defeated, and he continues to be rich."[321]

Not knowing that the predicament of oligarchy cannot be redressed within the compass of the appetite for wealth—say, by organizing society in such a way that the love of wealth (rather than the love of honor) may rule[322]—the riches allocated to solve these problems only exacerbate

---

[319] An early Christian analog to this view, found in the thought of Athanasius, should not be overlooked, for it is instructive of a significant difference between Plato and Christianity. His (Athanasius') understanding was that after the Fall, death was inscribed into human life and that this presented a Divine dilemma, to which the Incarnation was the only possible resolution. In his words: "Naturally, therefore, the Savior assumed a body for Himself, in order that the body, being interwoven as it were with life, should no longer remain a mortal thing, in the thrall of death, but as endued with immortality and risen from the dead, should thenceforth remain immortal. . . . Therefore He put on a body, so that in the body he might find death and blot it out. And, indeed, how could the Lord have proved to be the Life at all, had he not endued with Life that which is subject to death?" (*On the Incarnation*, trans. A Religious of C.S.M.V. [Crestwood, N.Y.: St. Vladimir's Orthodox Theological Seminary, 1993]), ch. VII, sec.44, p. 81). Through the Cross, there is both death and life, though here, life is achieved not by doctoring, but rather by Divine irruption, self-sacrifice, and resurrection. On Athanasius' view, the problem of the pagans was that they did not understand the extent to which death is inscribed into mortal life; nor, consequently, did they grasp the measures that were necessary to overcome the intractable difficulty. Here I am suggesting that Plato *does* grasp the magnitude of the difficulty, but does not recur to the answer Christians thought necessary, because the "divine rescue" of which he speaks involves an awakening in the soul of the Divine faculty of reason that is *already there*.

[320] Plato, *Republic*, Book IX, 577a. The passage occurs in the context of Socrates' discussion of the tyrant; his point about seeing beyond the appearances of power applies, however, to all defective types.

[321] Plato, *Republic*, Book VIII, 555a.

[322] This is the argument of Albert O. Hirschman, *The Passions and the Interests* (Princeton: Princeton University Press, 1977), an argument, I suggest in the Conclusion, that is in

them. Impoverishment is not resolvable by means of mortal currency, as the oligarch opines. Divine currency is the source of true wealth; it alone "can create unity and love [*homonoian kai philian*],"[323] Socrates says. Contrary to what Cephalus first suggested,[324] oligarchy can neither pay back nor, in this case, outgrow its debts.

To this catalogue of *visible* failings let us add some observations about what has begun to transpire out of sight—in the interstices of the oligarchic soul itself. While there is an appearance of strength in the soul for whom wealth is the orienting principle, in fact the oligarchic soul struggles to keep all other appetites bound up except the appetite for wealth. Yet these cannot be bridled because the reasoning part of the soul that can grant them their due—and so bind them—does not rule. The oligarch, consequently, is perpetually at odds with the unruly appetites he harbors.[325] Having crowned one appetite as king, the oligarch has no resources to ward off the rulership of all the rest. The true pilot of the soul has been inebriated, and now the appetites that show themselves only in sleep begin to appear on the borders of the oligarchic soul's golden world.[326]

Let it be granted, then, that oligarchy is a defective type. What is to be done? Perhaps the most remarkable thing about Book VIII is that time and again, even though the contradiction of each defective type is

---

accord with what I there call "the fable of liberalism." According to Hirschman, Hobbes wished "[to found] a state so constituted that the problems created by passionate men are solved once and for all" (p. 31); a thought Hobbes expresses, to be sure, in *Leviathan*, part I, ch. xiii, paras.1–8, pp. 75–76. Hirschman's intent is to show that Hobbes was part of an emergent tradition concerned with substituting interest (which was constructive) for the passion for glory (which was destructive). His reading of Locke is informed by the same thought. See ibid., pp. 53–54 *passim*. Understood in light of the claims of Book VIII of the *Republic*, Hirschman (like the son of the oligarchic father) sees that the passion for honor and victory is not an adequate principle on which to base justice; his defense of the love of wealth, however, fails to comprehend that it, too, is a defective type. The love of wealth rightly supersedes the love of honor, but the oligarchic son will have no fewer difficulties than did his timocratic father.

[323] Plato, *Republic*, Book I, 351d.

[324] See ibid., 331b: "Money enables [a man] to pay his debts."

[325] Where in timocracy there was faction, in oligarchy the rudiments of warfare appear. Worth noting is that as tyranny is approached the oppositions within the whole become progressively more antagonistic. The tyrant, the soul that Thrasymachus claimed "gets it all" (*Republic*, Book I, 343e), is unable to have anything because there is no unified center capable of action. See the section below on "The Inaction of the Divided Soul."

[326] It is worth pondering whether the explorations of the darker side of human desire that are to be found in the work of Freud and others at the close of the Industrial Age *must have* appeared when they did. Freud reveals the true incapacity of the oligarchic soul, which shows itself when the rule by one appetite begins to be supplanted by the rule of all appetites.

revealed and the son correctly apprehends that the father has not cor-
doned off what should rule from what should not, he (the son) redraws
the boundaries in a manner that only further reveals the secret harbored by all souls not oriented by the Good—that is, tyranny.[327] The son
recognizes that the father does not possess the real standard, but because
the son lacks the real standard, he looks in the wrong place for the corrective.

Only philosophy can save the son from the corruption of the father;
yet the oligarchic son, to take the type presently under consideration,
fights against the rule by one appetite that he sees enthroned in his father's soul without enlisting the one thing that could truly save him. The
son rightly recognizes that *one* appetite should not rule but concludes,
erroneously, that *all* the appetites must be liberated in order for him to
be happy. While he ostensibly rejects the father, the son honors him still
by looking in the same place (the Cave) to full the void in his soul that
only turning[328] can accomplish. Like Polemarchus, the son still remains
his father's heir.[329]

Notwithstanding the son's ostensible revolt, then, what is latent in the
father becomes patent in the son. The father looked in the wrong place.
Without the "pattern set up in the heavens,"[330] the son does no better.
Only the Good, which is the real source of the son's genesis, can help
him. The son rightly recognizes that wealth is inadequate, but not that
philosophy rather than the democratic rule of all waking appetites is the
way of correcting for the defect that the love of wealth shows forth.
Without philosophy, the appetitive part of the soul takes control ever
more firmly, and now demands that all its waking desires be gratified.
Here is the rallying cry for freedom.

Democracy

"A regime of distinction"[331]—so Socrates ironically characterizes
democracy. Here the rule by one appetite in the soul has been supplanted
by the equality of all appetites, the political expression of which is the
proclamation and ostensible presence of freedom, diversity, and tolera-

---

[327] Plato, *Republic*, Book V, 449a.
[328] Plato, *Republic*, Book VII, 518c.
[329] Plato, *Republic*, Book I, 331d.
[330] Plato, *Republic*, Book IX, 592b.
[331] Plato, *Republic*, Book VIII, 558c. Alternatively and more commonly, "a truly noble
regime." I take the locution to be concerned with the distinctions noble souls are disposed
to make rather than with nobility itself. The passages that follow indicate, in fact, that the
democratic regime is rather bad at drawing distinctions at all, hence the claim that Socrates
is being ironic.

tion.[332] The necessary appetites we have while we are awake have given way to the unnecessary ones, and, as in the movement from the moderate to the immoderate city at the outset of the *Republic*, there is an intimation that by moving toward this immoderation, philosophy becomes possible.[333] In a democracy, after all, is not 'each [appetite] rendered its due'? Under democracy we find for the first time among all the defective types a misunderstanding of justice—of "rendering each its due"—that allows for philosophy, though in a defective way. The timocratic, manly regime offered no place for philosophy; the regime that appeals to "boys and women"[334] seems to. The democratic soul, Socrates provocatively says, "bear[s] a likeness to philosophers [*homoious men philosophois*]."[335] The burden of my discussion of democracy here is concerned with the ambiguity of this likeness, which makes democracy at once the only defective regime, really, that has room for philosophy and which also make democracy anathema to philosophy. Either nodal understanding alone fails to comprehend both democracy and philosophy.

Let us begin with the observation that democracy is characterized by the absence of rulership. Absent such rulership, all parts take their turn in clamoring for the right to pilot the soul.[336] Where the oligarch insisted that a hierarchy in the soul is necessary (a faint remnant of the aristocratic insight, the real meaning of which he cannot capitalize on), the democratic soul demands that there be no distinctions, no boundaries, no rulership. In modern parlance, democracy demands "equality."

The failure to draw distinctions *within* the soul has the paradoxical effect of making possible the proliferation of different articulations *of* the soul, of "life-styles," each of which emanates from *a different appetite* and which, it is claimed, is equally legitimate, valuable, and worthy of

---

[332] Ibid., 557b–d.

[333] Consider Cephalus for a moment. Being an oligarch of sorts, the pleasures of the body make no claim on him (Plato, *Republic*, Book I, 329b–c). Might Socrates' subtle indication that the philosophical assent cannot occur without dwelling in the "city of pigs" suggest that of all the corrupt types, it is in a democracy, where the unnecessary appetites appear, that philosophy can first find a foothold?

[334] Plato, *Republic*, Book VIII, 557d.

[335] Plato, *Republic*, Book V, 475e.

[336] Cf. Plato, *Republic*, Book VI, 488a–489a. Hobbes, too, understood this problem. In the state of nature, he says, "the same man in divers times differs from himself, and one time praiseth (that is, calleth good) what another time he dispraiseth (and calleth evil); from whence arises disputes, controversies, and at last war" (*Leviathan*, part I, ch. xv, para.40, p. 100). He differs from Plato in that he sets forth not a philosophical resolution to the problem, but rather a covenantal one, where each accedes with every other to the rule of a sovereign who makes "mine and thine" possible—that is, who renders each its due. See ibid., part II, ch. xvii, para.1, p. 106.

expression. "[Democracy] is a many-colored cloak [*himation poikilon*], displaying all varieties of human character," Socrates says.[337] (In due course, we shall see what this cloak conceals.) What cannot be overlooked, however, is that while differences are present, *there are no real distinctions*—a thought echoed later in Tocqueville's insightful contrast between aristocracy and democracy.

> In aristocracies each man is pretty firmly fixed in his sphere, but men are vastly dissimilar; their passions, ideas, habits, and tastes are basically diverse. Nothing changes, but everything differs.[338]

In a democracy, Tocqueville elsewhere suggests, everything changes and nothing differs.[339] For Tocqueville, too, then, democracy is a "regime of distinction," a regime that seems diverse, but is not. The just soul is the one in which real distinctions obtain—among reason, honor, and the appetites. The democracy regime honors diversity, but such diversity is comprehended only under the category of the freedom *of the appetites* to express themselves without constraint or dishonor.

Socrates' playfulness with the ambiguous standing of distinctions within democracy is not an isolated instance. His discussion of "models" is no less ambiguous. Recall that the early education of the guardians relied on models of goodness, which they were to imitate. While these models were to be supplanted as our prospective philosopher moved from childhood to adulthood by the pattern "found somewhere in heaven for him who wants to see,"[340] the democratic soul seems not to understand the need for this "turn" toward the heavens at all. The democratic soul, Socrates says, "surely wouldn't lack for models."[341] The democratic soul is the first of the defective types discussed here to recognize the need for models—but seems unable to know where they can truly be found.

---

[337] Plato, *Republic*, Book VIII, 557c.

[338] Tocqueville, *Democracy in America*, vol. II, part III, ch. 17, p. 614.

[339] See ibid.: "[American society] is monotonous because all [its] changes are alike." This observation allows us to understand Tocqueville's curious invocation of Federalist No. 51 in *Democracy in America*. While he agreed with Madison about the danger posed by majorities, he disagreed that different interests would cancel each other out, as Madison suggested. Indeed, in the passage that Tocqueville quotes from Federalist No.51, he deliberately bypasses the section in which Madison makes that argument and picks up again after it is completed. Tocqueville saw distinctions without a difference, as it were, in Madison's idea of competing interests. See Tocqueville, *Democracy in America*, vol. I, part II, ch. 7, p. 260; and Madison, "Federalist No.51," in *The Federalist Papers*, p. 333.

[340] Plato, *Republic*, Book IX, 592b.

[341] Plato, *Republic*, Book VIII, 557e. The mimetic power of democracy is immense; here the "great and powerful beast" of public opinion (*Republic*, Book VI, 493a–b) reproduces itself in its own image, and the likelihood of escape is small.

The many models—let us call them "mortal models"—that democracy displays, moreover, seem to suggest a genuine ground for pluralism, for a unity of the different that seemed to be ruled out under both timocratic and oligarchic regimes. Is this the case? Is pluralism vouchsafed, in other words, by safeguarding these mortal models, as the democratic regime opines, or is "granting each its due" made possible, instead, only when a regime is oriented by the model set up in heaven for those who have eyes to see it? Those whose eyes cannot discern the Eternal Things and the Good that begets them, Socrates says, "wander about inspecting swarms of irrelevancies."[342] Are the models dispensed in democracy just such irrelevancies? Like any and all measures that fall short of reality,[343] might these models turn out to be no model at all, but rather kaleidoscopic apparitions that charm the kaleidoscopic soul[344] and lead to a very different place than the democratic regime imagines?

The possibility that these mortal models, which pretend to invite respect for "all kinds," cannot, in fact, underwrite pluralism is suggested by the utter absence of pluralism under tyranny, that regime type that is concealed within democracy. The narrative structure of Plato's fable is not, however, an argument in itself. So, we must ask, what is the mistake made under democracy—one, let us bear in mind, that comes tantalizingly close to getting it right—that invites the problems that follow?

The mistake made under democracy, already intimated by the preceding comments, pertains to where "the whole" is understood to be located. Under democracy "the whole" to which "pluralism," "freedom," "diversity," and "toleration" point is multiplex, expansive, and seemingly coherent expressions of the appetites that articulate themselves in time and space—in short, "the whole" comprises what the appetites, once unleashed, show forth in the world of coming-into-being-and-passing-away. This "whole," however, is not "the Whole" loved by the philosopher. Therein lays the proximity of the democratic regime to philosophy, and its divergence. To its credit, the democratic soul is the first of the defective types to recognize that the "whole" must be loved; not knowing how to profit from this insight, however, the whole it loves becomes the basis of its impoverishment. It does not look "up," where real refreshment can be found, and so wears itself out in trivial pursuits—a thought not lost to Tocqueville late in *Democracy in America*:

> People suppose that the new [democracies] are going to change shape daily, but my fear is that they will end by being too unalterably fixed with the same institutions, prejudices, and mores, so that mankind will stop pro-

[342] Plato, *Republic*, Book VI, 484b.
[343] Ibid., 504c.
[344] Plato, *Republic*, Book VIII, 561e.

gressing and will dig itself in. I fear that the mind may keep folding itself up in a narrower compass forever without producing new ideas, that men will wear themselves out in trivial, futile activity, and that for all the constant agitation humanity will make no advance.[345]

And elsewhere,

> There is a need for all who are interested in the future of democratic societies to get together and with one accord propagate throughout society *a taste for the infinite*, and appreciation of greatness, and a love of spiritual pleasures.[346]

While the idiom is slightly different, the insight Tocqueville offers is similar: Democratic souls always looks straight ahead, enchained and blindfolded, at the material world that promises to gratify their appetites. They do not, however, look "up." True greatness of soul requires "pathos of distance"[347]—but one far grander than any materialist can imagine.[348] For Plato, greatness is vouchsafed by the prospect of the "turning" that bridges the precipitous chasm between the all and the All, between the whole and the Whole—a chasm that among the defective types first dawns *as a possibility* for the democratic soul who, ruled by unnecessary appetites, loves "it all."

There are other tantalizing respects in which democracy furnishes, yet misunderstands, the rudiments of philosophy. Consider Socrates' remarks about the place of law in democracy.

> [Democratic citizens] end up by ignoring all laws, written and unwritten so that they may be spared the sense of having any master whatsoever.[349]

The resemblance of this remark to the apprehensions that Tocqueville[350] and Nietzsche[351] enunciate aside, the case against lawlessness that

---

[345] Tocqueville, *Democracy in America*, vol. II, part III, ch. 21, p. 645.

[346] Ibid., vol. II, part II, ch. 15, p. 543 (emphasis added).

[347] Nietzsche, *Beyond Good and Evil*, part IX, sec.257, p. 201.

[348] See Tocqueville, *Democracy in America*, Author's Introduction, p. 17: "[There are those] whose object is to make men materialists, to find out what is useful without concern for justice, to have science quite without belief and prosperity without virtue. Such men are called champions of modern civilization, and they insolently put themselves at its head, usurping a place which has been abandoned to them, though they are utterly unworthy of it."

[349] Plato, *Republic*, Book VIII, 563d–e.

[350] See Tocqueville, *Democracy in America*, vol. II, part III, ch. 12, p. 601: "The aim of democracy is to regulate and legitimatize necessary powers and not to destroy all power."

[351] See Nietzsche, *Genealogy*, Second Essay, sec. 12, p. 78: "Democratic idiosyncrasy . . . opposes everything that dominates and wants to dominate; [today] modern misarchism (to coin an ugly word for an ugly thing) has permeated the realm of spirit."

Socrates seems to be making in his remarks about the pathologies of democracy, like his assessment of the fathers, is not as unequivocal as it appears at first blush. In his discussion of the dialectic—that final component of philosophical education—Socrates had observed that "the current practice of dialectic is causing great harm . . . [because] its students have become lawless [*paranomias*]."[352] His worry there, however, is not with lawlessness per se, but rather with lawlessness that "lacks the requisite discipline."[353] Lawlessness, as it turns out, is integral to dialectic, but it yields "radical distrust of all that [was] formerly believed"[354] unless those who practice it have "orderly and steady natures"[355]— precisely what is lacking in democracy. The dialectic destroys opinions that are held dear; it is a kind of lawlessness that makes the sons unlikely to "continue to honor and obey what their fathers have taught them."[356]

Under democracy, for the first time in the descent toward tyranny, lawlessness appears. Its citizens are drawn toward it, rightly, it turns out, but cannot get the good of it because they do not know the way in which lawlessness and dialectical ascent are related. Like the orphan sons Socrates had discussed in Book VII, the lawlessness of the democratic soul ends in a perverse joy in refutation and in a dubiety about the existence of any measure other than the kaleidoscopic desires that call out for gratification.[357] Here, again, there is the rudiment of a correct insight—that lawlessness is necessary to move beyond sickness and toward human health—but it is grasped in the wrong way.

Consider, as well, Socrates' observation that in a democracy "each will pursue a way of life to suit himself."[358] Here the right insight—that each must find what is appropriate to itself—is understood to apply to the appetites alone, rather than to the soul as a whole. Where the philosopher understands that justice requires that each be "rendered its due" so that the entire soul may be unified, the (divided) democratic soul opines that "rendering each its due" means acceding to the entire palate of desires that emerges when appetites rule.[359] Justice for the democratic

---

[352] Plato, *Republic*, Book VII, 537e.
[353] Ibid., 539a.
[354] Ibid., 539c.
[355] Ibid., 539d.
[356] Ibid., 538d.
[357] Ibid., 538d–539a.
[358] Plato, *Republic*, Book VIII, 557b.
[359] This insight sheds peculiar light on Tocqueville's observation that the Southerner knows only hunting and war (*Democracy in America*, vol. I, part II, ch. 10, p. 347), while the New Englander is ruled by industrial callings (ibid., vol. II, part II, ch. 19, pp. 551–54). The repulsion to slavery in the North accords with Plato's suggestion that souls ruled by the appetites are the first to understand the need for equality.

soul means that each appetite expresses itself freely.[360] Justice for the philosopher means the right relationship between the parts of the soul, with (divine) reason ruling. In both instances, each is "rendered its due," but one manner of doing so is separated from the other by the chasm that divides things mortal and things divine. Under democracy, "rendering each its due" occurs. Without the awakening of divine reason, however, the outcome is not justice, but rather an invitation for the appetites that still sleep to awaken. In a word, not justice, but tyranny, ensues.

There is more. Everyone "minding their own business" in democracy suggests not only a sanction for expression, but also a kind of solitude, the full manifestation of which is revealed in tyranny (about which more below). The polis, that unity-of-the-different to which Socrates gave fabulous expression in the Myth of the Metals,[361] has already been shown to be a residual fiction in the previous stage of oligarchy,[362] where there were "rich" and "poor," but no "citizens." The oligarchic regime turned out to be *less* "political" than the timocratic regime. Under democracy, there is even less of a *polis*, of a unity-of-the-different. In democracy, each soul is even more on its own than were the previous types.

This thought is corroborated, as we have seen, in the Allegory of the Cave, where the enshackled prisoners can neither see nor talk to each other.[363] Moreover, the increasing appearance of individual isolation in the descent chronicled in Book VIII casts doubt on Thrasymachus' initial suggestion that the tyrant can benefit his friends, while the just man, in effect, stands alone.[364] Only the just man can have friends, as we shall see. Why, we may ask here, is the democratic soul isolated and on its own?

Let us begin with the observation that the democratic soul is correct to reject the fraudulent claims of oligarchic rule, but fails to understand that there must nevertheless be rulership if all is to go well. Instead, the democratic soul launches out on its own and denies that it need be taught by anyone—just as the sailors had done earlier in Socrates' parable of the pilot.[365] They are right, of course, that what they need cannot be taught; but instead of understanding this *philosophically*, to mean that others cannot bequeath the divine measure that they need,[366] they rest contented with the opinion that they need nothing at all, be it mortal or divine. Here they verge on philosophical understanding, but by miss-

---

[360] See Plato, *Republic*, Book VIII, 561c: "[The Democratic soul] repeats that one pleasure is as good as another and that all must be accorded equal status."

[361] Plato, *Republic*, Book III, 414d–415c.

[362] Plato, *Republic*, Book VIII, 552b–c.

[363] Plato, *Republic*, Book VII, 514b–515b.

[364] Plato, *Republic*, Book I, 343e.

[365] Plato, *Republic*, Book VI, 488b.

[366] Plato, *Republic*, Book VII, 518b–d.

ing the measure, they fall farther into the disorder that "equality" purports to overcome.

Having rejected the authority of others to teach it, then, the democratic soul is on its own and alone. Its loneliness is, of course, belied by ringing public proclamations of the equality of all to which everyone accedes in fraternal concord. Yet if Socrates' account in the Allegory of the Cave is a useful guide, each soul that remains in the shadow world of becoming and of lingering death is, in reality, without connection and adrift; it does not face others, nor understand them, nor hear them.[367] Democracy, that order where boundaries between persons seem most easily broken down, where distinctions are a great affront, in fact has very little on the basis of which persons may be gathered together—a thought not lost on Tocqueville, whose central thesis is that democracy tends to "[shut a man up] in the solitude of his own heart."[368]

There is an additional development within democracy that the previous defective types did not much evince, namely, an accelerating breakdown of the unity *within* the soul. The democratic man is kaleidoscopic, Socrates says, because his thoughts and actions are contextual. What he shows of himself is contingent upon where and with whom he finds himself.

> So [the democrat] lives his life day-by-day, indulging each appetite as it makes itself felt. One day he is drinking heavily and listening to the flute; on the next day he is dieting and drinks water only. Then he tries some exercise, only to lapse into idleness and lethargy. Sometimes he seems to

---

[367] Ibid., 514b.

[368] Tocqueville, *Democracy in America*, vol. II, part II, ch. 2, p. 508. See also Tocqueville's letter of January 1, 1856, to Madame Swetchine: "You can hardly imagine, honorable lady, how painful and terrible it is for me to live in this moral isolation, to feel as if I were living outside the intellectual community of my country and time, solitude in the desert would be no more difficult for me than this isolation in the midst of humanity. For, I will confess to you this weakness, isolation has always frightened me; and to be happy and even serene, I always had to live in a certain concord with others and to be able to count upon the understanding of my own kind—perhaps more than one can reconcile with wisdom. To me especially the line applies: 'It is not good to be alone' " (Alexis de Tocqueville, *Selected Letters on Politics and Society*, ed. Roger Boesche [Berkeley: University of California Press, 1985], p. 326). Also see Wilhelm Hennis, "In Search of the 'New Science of Politics,' " in *Interpreting Tocqueville's Democracy in America*, ed. Ken Masugi (Savage, Md.: Rowan & Littlefield, 1991), ch. 2, p. 49: "Tocqueville radicalizes the experience [of loneliness] suffered so much more prevalently in modern society by making this oldest pronouncement of our Judeo-Christian conception of human history the basis of his entire political thought. It is not only oppressive and sad, it is not good—it weakens and destroys spiritual strength and the soul of man if he is not torn from behind the walls of his ego into constant social and brotherly responsibility."

want to be a philosopher. More frequently, he goes in for politics, rising to say or do whatever comes into his head. If he develops an enthusiasm for military men, he rushes to join them; if for business, then he is of in at direction. His life lacks all discipline [*anagkē*] and order, yet he calls it a life of pleasure, freedom, and happiness and is resolved to stay the course.[369]

The democratic soul may proclaim its independence from all authority, and the right to a "life-style" of its own making, but in fact such a soul achieves whatever measure of coherent thought and action it does only by imitating others. In Nietzsche's ethic of resentment, the self is constituted in and through the other as *enemy*.[370] Here the self is constituted in and through the other as *model*. Not having a divine model by which his soul may be oriented, the democratic soul looks to others to supply the mimetic patterns. The patterns set forth by others, of course, are "no measure at all" within Plato's fable, and so the democratic soul is unable to hold fast to what is imitated.[371] So the democratic soul shifts to and fro, now reflecting this mortal measure, now that, all the while opining that it may find happiness in the diversity of its "experiences." Such a soul is rightly drawn to patterns; but without reason in command, without the divine faculty at the helm, the democratic soul has vision enough only to look to a multitude of false measures that pass, like the shadows on the wall of the Cave, in succession before it, which are without durability or form. Yet these are what the democratic soul longs to imitate, in the hope that through these it may resolve the inconstancies of its every moment—that through the security of one or another "life-style" the incoherence of kaleidoscopic life may be averted.

Disconcerting though this picture may be, however, we should note that the democratic, kaleidoscopic soul does bear a likeness to the philosopher, who is, in a different manner, refractory as well. The democratic soul responds to the models that pass before it by imitating them; the philosopher, because he must speak to each soul according to the degree to which its light of reason has been enkindled, *shows* himself to be kaleidoscopic too. Because the timocratic, oligarchic, democratic, and tyrannical souls each opine differently as to what goodness is, the philosopher must respond according to what each type opines, in order to draw them beyond their misunderstandings. Socrates speaks to the timocrat by appealing to his desire to found a city, to the oligarch by appealing to

---

[369] Plato, *Republic*, Book VIII, 561c–d.

[370] See Nietzsche, *Genealogy*, First Essay, sec. 10, pp. 36–39.

[371] See Charles Taylor, *The Ethics of Authenticity* (Cambridge: Harvard University Press, 1989), ch. VI, pp. 55–69, for a discussion of the rejection of mimesis and the turn toward subjectivity in the modern world.

his desire to find gold beyond measure, to the democrat by appealing to his desire for a freedom greater that the enshackled life in the Cave, and to the tyrant by appealing to his desire for a kind of power that exceeds his boldest dreams.[372] The Good is not manliness, gold, freedom, or power, of course; but the philosopher must work through all of these idioms—he must show himself in a kaleidoscopic manner—in order to speak to others. The philosopher may be just, and so be unmoved by the appeal of partial goods, but his interlocutors are not so blessed. The philosopher must, therefore, show himself in and through an appearance that others who know only appearance may recognize.

Having now considered a number of respects in which democracy "bears a likeness to philosophy,"[373] and in light of the attention I have given to the divine aspect of philosophy, it is worth noting here that the first mention of divine gifts in Book VIII occurs in Socrates' discussion of democracy.[374] Might he be suggesting, by this allusion, that the divine, so necessary for philosophy, is able to make its appearance for the first time within a democracy, when the soul is, paradoxically, most likely to "dwell with the Lotus Eaters"?[375]

This suggestion is neither as theoretically farfetched as it appears at first glance nor anomalous in the history of political thought. Indeed, Tocqueville seems to have had a kindred insight, *viz.*, that democratic peoples, prone as they are to be enchained to the material world,[376] are also, occasionally, a supremely religious people as well—more so, in fact, than the aristocratic peoples that precede them.[377] The soul dwells in a body, he says, but cannot be confined by it. The more the democratic soul seeks to gratify its appetites in the world, the more it anxiously intimates that the true source of its nourishment lies elsewhere.

---

[372] See Plato, *Republic*, Book I, 337a–c, 343a–344c.

[373] Plato, *Republic*, Book V, 475e.

[374] See Plato, *Republic*, Book VIII, 558b: "[I]n the absence of transcendent gifts [*huperbeblēmenēn phusin*] no man can become good unless from childhood on his play and all his activities are guided by what is fair and good."

[375] Ibid., 560c. The allusion is to Homer's *Odyssey*, book IX, 82–104, where Odysseus is entranced by the Lotus Eaters to forget his journey home. Understood in the context of Plato's fable, we would say that the democratic soul forgets about its journey home to the Good.

[376] See Tocqueville, *Democracy in America*, vol. II, part II, ch. 10, pp. 530–32.

[377] See ibid., vol. II, part II, ch. 15, pp. 542–46. Insofar as Plato's timocratic soul resembles Tocqueville's aristocratic soul—do they not both love honor and glory?—it can be said that both Plato and Tocqueville agree about the relative proximity of aristocracy and democracy to the Transcendent. Notwithstanding appearances, while democracy may render impossible a certain form of human flourishing that aristocracy brings forth, it also provides the *possibility* of being closer to transcendence, without, however, guaranteeing it.

The soul has needs, which must be satisfied. Whatever pains are taken to distract it from itself, it soon grows bored, restless, and anxious amid the pleasures of the senses.[378]

In Plato's idiom, when the soul seeks happiness in the world of things that come-into-being-and-pass-away, its success in "having it all" leads the soul to the dim intimation that the "all" that it possesses is not the measure it needs.

It is not, we should add, because the democratic soul is noble and strong that this intimation occurs, but rather because it is fragmented and weak. Honor-loving peoples—think of Nietzsche's Greeks[379]—know no such intimation. They are content with stories of nobility, passed down from father to son. An intimation of a transcendent home is revealed not to the noble man, but rather to the "defective" man, the pilgrim without a home in the world. With this thought Plato and Tocqueville, not to mention Nietzsche, agree. I consider this matter further in the second section of the Conclusion.

Tyranny

At the outset of the *Republic*, when Cephalus first appeared and pronounced his liberation from the appetites,[380] we had reason to suspect that his prompt departure from the discussion was intended by Plato to suggest that the appetites were, indeed, integral to the articulation of the soul into its parts, and to its subsequent ascent toward the unearthly light of the Good. Curious confirmation of the claim that human life cannot be adequately understood without recourse to the appetites is provided by Socrates' depiction of the tyrant at the outset of Book IX. Here, however, we are baldly confronted by that *other* possibility that the presence of the appetites portends, *viz.*, that they may lead to darkness unless properly enlisted and governed. Without appetitive transgression, we cannot proceed beyond the seemingly contented impasse of Cephalus; without *bounding* the appetites that have been unleashed, we cannot but move toward the frantic impasse of the tyrant.

Cephalus, recall, claimed to be "free from the savage masters" that seem to haunt the tyrant; yet this was so not because he had befriended and bound them, but rather because he did not have them to befriend and bind in the first place. Having unleashed the appetites after Cephalus

---

[378] Tocqueville, *Democracy in America*, vol. II, part II, ch. 12, p. 535.

[379] See Nietzsche, *Genealogy*, First Essay, sec. 11, pp. 39–43. This insight is confirmed, though with different intent, by St. Paul. See I Cor. 1:23 ("We preach Christ crucified, *to the Greeks foolishness*" [emphasis added]).

[380] Plato, *Republic*, Book I, 329c–d.

departed—in "the city of fever"[381]—Socrates now finally shows us where they lead *without* justice, namely, toward the pathologies of human desire of the sort that Freud so famously adumbrated.

> [When reason slumbers, then] the beastly and savage part, full of food and drink, casts off sleep and seeks to find a way to gratify itself. You know that there is nothing it won't dare to do at such a time, free of all control by shame or reason. It doesn't shrink from trying to have sex with a mother, as it supposes, or with anyone else at all, whether man, god, or beast. It will commit any foul murder, and there is no food that it refuses to eat.[382]

There is, in this account, something of a counterpoint to Glaucon, who earlier, in his exposition of the story of the Ring of Gyges,[383] depicted the appeal of acting without the sanction of reason or shame. In Glaucon's account, it seemed as if those who became the victims of the tyrant's injustice were dozing, or perhaps narcotized, so as to be unable to comprehend what was happening before their eyes in the very light of day. Here, Socrates intimates that it is not his "victims," *but rather the tyrant himself*, the one driven by appetites that show themselves when asleep, who dozes and is unable to comprehend what is really happening.

Beyond this outright reversal of the tale of the Ring of Gyges, there is a more subtle matter to which we must attend: On the one hand, the tyrant wishes to remain asleep, to avoid any prospect that others may intrude on its rampaging appetites (hence, the tyrant's proclivity to hide behind his "dazzling"[384] exterior); on the other hand, the tyrant desires to be recognized by others.

Both of these traits, recall, were revealed already in Book I of the *Republic*, in the quarrel between Socrates and Thrasymachus. There, Thrasymachus showed himself eager to be flattered,[385] but equally eager not to be exposed.[386] Only much later in the dialogue are these traits, which earlier might have been attributed to the accidents of Thrasy-

---

[381] Plato, *Republic*, Book II, 372e.

[382] Plato, *Republic*, Book IX, 571c–d. Cf. Sigmund Freud, *Civilization and Its Discontents*, ed. James Strachey (New York: W. W. Norton, 1989), ch. VI, pp. 75–82.

[383] The unjust man would "[take] what does not belong to him [and] steal with impunity in the very midst of the public market itself" (Plato, *Republic*, Book II, 360b–c).

[384] Plato, *Republic*, Book IX, 576d. See also Plato, *Gorgias*, 523a–524a. The tale Socrates recounts there is of judges who, dazzled by the outward appearance, fail to distinguish between those with good souls and those with evil ones. To judge well, he says, both the judges and those under judgment must be naked. "Once [the soul] has been stripped of the body, everything in the soul is manifest," he says (ibid., 524d). See also *Republic*, Book VII, 517e.

[385] Plato, *Republic*, Book I, 338c.

[386] That Thrasymachus blushes at one point in the argument (Plato, *Republic*, Book I, 350d) is revealing.

machus' personality, revealed to be essential attributes of the tyrannical soul.

In Socrates' more extended treatment of the tyrannical soul, this hiding from others and seeking recognition is shown to be a necessary manifestation of the soul's frantic search in the wrong place for nourishment. Knowing that its hunger cannot be sated, the tyrannical soul both seeks to hide its poverty from others *and* to receive from them recognition of the desirability of its manner of feeding—and this latter, in order to narcotize the doubts it knows to be warranted. The extent of his self-deception being more fully known by the tyrant than by the less defective types, the tyrannical soul is condemned to that purgatorial border—that "lingering death"[387]—to which the other defective types are not, as yet, fully exposed.[388] He hides as knower; he seeks recognition as self-deceiver.[389]

True though it may be that the tyrannical soul searches in the wrong place for nourishment, there are—as in the case of democracy—provocative intimations here that the tyrant has a familiar resemblance to the philosopher.

Consider, first, the matter we have just examined. The correlation of hiding and recognition shows itself not only in the tyrannical soul, but in the philosophical soul as well. The *way* in which this complex appears is different, of course, but the kinship is undeniable. Importantly, the manner of the philosopher's hiding is linked not to the dominion of the sleepful appetites (as it as in the tyrant's case), but rather to his being illuminated by the Good. Those who are ruled by the appetites are able to see only the exterior of things,[390] but not the soul in its elegant and beautiful simplicity; for this latter can be revealed only to the one who sees with other eyes and who is nourished by other food.[391] The unilluminated are

[387] Plato, *Republic*, Book III, 406b.

[388] It would be a mistake to conclude that this paradox is to be found only in the soul of the tyrant. The timocratic soul, that defective type that seems most removed from tyranny, also was involved in hiding (gold) and seeking recognition. The oligarchic soul is recognized for his wealth, but hides a desire to gratify all of his appetites. The democratic soul seeks to be recognized publicly in terms of his rights, yet hides a desire for power.

[389] See Reinhold Niebuhr, *The Nature and Destiny of Man* (New York: Charles Scribner's Sons, 1964), vol. I, ch. 7, sec. 4, p. 207: "If others will only accept what the self cannot quite accept, the self as deceiver is given an ally against the self as deceived."

[390] Plato, *Republic*, Book III, 402d–e.

[391] Plato, *Republic*, Book IX, 583b–586e. Socrates, we intimate, feeds on this true food. Thrasymachus suggested that Socrates was not fed by the same food on which those who are realistic are fed (see *Republic*, Book I, 345b: "Are you asking to be spoon-fed?"). He does seem to understand that Socrates is nourished by a food he cannot see—and so mocks him. Cf. John 6:32.

unable to "see" the philosopher; he is hidden from them.[392] While the tyrant seeks to hide, the philosopher is hidden. For both there is pathos of distance—the tyrant because he is a prisoner in his own home,[393] the philosopher because he knows of a home outside the prison.[394] Both the tyrant and the philosopher, moreover, rely on the shield that the pathos of distance provides between them and the people. Both purport to be a "friend of the people"—the tyrant in speech,[395] the philosopher in deed—yet each would, nevertheless, be killed[396] should he fall into the hands of the people of the city.[397]

Regarding the matter of recognition, where the tyrant looks toward others in order to conceal the emptiness of the pseudo-gratifications of his sleepful appetites, the philosopher knows that the Good alone can fill the soul's emptiness.[398] Moreover, this latter form of recognition, unlike the type the tyrant so desperately seems to want, is the basis of befriending others.[399] The philosopher seeks not recognition *from* others, but rather recognition *of* the Good. In Plato's fable, friendly relations, "lateral" relations, *between* persons require a "vertical" orientation *toward* the Good.[400] Without such an orientation, human beings face forward in the Cave without the possibility of recognizing others or of being recog-

[392] The philosopher seeks "a sheltering wall against the storm and blast of dust and rain" (*Republic*, Book VI, 496d). See also Plato, *Sophist*, 216c: "Certainly the genuine philosophers . . . take on all sorts of different appearances just because of other people's ignorance."

[393] Plato, *Republic*, Book IX, 579a.

[394] Plato, *Republic*, Book VII, 516d.

[395] Plato, *Republic*, Book VIII, 566e.

[396] See Plato, *Republic*, Book VI, 488a: "Now, nothing in all of nature can be found to match the cruelty with which society treats its best men."

[397] See Plato, *Republic*, Book VII, 517a; Book IX, 579a–b.

[398] Plato, *Republic*, Book IX, 585b.

[399] Augustine understood this problem of searching for recognition as well. See his *Confessions*, book II, ch. 1, p. 43: "[In this confession] I shall remind myself of my past foulness and carnal corruptions, not because I love them but so that I may love you, my God. . . . You gathered me together from the state of disintegration in which I had been fruitlessly divided. I turned from unity in you to be divided in multiplicity. At one time in adolescence I was burning to find satisfaction in hellish pleasures. I ran wild in the shadowy jungle of erotic adventures. 'My beauty wasted away and in your sight I became putrid' (Dan. 10:8), by pleasing myself *and by being ambitious to win human approval*" (emphasis added). Errancy from God is here linked to the search for approval from others—a thought not lost to Rousseau, who, in a different idiom, linked the "rage for distinction" (Rousseau, *First Discourse*, para. 40, p. 18) with human errancy from nature.

[400] The philosopher, insofar as his nature is revealed by the parable of the pilot, is not interested in the flattery and cunning of others, but rather wishes to attend to the stars. He alone, however, is capable of sustaining the others, even though they would wish to narcotize him. See Plato, *Republic*, Book VI, 488c–d. In a different idiom, the whole of Luther's social theory hinges on this distinction between "lateral" and "vertical" relations. See Joshua Mitchell, *Not by Reason Alone*, ch. 1, pp. 37–39 *passim*.

nized by them.[401] The philosopher appears to be alone and unreco-
gnized. Socrates seems to suggest, however, that such aloneness, which is
not to be confused with loneliness, is also the only basis for befriending
others, for recognizing them—notwithstanding their rejection of him.
The tyrant suffers a kindred aloneness, and would be rejected as well,
but he is neither able to befriend others nor to recognize them. There can
be no friendship or recognition in sleep.[402] His aloneness is lonely.

The tyrant and the philosopher, each in their own way, then, is cut off
and isolated from those around him. It would be a mistake, however, to
attribute to either condition a claustrophobic character. Where the oligarchic soul—who is exactly halfway between the best and the worst—is
stingy and small-minded, both the tyrant and the philosopher are accustomed to a far grander panorama before them. At the outset of the *Republic*, Thrasymachus had already alerted us to this matter:

> If you imagine that [in defending injustice] I am talking about ordinary
> purse-snatchers, I am ready to assert that even the lowest form of thievery
> is profitable if the thief is not caught. But I am not concerned with such
> petty activities; they do not compare with the kind of injustice on the scale
> to which I refer.[403]

No less is true of the scale of the philosophical enterprise, which has as
its object all that is knowable; that is, the domain beyond the totality of
things that come-into-being-and-pass-away. Both the philosopher and
the tyrant love the spectacle[404] of truth and of theater, respectively.

The grand scale of the enterprise of the philosopher and the tyrant
have as their common trait a desire to have "it all." This desire has already been encountered in democracy, to be sure; yet in this place there
is a peculiar aspect of the desire for "it all" which did not yet show itself
in democracy. In a democracy, recall, there was an ostensible commitment to the rights of each person, necessitated by the fact that democ-

[401] Because tyrants are not oriented by the Good, "they live their whole lives without
friends" (Plato, *Republic*, Book IX, 576a).

[402] Where, for Hegel, recognition entails the positing of the self, through an opposition
to the other in which the prospect of death is close at hand (see *Phenomenology*, para. 196,
p. 118), for Plato, recognition of the other is attended by a "wakefulness" of soul that only
rulership by (divine) reason—attentive, as it is, to the Good—makes possible. Levinas's attempt, in *Totality and Infinity*, to ground the possibility of the revelation of the Infinite on
recognition is perhaps an intermediate position between the two, for he begins, really, from
Hegel's *fearful opposition*, in the hope or arriving at Socrates' formulation that the Good is
higher than Being (*Republic*, Book VI, 509b)—and, therefore, that ethics is the highest
science.

[403] Plato, *Republic*, Book I, 348d. See also 344a–b: "[The tyrant deprives] others of their
property, not little by little but in wholesale lots." The philosopher, Socrates says elsewhere, is not stingy (*Republic*, Book VI, 486d).

[404] See Plato, *Republic*, Book V, 475e.

racy "tolerates all kinds"[405]—included, we may presume, the fathers. While the democratic man is distrustful of the authority of others, and so "lets no word of honest counsel [*alēthē*] come near the guardhouse [of his judgment],"[406] he is not yet *hostile* toward others—including, again, his father.

The democratic soul desires "it all" but does not yet fully understand, as the tyrant does, what this means with regard to the father. To grasp this point, recall the father's standing with respect to the son under oligarchy, under democracy, and under tyranny.

Under oligarchy, the son first imitates the father, and then turns away. Under democracy, on the other hand, the fathers and sons imitate each other.[407] Finally, under tyranny the son exhibits violence toward his father.[408] The oligarchic son, in turning toward clandestine company, keeps a distance from the father and, as it were, continues to respect him qua father. The democratic son, in virtue of his easy-going acceptance of any and all patterns, has, philosophically speaking, no "father"—no single model—at all.[409] Like everything else in democracy, father and son are equal. The tyrannical man, who is in no way easy-going, recognizes that having "it all" *sets each man against every other* in a struggle to gratify the limitless appetites in a world with limited resources.[410] The father is, for the tyrant, not one plausible model among infinitely many, but rather an impediment to be cast aside in the frenzied search amid the sleepy darkness for gratification. *Under tyranny, no models will do.* The apparent consonance between all models in democracy has given way; the father who in democracy was at least respected is here violently cast aside.

> [When tyranny comes to prevail], then the people will discover, by Zeus, what kind of monster they have reared in their midst. They will learn what it means when the father has become too weak to discipline the son.[411]

The question worth pondering here is why there is *no mention whatsoever* of models in Socrates' depiction of tyranny, and what this silence

---

[405] Plato, *Republic*, Book VII, 558d.

[406] Plato, *Republic*, Book VIII, 561b–c.

[407] Ibid., 562e.

[408] Plato, *Republic*, Book IX, 574b–c.

[409] Cf. Tocqueville, *Democracy in America*, vol. II, part III, ch. 8, p. 587: "[W]hen the state of society turns to democracy and men adopt the general principle that it is good and right to judge everything for oneself, taking former beliefs as providing information but not rules, *paternal opinions come to have less power over the sons*, just as his legal power is less too" (emphasis added).

[410] Cf. Hobbes, *Leviathan*, part I, ch. xi, para. 2, p. 58; ch. xii, para. 3, p. 75.

[411] Plato, *Republic*, Book VIII, 569b.

has to do with the violent rejection of the father by the son. Under democracy, recall, models that are put forth appear to be adequate unto themselves; each is purportedly a "life-style"[412] having its own internal coherence. Yet because any and all mortal models are necessarily partial, the soul oriented by them is bound to discover that they cannot provide what is needed.[413]

That is why the democratic soul is not entirely wrong in subsequently turning toward a kaleidoscopic existence. Its initial hope is to achieve a coherent existence by dwelling *sequentially* in the multiple though partial possibilities presented to it as models, in order to "get it all." This hope is, of course, chimerical, because the democratic soul is incapable of attending to anything whatsoever for a sustained period of time—and this, notwithstanding that the democratic soul is "resolved to stay the course."[414]

At some point, however, in the face of mounting evidence, the soul's resolve falters as the inner secret of the democratic search for models—that they are no models at all—is revealed.[415] Yet here, as in all the other cases where the son discovers the inadequacy of what he has inherited from his father, instead of looking for models "set up in heaven," the son now *wholly rejects the very idea of models* and turns instead to the spontaneous, disconnected, and random pleasures of the tyrant—to the iridescent possibilities lurking in kaleidoscopic existence. It is not by accident, at this point, that Socrates tells us that the tyrant will strike his father "for the sake of a blooming new-found *bel ami [neōsti philēs]*."[416]

The insatiable, tyrannical quest Socrates describes here, however, is

---

[412] This locution, to state the obvious, is a contemporary phrase intended to capture the sense in which Plato uses the term "models."

[413] Consider, in this regard, Max Weber's attempt to specify what he took to be the only existentially honest response to the absence of God in the modern world, namely, a coherent life commitment to one or another "value sphere," several specific explorations of which are to be found in his two essays, "Politics as a Vocation" and "Science as a Vocation." Worth considering is whether the Weberian distinction between autonomous spheres, which underwrites the grand dream of specifying a basis of existential coherence in a democratic age without God, collapse by virtue of the *density of appetitive desire* (about which more shortly) that tyranny reveals. See Max Weber, "Politics as a Vocation," in *From Max Weber*, ed. H. H. Gerth and C. Wright Mills (New York: Oxford University Press, 1946), pp. 77–128; and Max Weber, "Science as a Vocation," in ibid., pp. 129–56.

[414] Plato, *Republic*, Book VIII, 561d.

[415] Worth considering here is whether this line of thinking can illuminate the fragmentation of "party politics" in America into single-issue politics. Party politics represents more or less coherent models of political commitment. Yet such models are eventually rejected in a democracy, in favor of commitments to intense, yet short-lived issues. There have, of course, been periodic "realignments," when relatively coherent models emerge anew. Yet on Plato's view, it is only a matter of time before single-issue politics comes to prevail and party politics falters.

[416] Plato, *Republic*, Book IX, 574b–c.

not for a democratically sanctioned "life-style" on the basis of which the happiness of all—both the fathers and the sons—can purportedly be found. Rather, the longings that now drag the son to and fro[417] render such purportedly coherent "life-style" models impossible. Here, the *density of desire* leaves no space for such models to retain their independence, mutual distance, and coherence. Nothing holds them integrally apart, and nothing gathers them together. The "space" necessary for "pluralism," "freedom," "diversity," and "toleration" now collapses; and the son opines that everything that the father does or counsels is a threat to his so-called happiness.

What Plato's fable seems to be indicating is that what characterizes the movement from democracy to tyranny is the rate and intensity at which appetitive desires "come at one"[418]—whence the phrase "density of desire," immediately above. In a democracy, Socrates says, appetites are celebrated, yet their frequency and amplitude are (still) manageable. On the cusp of the transition to tyranny there are foreboding signals, however, of their unmanageability. (Freud, who during the Cold War was sometimes purported to have merely exposited the inner contours of the democratic soul,[419] may better serve to illuminate the contours of this transformation about which Socrates is concerned here. In the light of Plato's fable, Freud's exposition of the "economics of the libido"[420] depicts the soul that is confronted by the *near*-impossibility of mediating between conflicting desires.) At great expense, nevertheless, the soul periodically manages to establish a delicate balance, to find ephemeral "happiness." Desire, while somewhat difficult to manage, is not yet an uncontrollable beast; there is, moreover, still room for "spontaneity," for

---

[417] See Plato, *Republic*, Book X, 589a, where the one who recommends rulership by the appetites "offer[s] a recipe that will starve the human being within him to the point were he can be dragged wherever the other parts of the soul want to go."

[418] Hans Blumenberg (*Work on Myth*, trans. Robert M. Wallace [Cambridge, Mass.: MIT Press, 1985]), suggests that the achievement of upright posture so extended the horizon from which reality can "can come at one" (part 1, ch. 1, p. 5) that it became necessary for the imagination to arrest the "existential anxiety" (p. 6) that ensued when the human being nakedly faced the unoccupied, unnamed, horizon. Myth fills that horizon and arrests anxiety. For Socrates, one of the differences between democracy and tyranny is that in the later there is no arrest from such existential anxiety. Here, persuasion by myth—"the telling of tales and recounting of fables" (*Republic*, Book II, 376d)—may have its greatest power.

[419] See Niebuhr, *Nature and Destiny*, vol. I, ch. 2, p. 53: "Freudianism is a typical product of the uneasy conscience of that portion of the upper middle class which has discovered the realm of chaos under the pretenses and partial achievements of rational order and discipline, but is unable or unwilling to find a basic solution for the problem which it has discovered."

[420] Freud, *Civilization and Its Discontents*, ch. II, p. 36n.

appetites whose burden is both light and infrequent enough so as not to be overwhelming.

The fall into tyranny is marked by a change in the density of desire: In this phase of the soul's descent, nothing can banish the beast from governing. The cautious joy of spontaneity defended by the democratic soul has given way to the terror of incessant appetitive demand. Where having "it all" in a democracy meant the (undeliverable) *promise* of having an infinite variety of "life-styles" available, under tyranny the density of desire reveals the capriciousness of such democratic pleasantry; having "it all" now means what Thrasymachus intended[421] by that phrase at the outset of the *Republic*: not tolerance, but dominion; not the right *to*, but rather the power *over*.

While Socrates does not mention it, we are, at this point, able to understand that the seemingly innocent distinction that he offered to Glaucon near the end of Book V—between the philosopher, who loves Beauty itself, and the philosopher's likeness, who enjoys the multiple manifestations of beauty[422]—is not without important implications for "the real question before us, the question, that is, how each of us may live the best life."[423] Glaucon himself did not intimate that loving "all" the manifestations of beauty rather than loving Beauty itself leads to the son striking the father. We, on the other hand, are now able to apprehend the connection.

The tyrant's love of "every new-found *bel ami*,"[424] like Glaucon's desire "[not to] risk losing a single one of the young flowers,"[425] supposes that there is no divine model of Beauty, in which beautiful things only partially participate. The tyrannical son, as we know, strikes his father because he sees him as an obstruction to having "it all." Glaucon is not, of course, a tyrant. Yet by virtue of his dim vision, his inability to grasp *where* his desire to have "it all" may be truly nourished without injustice, we are able to understand that it is only a question of time before the inner secret that he (and every other soul) harbors[426] emerges into view, namely tyranny. Glaucon's seemingly guileless relationship to his "young flowers," when fully unfolded, amounts to destructive fury of the sort about which we read in Book IX.

---

[421] Plato, *Republic*, Book I, 343e.

[422] Plato, *Republic*, Book V, 474d–475e.

[423] Plato, *Republic*, Book I, 344e. See also Book IX, 578c: "[A]fter all, we are here addressing the greatest of all questions: the difference between the good life and the bad."

[424] Plato, *Republic*, Book IX, 574b–c.

[425] Plato, *Republic*, Book V, 475a.

[426] See Plato, *Republic*, Book II, 360d: "[F]or every man believes in his heart that injustice will profit him more than justice."

What Socrates does *not* say—perhaps necessarily, because of the grave misunderstanding to which it is prone—is that the son is in no small measure *correct* in "striking" the father, in utterly rejecting him. Throughout the *Republic*, of course, Socrates has gone to considerable lengths to uphold the father; yet there is good reason to believe that his portrayal of the son's relationship to the father under tyranny reveals something fundamental about the mortal condition in shadowy times, something that should perhaps be *explicitly* conveyed with the greatest of care, as a remark much earlier in the *Republic* had already intimated:

> [Think of the stories about what] Uranus did to his son Cronos and how Cronos revenged himself on his father. Then there is the tale of Cronos's further doings and how he suffered in his turn at the hands of his own son, Zeus. Even were these stories true, they ought not to be told indiscriminately to young and thoughtless persons. It would be best if they could be buried in silence. *If they absolutely must be retold, it should be only to a chosen few under conditions of total secrecy* [*di' aporrētōn akouein*].[427]

The secret that Socrates has in mind here is that the son must repudiate his father, no less than the prisoners must be "turned" aside from all mortal models in the Cave in order to come unto the divine model set up in the heavens. Both must leave their father's house, so to speak, in order to come unto their true Home. Here, deference and loyalty, of the sort we witnessed at the outset of the *Republic* in the comportment of Polemarchus toward Cephalus,[428] is no longer desirable or possible. A complete break is needed. The philosopher understands this. The proud son who would honor his father (the timocrat), the disciplined son who would respect his father (the oligarch), the tolerant son who would accommodate his father—these do not. The tyrant is the first of the defective types who *might* also understand.

The philosopher, as we have said, looks elsewhere for a pattern capable of guiding him, for the father cannot give him what he needs. He (the philosopher) knows that he is, in effect, *fatherless*. So, too, is the tyrant;

---

[427] Ibid., 377e–378a (emphasis added).

[428] Plato, *Republic*, Book I, 331d. Polemarchus, as I have said, does not listen to Socrates; he attends only to his father. We are given hints, however, that Thrasymachus *does* listen. While Thrasymachus, the tyrant, and Socrates are initially at odds, Thrasymachus seems to understand a great deal more than does Glaucon by the beginning of Book V, where Thrasymachus longs for more than the fool's gold with which Glaucon seems to be satisfied at the outset of Book IV. "Do you think we have come here looking for fool's gold or for genuine discourse?" he asks (Book V, 450b). Finally, near the end of Book IX (588b), Socrates says, "Someone, I recall, said that the unjust man will find injustice profitable provided he has a reputation for justice." There, Thrasymachus does not speak up to claim his earlier thought.

but he does not yet understand the meaning of his orphanhood. The philosopher, having been "turned," knows that beyond this mortal condition of orphanhood, he has a true Home. The tyrant approaches more nearly to this insight about his orphanhood than any other defective soul, since he alone among them repudiates his father. Nevertheless, he falls short because he does not know where to look for his true Home, or even that he has one. Both he and the philosopher repudiate their "inheritance." But whereas the philosopher does this by turning toward divine reason,[429] the tyrant does this with intemperate destruction. For the philosopher to emerge, Socrates said, "the record of the city and its citizens [must be wiped] clean,"[430] and this, because the mortal city that until then had been discussed was not capable of accommodating divine reason to which we were shortly thereafter introduced. When the tyrant emerges, his unrelenting appetites do just this—they wipe the city clean—though not with the same beneficent results. Both the philosopher and the tyrant "strike the father in order to have it all," to invoke the generic formulation Socrates seems to have in mind. The one does this with a view to the Eternal World, the other with a view to the world of coming-into-being-and-passing-away. Therein lays the chasm that separates the philosopher from the tyrant, the life of justice from breathless frenzy of injustice.

"In a perverted way," Augustine says of God, "all humanity imitates you."[431] No less can be said of the tyrant's relation to the philosopher. The tyrant is a perverse imitation, simultaneously farthest and closest; a mortal correspondent to a divine type, which goes horribly wrong in virtue of its very proximity to philosophy.[432]

This conclusion, recall, was already foreshadowed in the section above on "The Origin of the City" when Socrates had suggested that the precondition of the emergence of justice, of granting each its due, was the strife and appetitive transgression that seems so anathema to the philosophical enterprise. Who, more than the tyrant, is exposed to and

---

[429] Recall that the "first wave" of Book V (450b–457c) was about the need for philosophic reason and the inadequacy of convention.

[430] Plato, *Republic*, Book VI, 501a.

[431] Augustine, *Confessions*, book II, ch. vi, p. 32.

[432] For heuristic purposes, consider the contours of Marx's historical dialectic. While the first historical stage of primitive communism *looks like* the last stage of true communism, true communism is arrived at only after passing through various stages of history in which primitive communism's internal contradictions are progressively exposed. Only in the hideous and penultimate stage of late capitalism are these contractions fully borne out. In the abject poverty of this condition, which appears to be most *unlike* true communism, is to be found the basis for the "turn"—Marx would say "revolution"—to true communism.

caught up in just such strife? And to extend the paradox, who knows less of such strife than the honor-loving timocrat, the one who is, in order of defection, closest to the philosopher? In the very darkest of places, in the conflicted enclosure of the tyrant's soul, is revealed an impotence and enchainment of which the timocratic remains yet unaware.

On the one hand, then, Book VIII of Plato's fable has as its purpose the disclosure of what sort of life, what sort of stumbling, shows itself when the "turn" to the Good does not occur. On the other hand, however, the larger contours of the fable intimate that stumbling of the sort encountered in the more defective types may be necessary for the ascent itself.

The soul oriented by honor will reject this conclusion, to be sure. For such a soul is satisfied that the resolution to the ills of the soul and of society can be cured only by the "truly noble concept of education"[433] that Socrates ironically praised earlier, in Book III:

> Should we conclude, then, that our supervision should be confined only to the poets, compelling them to summon up the image of goodness in their poems or else forgo writing poetry among us? Or should we extend our guidance to those in the other arts and forbid representations of any kind of evil disposition—of what is licentious, illiberal, and graceless—whether in living creatures, in buildings, or in any other product of the arts of man? Here, too, we would penalize disobedience by excluding them from the practice of their art in our city. *In this way we could protect our guardians from growing up in the presence of evil,* in a veritable pasture of poisonous herbs where by grazing at will, little by little and day by day, they should unwittingly accumulate a huge mass of corruption in their souls.[434]

While souls ruled by honor will seek to convey virtuous and manly tales so that the city may be well ordered,[435] democratic and tyrannical souls are under no illusion that an education of this sort will be effective. It is they, I suggest, who are closest to intimating the "prisoner's dilemma" in which they find themselves—a dilemma that no noble education can resolve.

---

[433] Plato, *Republic*, Book III, 401d.

[434] Ibid., 401a–c (emphasis added).

[435] See Titus Livius, *History of Rome*, trans. Canon Roberts (London: J. M. Dent & Sons, 1905), vol. I, preface, p. 1: "There is this exceptionally beneficial and fruitful advantage to be derived from the study of the past, that you see, set in the clear light of historical truth, examples of every possible type. From these you may select for yourself and your country what to imitate, and also what, as being mischievous in its inception and disastrous in its issues, you are to avoid. Unless, however, I am misled by affection for my undertaking, there has never existed any commonwealth greater in power, with a purer morality, or more fertile in good examples" (emphasis added).

The Prisoner's Dilemma

Wisdom, then, seems to be of a order different from those other things that are also called virtues of the soul. They seem more akin to the attributes of the body, for when they are not there at the outset, they can be cultivated by exercise and habit. *But the ability to think [phronēsai] is more divine.*[436]

Without wisdom, itself a divine gift, there is no way for the soul to understand that there is *another* pattern by which it must be oriented, one different from the patterns reproduced mimetically in the (Cave) world. Within the confines of this darkened world, the invocation in speech of a divine pattern will seem, as it did to Thrasymachus in Book I, like the sniveling of a fool. "By every measure," Socrates says, "reality for the prisoners would be nothing but shadows cast by artifacts."[437] The answer most needed to the question of how to live well cannot but be ruled out by Thrasymachus and his heirs. What the prisoners most need to understand, they cannot understand.

It was this difficulty of showing his interlocutors what they could *not* see, I suggested, that brought Socrates to his exposition in Book VIII. By virtue of the fact that the Good is an *unspeakable* "radiant manifestation,"[438] he cannot show his dim-visioned interlocutors what the Good *is*. He can, nevertheless, intimate to them where a life led *without* an orientation toward the Good leads—namely, to tyranny. The divine pattern cannot be shown to merely mortal eyes; what lurks in any and all defective patterns perhaps can be. The account of the decline in Book VIII is meant to convey just this.

We may, of course, find some measure of satisfaction in this account. The luminousness of the Good is vouchsafed and averred by the disclosure of what it is not. Yet in light of Socrates' dubiety about the man who is more interested in "[polishing] his own intellect"[439] than in directing his attention to the problem of living well, we are justified in wondering whether this formulation remains deficient as it stands. After all, could not the man who is drunk, as easily as the one who is sober,

---

[436] Plato, *Republic*, Book VII, 518d–e (emphasis added).

[437] Ibid., 515c.

[438] Ibid., 518c–d. About the unspeakable nature of the Good, see Augustine, *City of God*, vol. 7, book IX, ch. 16, p. 102: "[Plato's teaching was that God] is the only being who cannot be described, in any language, because of the poverty of human speech; and that even among the philosophers whose force of mind sometimes lifts their spirits as far as possible above matter, an understanding of God is but an intermittent glimmer, like a rapid flash of a dazzling light in utter darkness" (*CG*, p. 362).

[439] Plato, *Republic*, Book VI, 500d.

accede to it? Because Socrates' hope is that mortal man emerges from that drunken condition in which "he has no idea where he is,"[440] this distinction is not trivial. We must therefore go further; for the challenge before us is to convince the man whose intellect is "highly polished" and who professes to understand what Socrates has said that he is, nevertheless, *drunk rather than sober, dreaming rather than waking.*

Just *who* is awake and who is sleeping is, of course, an important question of the *Republic*, akin to the question of who is enchained and who is not. While Thrasymachus would have it otherwise, the Allegory of the Cave indicates that those who have not been illuminated by the radiant light of the Good are the ones who are drunk, asleep, and enchained. In Socrates' sustained account of their condition there is, interestingly, no reference to the pain to which such souls are exposed by virtue of their condition as prisoners "shackled [and] confined to the same spot."[441] Socrates speaks only of the pain experienced by the person who is "turned" toward the Good. In fact, however, the "unturned" prisoners feel pain as well. They may well be inebriated and dozy, and so protected—as if in a womb—from a full exposure to their pain; but wholly inured from it they are not. It *appears* as though the philosopher alone suffers, but the reality is otherwise.

The prisoner's dilemma revolves around this silence in Plato's fable, and can be formulated in the following precise way: which pain is worse, the pain of "death" known by the reoriented soul, or the pain of staying put, surrounded by the apparent satisfactions of the Cave? The drunk, sleepy, prisoner chooses the latter satisfactions, as we know. Yet it is worth pondering whether a *sober* view of his situation would make the case against staying put much more equivocal than it at first appears to be. With that task in mind, I turn now to a catalog of the malefactions to which the prisoner's life is prone, with a view to attending soberly to the pain that is entailed by them. While not every one of them pertain to each of the defective types, we may nevertheless conclude that the items in this catalog are to be reckoned among the attendant though obscured costs that appear when reason has been deposed and delirium prevails in the world of shadows.

---

[440] Plato, *Republic*, Book III, 403e. In the earlier discussion of the "noble lies" I indicated that they were to be understood as antidotes to lies harbored in the soul and that the good doctor-philosopher knows how to treat them, while the sophist does not. Here it can be said that such fables are the proper idiom to use when addressing those who are drunk or who are somewhere between sleep and wakefulness. Those who are narcotized and sleepy are addressed to in one way, those who are wide awake in another.

[441] Plato, *Republic*, Book VII, 514b.

Envy

Notwithstanding the apparent concord among the inhabitants of the Cave below, we are also informed of two strangely juxtaposed aspects of this life of feasting on crumbs and being comforted by dim light and distant warmth. On the one hand, by virtue of wearing blinders that point them straight ahead, the prisoners can seem scarcely capable of envy. The minimal requirement for envy, after all, is the ability to glance toward others with vision just keen enough so that comparisons—well founded or otherwise—may be fabricated. Are not our prisoners alone, and therefore incapable of envy? On the other hand, it is precisely because their gaze is directed "horizontally" rather than "vertically" that the problem of envy arises at all. Unable to look upward, to the "higher things,"[442] in order to gauge themselves by the true, divine measure, they spend their time measuring themselves against others whose measure they are unable to truly take. Measure, souls must; but by dim light they do it poorly, and incessantly—or rather, the frequency of this measuring called envy increases in proportion to the respect in which the other souls that are measured bear a likeness to the one who measures. The healthy soul recognizes its likeness (through love) to the divine; the diseased soul recognizes its likeness (through envy) to others. Likeness, all souls seek; the democratic soul—the soul that proclaims fraternity, tolerance, and, above all else, equality—finds such likeness available as it shifts its blinder-donned gaze from side to side suspiciously among its kindred. Democratic sensibilities, predicated as they are on the equal right of all the appetites to express themselves, seem to provide an ideal basis for concord; yet far from reducing envy, equality actually increases it.[443] As the tyrant within comes more and more to rule in the souls of

[442] Ibid., 529a–c. Rousseau, too, seems to understand that the true measure is not time-bound when he speaks of the state of nature, "which no longer exists, which perhaps never did exist, which probably never will exist, and about which it is nevertheless necessary to have exact notions in order accurately to judge our present state" (*Second Discourse*, Preface, para. 4, p. 128).

[443] See Rawls, *Theory of Justice*, part 3, ch. IX, secs. 80–81, pp. 530–41. Rawls there treats the problem of envy (see esp. p. 535), but reverses Tocqueville's insight that envy becomes acute precisely when social distance is diminished (see *Democracy in America*, vol. II, part II, ch. 13, p. 538). Rawls argues that the general condition of equality established by the original condition circumscribes the envy that would arise were gross inequalities present (*Theory of Justice*, part 3, ch. IX, sec. 81, p. 536). Cf. Tocqueville, *Democracy in America*, vol. I, part II, ch. 10, p. 355, on the principle of "relative justice"; and ibid., vol. II, part IV, ch. 3, p. 673, where he suggests that increasing equality causes envious citizens to "favor the gradual concentration of all political rights in those hands that alone represent the state." Plato might say that while Rawls's "Difference Principle" (*Theory of*

the prisoners, envy increases in proportion as the noble, timocratic soul recedes.[444] Democracy is the unstable equilibrium that the soul for a time achieves when this pathology first emerges. On *this* point, at least, Socrates and Nietzsche are in accord—the difference between them being that while Nietzsche would have us chose timocratic nobility instead, Socrates is under no illusion that the prisoner's dilemma can be averted simply by embracing a *different* defective form.

Sadomasochism

Gratuitous though it may sound, Socrates' analysis of the pleasures of those who, without real gratification, feast here below warrants elaboration along the lines indicated by this provocative heading. By this I do not intend to suggest that every prisoner experiences every pleasure explicitly under this guise, but rather that the inner secret of all pleasures *except the pleasure known uniquely by the philosopher* is that they are unavoidably mixed up with pain.[445] As such, the claim made here is that sadomasochism is that form of "pleasure" that best reveals what is yet hidden in all other forms of pleasure that are not, strictly speaking, philosophical.

It is pertinent to recall that notwithstanding the seeming stability of the other defective types, Socrates' account leaves us really with only two real alternatives: either tyranny or philosophy. All the others, in truth, conceal tyranny. By extension, we may conclude that there *really* are only two sorts of pleasures: those that are essentially mixed (sadomasochism) and those that are not (the pleasure known by the philosopher).[446] All pleasures other than the latter, in truth, conceal the mixed

---

Justice, part 1, ch. I, sec. 13, pp. 75–83) eliminates the distance between the rich and the poor in an oligarchy, democracy introduces new cleavages altogether, which make up in extent what they lack in amplitude. Envy is a democratic, not an oligarchic, phenomenon—for the simple reason that the chasm between rich and poor is too vast for it to emerge. Envy is the vice of those who rub shoulders.

[444] See Nietzsche, *Genealogy of Morals*, First Essay, sec. 10, p. 39: "To be incapable of taking one's enemies, one's accidents, even one's misdeeds seriously for very long—that is the sign of strong, full natures in whom there is an excess of the power to form, to mold, to recuperate and to forget."

[445] Cf. Plato, *Phaedo*, 60b: "What a strange thing that which men call pleasure seems to be, and how astonishing the relation it has with what is thought to be its opposite, namely pain! A man cannot have both at the same time. Yet if he pursues and catches the one, he is almost always bound to catch the other also, like two creatures with one head."

[446] The philosopher, like the soul who cleaves to God, knows that "the eye is not satisfied with seeing, nor the ear filled with hearing" (Eccles. 1:8). The tyrant, like the soul that seeks satisfaction in the world, knows only the pleasures the senses disclose—that is, those pleasures associated with things that come into being and pass away.

pleasure of sadomasochism. In a world of shadows, where things neither *are* nor *are not*,[447] where our pleasures have pain as their necessary counterpoint, has not the man who has renounced the futile attempt to find pure pleasure in that domain where it cannot exist[448] simply more honest about what can be found in such a world? If, as Socrates tells us, "[his] pleasures must [*anagkē*] be mixed with pain,"[449] then is not he who still believes that pleasure and pain are unrelated deluding himself about *where* the purity he seeks may be found? In a shadowy world, no such purity exists.[450]

Said otherwise, the prisoner's search for true pleasure in the Cave is no less futile than searching for the Good or for Being among the shadows: Both strategies betray a fundamental misunderstanding that in the world below, prisoners are perennially confronted by the "relativity of all things." The sadomasochist, like the tyrant, knows something that the others do not.

Rights and the Relativity of All Things

The failure of the timocratic type, I suggested some time ago, was that while it correctly held that death was not to be feared, the sort of death that was practiced was not philosophical. The oligarchic type, on the other hand, correctly held that gold was to be worshipped, but misunderstood that the kind of currency to be worshipped was divine rather than mortal.[451] The democratic type correctly holds that the models given by the fathers are inadequate guides, but incorrectly proceeds to reject the possibility of a divine rather than mortal model. Instead, it looks to cordon off domains of relative stability and coherence where *all* models may flourish. Within the confines of Plato's fable, we may speculate that the invocation of the category of "rights" occurs as a way of securing a protected space for the prolific novel claims of the appetites that emerge once the models given by the father have been rejected. Here, a compromise of sorts has been reached between the desire to reject the very idea

---

[447] Plato, *Republic*, Book V, 478c–d.

[448] See Plato, Book IX, 586a: "Confined to these limits, they never look upward to what is truly above them; nor have they been borne upward. Never have they been refreshed by reality's essence; never have they tasted pleasure which is pure and cannot deceive."

[449] Ibid., 586b.

[450] See Hobbes, *Leviathan*, part II, ch. xxxi, para. 40, p. 243: "There is no action of man in this life that is not the beginning of so long a chain of consequences as no human providence is good enough to give man a prospect to the end. And in this chain there are linked together both pleasing and unpleasing events, in such a manner that he that would do anything for his pleasure must engage himself to suffer all the pains annexed to it."

[451] See Plato, *Republic*, Book III, 416e–417a.

of models, which we find when tyranny rules, and the vestige of a belief that was still taken for granted in timocracy and to a lesser extent oligarchy: namely, that life involves "imitating"—and hence that *what* is imitated is, in a fundamental sense, unassailable.[452] In democracy, strangely enough, aspects of both are held together in the idea of rights: the collapse of the idea of imitating the models of the fathers clears the way for the idea of rights to emerge; yet the very *unassailability* of the idea of rights is a *vestige* of a typology (oriented by imitation) that becomes incoherent once the idea of rights in democracy gains ascendancy.

This fortuitous convergence of incompatible elements invites the criticism that the idea of rights is but an unstable equilibrium, of the sort that democracy itself evinces. Let us concede that this is a warranted appraisal, one to which I return shortly. Such a conclusion, however, ought not to blind us to the fact that the idea of rights is a response to the *failure* of the models set forth by timocracy and oligarchy. The democratic sons rightly understand that what they have been given by the fathers is inadequate, but wrongly understand where to turn to correct their fathers' errors. The love of honor is no less imperfect than the love of wealth: The failure of both to generate anything other than faction yields the democratic idea of rights—that last bastion of things unassailable that promises to offer a basis for political unification.[453] As a response to the failure of the fathers, the idea of rights is understandable, even commendable. The problem lies less in the justification the sons offer *against the fathers* than in where the idea of rights leads or, should I say, where it leads unless philosophy comes to the rescue.

The problem with the idea of rights is not with the idea of things unassailable but, rather, that in trying to comprehend human life *wholly* in terms of the verities of the prisoner's Cave, the basis for making *any* unassailable claims is dubious.

> [W]ill not any of these beautiful things sometimes appear ugly and base? And of the things that are just, will not they sometimes seem unjust? Of holy things, will they not sometimes seem unholy?[454]

[452] True, the sons of the aristocratic and timocratic fathers reject what their fathers bequeath them, but they do not yet attempt to fashion their own unique "life-style," as the democratic son does.

[453] Rawls well understands the problem: "In a well-ordered society citizens hold the same principles of right and then try to reach the same judgment in particular cases. These principles are to establish a final ordering among the conflicting claims that persons make upon one another *and it is essential that this ordering be identifiable from everyone's point of view*, however difficult it may be in practice for everyone to accept it. On the other hand, individuals find their good in different ways, and many things may be good for one person that would not be good for another" (*Theory of Justice*, part 3, ch. VII, sec. 68, pp. 447–48, emphasis added).

[454] Plato, *Republic*, Book V, 479a (emphasis added).

In our own time—for the purpose of illustration—the idea of rights suffers from the very difficulty that haunts all justificatory projects of the sort that originate from souls who dwell with the Lotus Eaters, who have forgotten about their journey Home. Here the absence of self-evident grounds for justification for the idea of right is the unspoken embarrassment around which thought is invariably contorted. Tocqueville understood the problem, even if his proposal for resolving it falls short:

> Do you not see that religions are growing weak and that the conception of the sanctity of rights is vanishing? Do you not see that mores are changing and that the moral conception of rights is being obliterated with them? Do you not notice how on all sides beliefs are giving way to arguments, and feelings to calculations? If amid this universal collapse you do not succeed in linking the idea of rights to personal interest, which provides the only stable point in the human heart, what other means will be left to you to govern the world, if not fear?[455]

Here, as with so many other formulations in the modern world, the transcendent ground of rights has fallen into disrepute, compelling thinkers to scurry about in search of other means of authorizing the idea. Now, several hundred years into this project, the alternatives coalesce into two possibilities, one conspicuously German, the other distinctly English: justification either on the basis of the notion of intersubjectivity and the universals to which, in principle, the self may accede,[456] or by virtue of historical accident.[457] With respect to the German variant, at any rate, Nietzsche's phrase "it is the church, and not its poison, that repels us"[458] is worth remembering. Even though the idea of transcen-

---

[455] Tocqueville, *Democracy in America*, vol. I, part II, ch. 6, p. 239.

[456] See Jürgen Habermas, *Between Facts and Norms*, trans. William Rehg (Cambridge, Mass.: MIT Press, 1996), ch. 3, p. 99: "[H]uman rights and the principle of popular sovereignty . . . represent the precipitate left behind, so to speak, once the normative substance of an ethos embedded in religious and metaphysical traditions has been forced through the filter of post-traditional justification." From Kant we get the rudiments of rights; from Rousseau we get the rudiments of popular sovereignty. "Both conceptions," Habermas says, "miss the legitimating force of a discursive process of opinion- and will-formation, in which illocutionary binding forces of a use of language oriented to mutual understanding serve to bring reason and will together—and lead to convincing positions to which all individuals can agree without coercion" (ibid., p. 103).

[457] See John Gray, *Two Faces of Liberalism* (Cambridge, U.K.: Polity, 2000). Gray argues that liberal theory has largely, and mistakenly, turned to Kant for its justification, but that Hobbes provides warrant for a kind of liberalism that is pluralistic and supports the idea of rights without the need for grand theoretical justification.

[458] Nietzsche, *Genealogy of Morals*, First Essay, sec. 9, p. 36. See also Leo Strauss, "The Dialogue between Reason and Revelation," in *The Rebirth of Classical Political Rationalism* (Chicago: University of Chicago Press: 1989), p. 240: "Nietzsche's criticism can be reduced to one proposition: modern man has been trying to preserve Biblical morality while abandoning Biblical faith. That is impossible."

dence has been repudiated by the "free spirit" of today, its poison—in this case, the idea of rights—still lingers on, though without any justification that can, *in all honesty*, be upheld. The philosophical project of the future, he thought, was to understand what accepting the relativity of all things *really* meant. The implication that this acceptance has for the idea of rights has yet to be fully thought through. The "twelve beats of noon [have sounded, and we still ask,] 'what really was that which just struck?' "[459]

I recognize that I am being rather harsh here. Yet for Socrates, the unassailable claim made in democracy about the sanctity of rights is a sort of atavism, a pretense to have found something unmovable in a world where all things are on the move. The idea of rights that reverberates in a democracy is superior, to be sure, to the *defective* idea of the Good that is opined by the timocratic and oligarchic fathers. Its superiority, however, is only juxtapositional: So long as philosophy—the object of which is the divine pattern that the fathers *cannot* give the sons— is ruled out, the idea of rights is subject to unending expansion as more and more appetites emerge from the shadows and demand to be accorded their due.

The promise that the idea of rights is able to provide a way to mediate between the urgent and increasingly factional claims about what each is due, cannot, finally, be delivered, for the simple reason that the light in the prisoners' Cave is too dim to establish a fixed and unwavering basis for the justice that is sought. What begins as an attempt to find an unassailable basis of unification ends by providing a justification for holding citizens apart, hermetically sealed in worlds where, like Polemarchus in the opening exchange of the *Republic*, they are self-assuredly able to say, "[How] could you persuade us if we won't listen?"[460] As one recent commentator put the matter:

> For [the man who claims rights] there is no longer any differential tension between empirical and completed being, between potency and act, between what is fulfilled and desired. Whether rights are guaranteed or scoffed at, it is in any case the empirical being himself who holds them. The one who seeks justice, wisdom, or truth knows that he does not possess them, *but the one who declares his rights and demands that they be respected knows that he possesses them, and that nothing he or anyone else does can change anything about this possession.*[461]

---

[459] Nietzsche, *Genealogy of Morals*, Preface, sec. 1, p. 15.

[460] Plato, *Republic*, Book I, 327b.

[461] Pierre Manent, *The City of Man* (Princeton: Princeton University Press, 1998), ch. IV, p. 136 (emphasis added). See also p. 145: "[T]he language of rights is the only language for anyone who wants to organize the human world with positing or accepting *a priori* any

Perhaps it can be said that this transformation of the idea of rights into a device by which we are insulated from one another, and need not listen, is bound to occur because the ethical disaster toward which the relativity of all things points must be arrested before it occurs. The idea of rights, understood protectively, provides just such a bulwark.

For Socrates, however, this effort at protection cannot be successful—and this, because the rulership of the appetites that led to the affirmation of the relativity of all things and to the initiation of the idea of rights in the first place *increases* without attenuation so that eventually protections even stronger than rights come to be needed. For this task the prisoners turn *away* from the idea of rights for protection, and *toward* a tyrant, "the root and foundation of [whose] power [is] his initial role as protector."[462] From protections to protector they go. Amid the relativity of all things, there are no safeguards—something the prisoners soon discover after they willingly trade the tenuous protection afforded by rights for the illusory protection offered by the tyrant.

Averting Ruptures

"By every measure [*pantapasi*]," Socrates says, "reality for the prisoners would be nothing but shadows cast by artifacts."[463] The problem of ruptures—here understood to be disconcerting evidence that another, divine measure actually obtains—therefore ought not to appear at all. For how can ruptures of this sort occur if reality is a closed system that precludes such a measure from obtruding? After all, the world in which the prisoners dwell is, as we know, womb-like; and like a mother's womb, it is a barrier of sorts against the world outside—a world of which the unborn knows nothing. Are not the prisoners, then, safeguarded against irruptions of this, for them, unmeasurable measure of all things?

We are wrestling here with a matter of great importance, *viz.*, whether even in this insular fetus-like condition of dreaming, the divine measure that betokens wakefulness and illumination beckons without announcing itself,[464] and whether this beckoning that is resisted and ruled out by

---

idea of human nature of Law by which man is bound to direct his life. The principle of human rights is the only reflexive principle of action of a man who has no ends." See also Alasdair MacIntyre, *After Virtue* (Notre Dame: Notre Dame University Press, 1984), ch. 6, p. 70 *passim*.

[462] Plato, *Republic*, Book VIII, 565d.

[463] Plato, *Republic*, Book VII, 515c.

[464] See Charles Taylor, *Sources of the Self* (Cambridge: Harvard University Press, 1989), ch. 25, p. 505: "Goods . . . can't be demonstrated to someone who really is impervious to them. One can only argue convincingly about goods which already in some way impinge on people, which they already at some level respond to but may be refusing to acknowledge."

the prisoners takes the form of a *peculiar relationship* that the prisoners have to what is present at hand in the Cave. By way of illustration, a lengthy passage from Heidegger is helpful:

> Certainly among readily familiar things there are also some that are puzzling, unexplained, undecided, questionable. But these self-certain questions are merely transitional, intermediate points in our movement within the readily familiar and thus not essential. Wherever the concealment of beings as a whole is conceded only as a limit that occasionally announces itself, concealing as a fundamental occurrence has sunk into forgottenness. But the forgotten mystery of Dasein is not eliminated by forgottenness; rather, the forgottenness bestows on the apparent disappearance of what is forgotten a peculiar presence. By disavowing itself in and for forgottenness, the mystery leaves historical man in the sphere of what is readily available to him, leaving him to his resources. Thus left, humanity replenishes its "world" on the basis of the latest needs and aims, and fills out that world by means of proposing and planning.[465]

To put the matter in terms of Plato's fable: Just because the prisoners do not have a measure by which they are able to comprehend their true situation—a situation which, by virtue of drinking from the waters of Lethe, they have forgotten[466]—does not mean that they proceed in a manner completely consistent with the defective measures at hand. On the contrary, the presence of this, to them, invisible measure confirms itself to be what it is precisely in the *disproportionate evasions* that the prisoners evince when they are approached by this *other* possibility that is to them unimaginable.

Adeimantus evinces this trait when he asks Socrates how this city, which he has been told is only an allegory meant to guide us toward and understand of justice, divine reason, and the Good that illuminates it, is to be "managed."[467] And then, later, there is poor Glaucon, who never really understands anything that Socrates has told him, and who, when brought to the precipice where that most luminous of things, the Good, may be sighted for the first time in the *Republic*, prattles on and is unable to "be still."[468]

In these two instances Socrates seems to be intimating something about the prisoner's situation in the Cave: "Management" and "idle talk,"[469] if you will, have in common that they are ways in which the

---

[465] Martin Heidegger, "The Essence of Truth," in *Martin Heidegger: Basic Writings* (New York: Harper & Row, 1977), p. 134.

[466] Plato, *Republic*, Book X, 621a.

[467] Plato, *Republic*, Book V, 449d.

[468] Plato, *Republic*, Book VI, 509a.

[469] See Heidegger, *Being and Time*, Division I, ch. 5, para. 35, pp. 211–14.

divine measure may be averted, its fecundity and stillness temporarily overwhelmed by the contrived resonances of man in motion.

Now as it turns out, "management" and "idle talk" may be said to correspond to the defective types of oligarchy and democracy, respectively: The oligarch draws resources together for the purpose of increasing his wealth so that nothing may break in on his manufactured contentment; and the democrat is forever involved in chatter that fills all voids and names all things. This formulation, which superimposes these two modes of averting ruptures onto two defective regime types, is helpful, I suggest, because it illuminates the differences between Plato and Heidegger on this matter of averting ruptures, which I pause to consider here briefly. I do so because Plato and Heidegger are, together, the two philosophers in the West who have thought most deeply about this mortal propensity to avert ruptures. Locating Heidegger's thinking on this matter within the confines of Plato's fable further sheds light not only on this peculiarity itself, but also on Plato and Heidegger's manner of understanding it.

Heidegger does, to be sure, alert us to the two modes of averting ruptures I identified above, namely, "management" and "idle talk." His preeminent concern, however, is with the "oligarchic" concealment that is "proposing and planning"—in a word, with the constellation of technology for which "management" is the solution.

For Plato, however, the purported unconcealment that the closure wrought by technology affords[470] does not occur in the manner that Heidegger imagines. What is unconcealed to and in spite of oligarchic "management" is not the luminousness of Being, but rather *the next defective form*, namely, the kaleidoscopic democratic soul. The attempt to avert ruptures is an attribute shared by all defective types, but just what is unconcealed is type-specific; that is, it is contingent on what is *immediately hidden in each type*. The manner of averting ruptures that Heidegger purports discloses man's being-in-the-world turns out to be specific modalities endemic not to *Dasein* itself, but rather to a distinctive "type," namely, the oligarchic, money-loving soul, amply in evidence in Heidegger's Germany during the early twentieth century. It is hard to imagine, for example, Heidegger purporting that the modality of 'proposing and planning' characterizes the timocratic soul. Indeed, Heidegger accounts for just this timocratic soul by locating him, temporally,

---

[470] See Martin Heidegger, *The Question Concerning Technology*, trans. William Lovitt (New York: Harper & Row, 1977), p. 12: "If we inquire, step by step, into what technology, represented as means, actually is, then we shall arrive at revealing. The possibility of all productive manufacturing lies in revealing. Technology is therefore no means. Technology is a way of revealing. If we give heed to this, then another whole realm for the essence of technology will open itself up to us. It is the realm of revealing, i.e., of truth."

prior to Plato, with the pre-Socratics, for whom, he claims, the "question of being" had not yet been closed off.[471] Understood in terms of Plato's fable, Heidegger's claim is that the timocratic (pre-Socratic) soul was not a defective type at all, but rather the one in whom the averting of ruptures did not occur. In Plato's fable, on the other hand, *all* defective types are involved in the attempt to avert ruptures, and this because mortal life in the Cave world of coming-into-being-and-passing away always entails it. Heidegger grants to timocracy (but not to oligarchy or democracy) a privileged status, something Plato's fable rules out. The philosopher alone—the one in whom divine reason rules—is privileged, however; all the rest possess a divine spark that is not yet enkindled and, so, may be said to be merely mortal.

Since the language of luminousness pervades both Plato and Heidegger's writing, it is worth remembering that luminousness is, for Plato, an attribute not only of the Real World that is bathed in Light (which the eye of the philosopher alone can behold), but also of the darkest recesses of the Cave world, where we find the iridescent light of the tyrant[472] to which we are drawn. Both the philosopher and the tyrant have the attribute of luminousness; only the philosopher can distinguish rightly between them.

The prisoner's dilemma, in this light, is that while averting ruptures is the impossible task to which the anxious energy of man is perennially directed, conferring dignity, under the purported guise of philosophy, on "letting Being be," as Heidegger does,[473] may well betray a fatigue of the soul, through which man is less liberated from his chains than delivered, ultimately, unto a more profound bondage that being captivated by the iridescent spender that tyranny involves. The unconcealment to which we are invited through Plato's fable is the unconcealment that, through the practice of death rightly understood, philosophy alone confers. As we shall see in the section below on "Ethics as First Science," this is the purview of ethics. Short of ethical inquiry, luminous unconcealment leads only to tyranny.

The Pathos of Measurement, and Power

Inside the Cave, the prisoners opine that all things that can be measured can be managed, and therefore turned to their own "advantage." Outside

---

[471] See Heidegger, *Being and Time*, Introduction, I.I, p. 21.

[472] See Plato, *Republic*, Book VIII, 568d: "The tyrant [is surrounded by] his splendid, iridescent, numerous, and ever-changing bodyguard."

[473] See Martin Heidegger, "Letter on Humanism," in *Basic Writings*, pp. 193–242. Thinking, Heidegger says, "lets Being—be" (ibid., p. 236). See, in this regard, John D. Caputo, *The Mystical Element in Heidegger's Thought* (New York: Fordham University Press, 1978), ch. 4, sec. 5, pp. 173–82.

the Cave, the freed man knows that the divine measure has no correlative. It can neither be managed nor manipulated. Man has no leverage with respect to the divine measure, no point of purchase, no manner of turning it to his own advantage. The luminous divine measure elicits from man no plan and no contrivance; here one can do nothing other than "be still."[474] The attempt to take the measure of what has been seen convicts its author of misunderstanding what he has witnessed.

In the Cave, however, no such repose is to be found. Here below, the prisoners seek to measure "it all" because they want "it all." Is it an accident that Plato's fable embodies this collusion between the desire for precision and the desire to have "it all" in the character of Thrasymachus? I think not. Plato is much too careful for this conjunction to be mere inadvertence. The irony surrounding the character of Thrasymachus, of course, is that in dwelling in the world of shadows, what he purports to measure can never be rendered with the sort of precision he desires. The ambiguity of which he accuses Socrates pertains, finally, to his own poorly illuminated world, not that world "above" whose light clearly delineates the outline of Things—were he to have eyes capable of seeing them. Thrasymachus forever seeks an unambiguous measure to measure a world that is forever ambiguous.

The measure he sets forth, the one that he proudly yet impatiently presents in order to circumvent this seemingly endless talk that wastes his precious time—for time is all that he has—is power. Power is the measure of all things. The ambiguous measures of honor, wealth, and freedom—all of these are reducible to power, the sole and solitary substance.[475] Power debunks the pretense of all things "higher" than itself and mocks the idea of the Good, that Higher Thing of a different order altogether. By such bebunking, kindred defective measures are revealed to have their roots in power itself; and the idea of a divine measure is mocked for being beyond the wildest flights of fancy. The idea of the Good is less *exposed* (as are honor, wealth, and freedom) than *ridiculed*.[476]

---

[474] "Being still" is the confirmation that one has understood what has been witnessed. That Socrates is found at the beginning of the *Republic* "down at the Pireaus" (Book I, 327a) and that his response to the Delphic oracle's claim that he was the wisest man alive was to question those around him in an effort to refute the oracle (see Plato, *Apology*, trans. G.M.A. Grube, in *Plato: Complete Works*, 20e–22e) suggests that the philosopher is not called on to remain still and to say nothing.

[475] In this regard, Hobbes may be paradigmatic. See *Leviathan*, part I, ch. viii, para. 15, p. 41: "The passions that most of all cause the differences of wit are principally: the more or less desire of power, of riches, of knowledge, and of honour. All of which may be reduced to the first, that is, desire of power. For riches, knowledge, and honour are but several sorts of power."

[476] Again, see ibid., part I, ch. v, para. 7, p. 24: "[Man has] the privilege of absurdity, to which no living creature is subject but man only." This "privilege" obtains because man

In order for the man whose soul is ruled by the love of power to prove that power is the measure of all things, the ambiguity and insufficiency of all of other measures must be shown. This is the tyrant's epistemic project. To complicate matters somewhat before proceeding further, we would do well to recall that Plato is not entirely unsympathetic to this project. In Book VIII, after all, he has every one of the sons reject the illusory pretensions of their respective fathers in favor of a measure that is seemingly more "realistic." All the sons come to think that the measures by which their fathers have lived—honor, wealth, and freedom—are vacuous. In this *specific* respect all the sons resemble the tyrant.

Socrates is not satisfied with the ephemeral measures of honor, wealth, and freedom either, of course; and his task, no less than that of Thrasymachus, is to debunk the pretensions of these measures. It is one thing, however, to call opinions into question for the purpose of intimating—but never precisely demonstrating—the existence of a divine measure beyond all defective measures, and quite another to discredit such opinions with a view to demonstrating precisely that power is the only measure. The philosopher does the former, the tyrant does the latter. Their divergence is attributable not to their different assessments of honor, wealth, and freedom but to what is to be done once these measures have been shown to lack a stable foundation.

At the outset, the tyrant's project seems promising, and its conclusions inescapable, because those who are ruled by the measures of honor, wealth, and freedom have no precise way of measuring these things or of proving that they are not reducible to another, more rudimentary, scale. The tyrant need only establish the absence of precision of these other measures, and the contest is summarily decided in his favor.[477] The burden of proof rests elsewhere. To make the case more troubling still, if Plato's account of the Myth of Gyges is to be trusted, then every man is secretly a tyrant anyway, and therefore is himself unswayed by the very (imprecise) measure he purports to call his own. The capitulation that occurs by those whose measure is honor, wealth, or freedom is perhaps begrudging; it is, nevertheless, advertent. Nothing is taken from them that they have not already secretly renounced. In discrediting imprecise measures, the tyrant aggrieves no one. It is only Socrates who complains, after all, that Thrasymachus has pounced on him like a wild beast

---

uses words that are designated by ideas for which there is no empirical referent, such as Eternity, Infinite, and Good. According to Hobbes, the violent dissensions this privilege produces make an awful Leviathan necessary.

[477] Corrupted reasoning, Rousseau says, "turns out to be good only at destructive criticism" (*Emile*, book IV, p. 268).

(*thērion*).[478] The other interlocutors are surprisingly unperturbed by Thrasymachus' denunciations.

All indications are, then, that the tyrant's measure of power will prevail. When capricious measures abound, the calculus of power is an enticement for the weary soul, an invitation to lucidity of thought and coherency of action in a world of enslaved men who neither think nor act well. *Relative to* other defective measures, nothing can measure up to power; every other measure sooner or later bows deferentially before it.

Yet the project of reducing all ambiguous measures to a single measure turns out to be promising less as a *constructive* project than as a critical one. Absent the comparisons with other defective measures that give it voice, the measure of power is unable to give an adequate account of itself and is reduced to silence—as is Thrasymachus at that mere resting place called Book I in the hunt for justice. The measure of power can expose the shadowy dreams of honor, wealth, and freedom, but cannot show us where to turn in order to live well. To do that requires the light of the Good, by which reason is empowered, justice made possible, understanding made precise, and action made authorial. Notwithstanding the efforts of the tyrant, the critique he offers cannot touch divine reason, which is of a higher order and which makes even that *trace* of justice evinced among thieves possible.

> If we observe, nevertheless, that unjust men sometimes cooperate successfully in some joint endeavor, our powers of observation are at fault. If such men [whose only measure is power] had been completely unjust, nothing would have prevented them from wronging each other. *So there must have been some element of justice in each* [that] prevented them from treating one another in the way they treated their victims. It is this element of justice [that] must have brought them that degree of success they were able to achieve. They must have been only half corrupted when they initiated their misdeeds, since utter villains are completely unjust and would therefore be totally incapable of effective joint action.[479]

The prisoner's dilemma with respect to the tyrant's measure is that while power is the more *immediately* inviting measure to adopt, doing so can succeed only in clearing away the defective measures of honor, wealth, and freedom. Yet power in itself is mute with respect to the question of how to live well. *This* question, however, for which the reward is disorientation of a grave sort, seems to the tyrant senseless to pose. Besides, is not the project of disposing with the measures of honor,

---

[478] Plato, *Republic*, Book I, 336c–e. The tyrant, Socrates says elsewhere, "trade[s] his humanity for the life of a wolf [*lukō*]" (Book VIII, 566a).

[479] Plato, *Republic*, Book I, 352c–d (emphasis added).

wealth, and freedom enough to involve and deflect all of man's attention? Why attend to the difficult question of how to live well, when there is so much joyous labor in helping others discover that the measures they un-reflectively adopt as their own are naïve, disingenuous, and inadequate?

The discernible comparisons that can be made between, on the one hand, this initially promising but ultimately barren strategy of debunk-ing that the prisoners choose to follow and, on the other, certain facets of Enlightenment thought during the modern period, I leave for the reader to consider.[480]

Trivia

Those who are not philosophers, Socrates says, "wander about inspect-ing swarms of irrelevancies."[481] This observation, as we know, occurs in the midst of his attempt to illuminate the nature of philosophical inquiry for his dim-visioned interlocutors and to distinguish such an inquiry from the search for knowledge of things on which the Good—that high-est object of philosophical inquiry—seems to have no bearing. Why does inquiry directed singularly toward *things* yield irrelevancies, we may ask?

One immediate and well-known reply has been considered already.

> However much we may know about other things will avail us nothing if we do not know [about the Good]. Neither would any kind of possession profit us if we had not the possession of the Good. Or do you think there is any profit in possessing everything except that which is good? Or in under-standing and knowing everything, but understanding and knowing nothing about the good and the beautiful?[482]

The light of the Good confers upon things their pertinence. Things may be objects of inquiry, but knowing them *as things* in no way assures that the prisoners will get the good of them. The goodness of the things pos-sessed by the prisoners derives not from the knowledge that the *posses-sion* of them confers—not, that is, from the art or science that through its elaborations grants such *things* to us—but rather from that Source of all things that itself cannot be possessed: the Good.

There is an obvious objection here, namely, that this distinction be-

---

[480] See Max Horkheimer and Theodor W. Adorno, *Dialectic of Enlightenment*, trans. John Cumming (New York: Continuum, 1987), ch. 1, p. 9: "Myth turns into enlighten-ment, and nature into mere objectivity. Men pay for the increase in their power with alien-ation from that over which they exercise their power. Enlightenment behaves toward things as a dictator toward men."

[481] Plato, *Republic*, Book VI, 484b.

[482] Ibid., 505a–b.

tween the goodness that cannot be possessed, on the one hand, and the art or science that generate the things that the prisoners can and do possess, on the other hand, is specious. What are we to make, for example, of the nascent scientific ruminations of Bacon, Descartes, and Hobbes, who, each in their own way, reject the notion that the Good has any bearing whatsoever on our knowledge of things and argue that mankind would benefit precisely by proceeding *without* recourse to the Good?[483] Do they not handily answer Socrates' provocation? Has scientific knowledge not generated wealth beyond measure, and therefore great benefit?

To address this question we would do well to recall the decline from timocracy to oligarchy that Socrates traces in Book VIII, and to invoke it as a heuristic model in order to understand the sort of knowledge against which Bacon, Descartes, and Hobbes were writing. Notwithstanding the differences between these authors, each sought to discredit the "useless" measures of glory and honor they had inherited, so to speak, from their fathers. In the terms of Plato's fable, the sons grew impatient with spiritedness as a ruling principle of the soul and with the noble accouterments that can be bestowed upon only a few. They sought, instead, a more precise and useful measure, a measure appropriate to souls "alloyed with brass and iron,"[484] that is, to "craftsmen" ruled by appetites. In Bacon's words:

> [I]t will be thought, no doubt, that the goal and mark of knowledge which I myself set up . . . is not the true or the best, for that the contemplation of truth is a thing worthier and loftier than all utility and magnitude of works; and that this long and anxious dwelling with experience and matter and the fluctuations of individual things, drags down the mind to earth . . . remov-

---

[483] See Francis Bacon, "The New Organon, or True Directions Concerning the Interpretation of Nature," in *The New Organon and Other Writings*, ed. Fulton H. Anderson (New York: Macmillan, 1960), Aphorisms [Book One], I, p. 39: "Man, being the servant and interpreter of Nature, can do and understand so much and so much only as he can observe in fact or in thought of the course of nature. *Beyond this he neither knows anything nor can do anything*" (emphasis added). See René Descartes, *Rules for the Direction of the Mind*, in *The Philosophical Writings of Descartes*, Rule Two, pp. 12–13: "[We should not conclude] that arithmetic and geometry are the only sciences worth studying, but rather that in seeking the right path of truth we ought to concern ourselves only with objects which admit of as much certainty as the demonstrations of arithmetic and geometry." See Hobbes, *Leviathan*, part I, ch. v, para. 20, p. 26: "[T]he light of human minds is perspicuous words, but by exact definitions first snuffed and purged of ambiguity; reason is the pace; increase of science, the way; and the benefit of mankind, the end. And on the contrary, metaphors, and senseless and ambiguous words are like a [fool's fire], and reasoning upon them is wandering among innumerable absurdities; and their end, contention and sedition, or contempt."

[484] Plato, *Republic*, Book III, 415c.

ing it and withdrawing it from the serene tranquility of abstract wisdom, a condition far more heavenly. Now to this I assent. . . . For I am building in the human understanding a true model of the world.[485]

As Descartes put the matter:

> I thought very little of the glory [that] I could hope to acquire only through false pretences [of the dubious sciences of my day]. . . . For it seemed to me that much more truth could be found in the reasonings which a man makes *concerning matters that concern him* than in those which some scholar makes in his study about speculative matters.[486]

Hobbes, whose Leviathan draws all honor and glory unto himself, so that by contrast citizens appear to have none,[487] also provides a warrant for the oligarchic sons.

> The Nutrition of a commonwealth [over which the Leviathan rules] consisteth in the *plenty* and *distribution* of *materials* conducing to life; in *concoction* (or *preparation*); and (when concocted) in the *conveyance* of it, by convenient conduits, to the public use.[488]

In each case, what was hoped for was a way of proceeding that liberates man from the shackles set upon him when spiritedness rules and reason has lost its sight; what was promised was an *improvement* of human life that paradoxically involves turning a blind eye to the Good.

In what sense, though, can it be said that the knowledge thus gained, the new measure employed, amounts to no more than "swarms of irrelevancies," from which no benefit may be credited? Does no goodness at all come from the new, oligarchic measure of knowledge concerned with increasing wealth? Clearly, there is *some* good that accrues from this turn away from the defective timocratic measure. What sort of account of this can be given?

It is helpful to recall here that as the prisoners move toward the "lower" defective types, they *increasingly* use up the interest on the principal, so to speak, until finally, when tyranny is reached, "the tyrant will sell [*analōsei*] the city's sacred treasures, if it has any."[489] *Prior* to the appearance of the tyranny, however, the sacred treasure is not yet exhausted, and

---

[485] Bacon, "The New Organon," Aphorisms [Book One], CXXIV, p. 113.

[486] Descartes, *Discourse on the Method*, part I, p. 115 (emphasis added).

[487] See Hobbes, *Leviathan*, part II, ch. xviii, para. 19, p. 117: "As in the presence of the master, the servants are equal, and without any honor at all, so are the subjects in the presence of the sovereign."

[488] Hobbes, *Leviathan*, part II, ch. xxiv, para. 1, p. 159 (emphasis in original).

[489] Plato, *Republic*, Book VIII, 568d. In light of the fact that we have been told already by Socrates that the only treasure worthy of the name is that divine gold of reason that

so the knowledge associated with the "higher" defective measures—which within Plato's fable should really be called "opinings"—yet brings *some* sustenance. While the tyrant spends *all* of the "sacred treasure," the oligarch, Socrates says, "defile[s the] temple"[490] but does not yet exhaust it.

Oligarchic knowledge, then, is *not yet* a "swarm of irrelevancies." Rather, it bequeaths some "benefit" even while it continues to draw interest on the principal. Only when oligarchic knowledge is replaced by the knowledge that attends the emergent forms of democracy and tyranny, as it will be unless philosophy comes to the rescue, can what emerges be indicted on the charge that Socrates levels. Said otherwise, the quest for knowledge in the Cave that is both useful and durable *degenerates* into a game of trivial pursuits unless the prisoners are turned toward the light of the Good, toward knowledge of what is *truly* useful and *truly* durable.

If oligarchic knowledge is not the stable thing its defenders wish it to be, then what happens to it? Let us briefly trace the path of its decay. For heuristic purposes let us consider an observation from Tocqueville who, in his own way, was concerned with just this problem:

> As men grow more like each other, a dogma concerning intellectual equality gradually creeps into their beliefs, and it becomes harder for any innovator whosoever to gain and maintain great influence over the mind of a nation. In such societies sudden intellectual revolution must therefore be rare. For taking a general view of world history, one finds that it is less the force of an argument than the authority of a name [that] has brought about great and rapid changes in accepted ideas.[491]

For Tocqueville, importantly, the great advances in knowledge during the modern period can be attributed to *lingering* sites of authority that were the vestiges of aristocracy or, in the terms of Plato's fable, timocracy. This thought is not Tocqueville's alone, of course. Hobbes,[492] Rousseau,[493]

---

already resides in the soul, we may conclude that the "sacred treasure" that is finally squandered by the tyrant is just this currency. See *Republic*, Book III, 416e: "Gold and silver, we shall tell [our guardians] they already have in their souls in divine measure from the gods."

[490] Plato, *Republic*, Book VIII, 552d.

[491] Tocqueville, *Democracy in America*, vol. II, part III, ch. 21, p. 641.

[492] See Hobbes, *Leviathan*, part II, ch. xxvi, para. 41, p. 188: "[F]or if men were at liberty to take for God's commandments their own dreams and fancies, or the dreams and fancies of private men, scarce two men would agree upon what is God's commandments." The passage here is concerned with religion, which is a particular instance of the general problem of authority for Hobbes. On his account, if each man is left to his own devices in the state of nature, then no durable knowledge of any sort is possible.

[493] See Rousseau, *First Discourse*, part II, para. 59, p. 27: "If a few men are to be allowed to devote themselves to the study of the Sciences and the Arts, it must be only those

Nietzsche,[494] and, more recently, Polanyi,[495] each wrote about the crisis of knowledge that would occur when these vestigial sites disappeared. For each, the *dissipation* of knowledge coincides with the demise of the timocratic vestige of the honor that authoritatively gathers together.[496]

Honor is not, however, renounced overnight. The remaining *trace* of honor that has been officially rejected by oligarchy is carried forward into oligarchy itself in the institutional forms concerned with amassing the knowledge it purports to need: namely, the scientific communities and the wealth generating apparatus that attends them. It is, moreover, the vestiges of these authoritative sites that *preserve* knowledge from becoming trivia, from becoming knowledge that leverages nothing. Knowledge is always and only privileged; absent "gatherings" of one sort or another, there can be no purchase on useful knowledge.

If the useful knowledge within oligarchy requires the atavism of honor from timocracy, then we should expect that the degeneration into democracy ought to be accompanied by the emergence of a new, more egalitarian, criterion of what constitutes knowledge—something less privileged than the useful knowledge that still harbors honor even while it professes to provide a universal method available to all.[497]

That new criterion, which bears a resemblance to ethics but which ought not to be confused with it, is the criterion of *meaningfulness*. Meaningfulness is an intermediary criterion of knowledge between oligarchic usefulness and tyrannical trivia. It presupposes usefulness—

---

who feel they have the strength to go forth alone in their footsteps, and to overtake them: It belongs to this small number to raise monuments to the glory of the human mind. . . . Only [when you do this] will it be possible to see what virtue, science and authority, animated by a noble emulation and working in concert for the felicity of Mankind, can do."

[494] See Nietzsche, *Beyond Good and Evil*, part 6, sec. 204, p. 121: "The scholar's declaration of independence, his emancipation from philosophy, is one of the more refined effects of democratic order—and disorder: the self-glorification and self-exaltation of scholars now stands in full bloom." The scholar is one instance among many of the degradation of man. For Nietzsche, the scholar is a pale imitation of the genius (see ibid., sec. 206, p. 125).

[495] See Michael Polanyi, *Meaning* (Chicago: University of Chicago Press, 1975), ch. 12, pp. 183–84: "Many advocates of free societies . . . failed to realize that a free society *rests upon a traditional framework* of a certain sort; and, in their mistaken notion that a free society is an open one, they threw out the baby with the bath water" (emphasis in original).

[496] Tocqueville, *Democracy in America*, vol. II, part II, ch. 5, p. 517: "In democratic countries knowledge of how to combine is the mother of all other forms of knowledge; on its progress depends that of all others." Bear in mind here that for Tocqueville voluntary associations fill the vacancy left by the demise of the honor-loving class.

[497] The ruse in contemporary social science is that there is a "method" that is available to all practitioners and that levels the differences among those universities whose standing is still predicated on honor.

more precisely, it relies on the goods and services that oligarchic knowledge generates—but marks the beginning of that movement toward soliloquy and isolation into which the criterion of meaningfulness *ultimately* devolves.

An example, in our own day, of this nascent criterion is the claim that the love of material "gain," underwritten as it is by oligarchic uselfuless, is being supplanted by the post-materialist search for meaning.[498] The love of wealth has lost its luster, and we have "discovered" that the soul actually has a hierarchy of needs, the highest of which is the achievement of meaning.[499] In this development lurks a tacit censure of oligarchic knowledge, while at the same time a reliance on it as a precondition for embarking on the path toward (individual) meaning. "Meaning," a term that had no currency whatsoever in the canonical texts of the early modern, oligarchic period, is something that only the democratic soul understands.

There are, to be sure, cleavages that appear once meaningfulness becomes the criterion of knowledge: cleavages among generations, among men and women, among different ethnic, racial, sexual, and religious affiliations—all of which, it is hoped, can be ameliorated by a sort of sympathetic indwelling or sensitivity on which democratic education must place such a strong emphasis. Notwithstanding these cleavages that occasionally seem unbridgeable, however, the criterion of meaningfulness has as its correlate the requirement of *coherence*, and so is saved from more profound fragmentation that emerges when trivia—the tyrannical criterion of knowledge—appears.

I have said that the oligarchic criteria of usefulness, which purported to be universal, still retains aspects of authority. The move to meaningfulness is, on the one hand, a rejection of such authority; on the other hand, it is purported to be the true universal because *everyone* is capable of searching for it, without regard for the rigors and discipline that oligarchic knowledge presupposes. One need merely look inward to find meaning. Here is self-knowledge without cost, to which all are privileged. No authority but one's own need be consulted.

---

[498] See Ronald Inglehart, *Culture Shift in Advanced Industrial* Society (Princeton: Princeton University Press, 1990), and, more recently, *Modernization and Postmodernization* (Princeton: Princeton University Press, 1997), ch. 11, p. 325: "In Postmodern society, emphasis on economic security and economic growth is giving way to an increasing emphasis on quality of life. *The disciplined, self-denying, and achievement-oriented norms of industrial society are yielding to an increasingly broad latitude for individual choices of lifestyles*" (emphasis added).

[499] See Abraham H. Maslow, *Towards a Psychology of Being* (New York: Van Nostrand Reinhold, 1982).

In Plato's fable, however, there is an intimation that even this task of establishing a meaningful life proves to be too difficult a task.[500] As we have already seen in the section above on "Democracy" democratic models turn out to be unsustainable, because the appetites that rule soon make demands that subvert the disciplined commitment to one life-style or another. The matter before us at the present moment, though related, is more explicitly concerned with knowledge: How and why does meaningfulness as a criterion of truth devolve into trivia?

The increasing demand of the appetites provides an answer to this question. The more the appetites call out for gratification, the louder their pleas become, since they are in competition with all the rest. Whereas the criterion of meaningfulness presupposes that there is the possibility of an agonistic[501] but ordered internal conversation among the appetites, the advent of trivia presupposes that conversation has given way to cacophony: Now the soul can grasp only passing "bits" of information in a whirlwind of meaningless noise. The democratic soul proudly braves the wind, but is unprepared for the torrent that will soon overwhelm it. The tyrannical soul loses its footing and is hurled about, as in a dream, where fragment follows fragment without repose. Here, neither the coherent and ordered *privileged* knowledge of science and its attendant arts that oligarchy sets forth nor the coherent and ordered *egalitarian* knowledge of meaningfulness privileged by democracy is possible. The studied, distant, scientific knowledge of oligarchy, which gives way to an intimate search of meaningfulness, ends in an exposed encounter with those "swarms of irrelevancies"[502] that one merely rides out, as in a storm. The *initial* response by the democratic soul on the cusp of the transition to tyranny is perhaps a kind of playfulness with the first gusts of this impending torrent. Those who celebrate this playfulness do not, however, "know where their laughter leads."[503]

---

[500] Weber, on the other hand, thought such coherence, while difficult to achieve, was still possible. See Max Weber, *The Methodology of the Social Sciences*, trans. Edward Shils and Henry Finch (New York: Free Press, 1949), ch. I, p. 18: "The fruit of the tree of knowledge, which is distasteful to the complacent, but which is, nonetheless, inescapable, consists in the insight that every single important activity and ultimately life as a whole, if it is not to be permitted to run on as an event in nature but instead be consciously guided, is a series of ultimate decisions through which the soul—as in Plato—chooses its own fate, that is, the meaning of its activity and existence." Weber's idea of coherent personality is not quite democratic, in the sense conveyed in Plato's fable, because of his (Weber's) indebtedness to Kant, whose idea of autonomous value-spheres constrains the range of coherent models that are possible.

[501] See William Connolly, *Identity/Difference* (Ithaca, N.Y.: Cornell University Press, 1991), ch. 6, pp. 178–79 *passim*.

[502] Plato, *Republic*, Book VI, 484b.

[503] Plato, *Republic*, Book V, 457b.

Medical Crises, Legal Gridlock

To take the true measure of life, Socrates says, "[we] must probe into its *every* corner and at all levels."[504] Having been told that the dialectic is concerned with seeing the relationship of *all* the parts,[505] this claim should not surprise us; yet what that might mean here is not immediately apparent. Why do medical crises and legal gridlock *necessarily* become a problem for the prisoners? Moreover, in what way are the two problems related? In what way do they reveal the condition of the whole?

Let us take up medical crises first, and return to the two doctors whom we considered earlier: Asclepius and Herodicus. The just citizen, the one ruled by reason, would want Asclepius—the "real politician"[506]—to be his doctor. The divided soul ruled by the appetites, on the other hand, looks to Herodicus for "cures" that ameliorate the symptoms of his various ailments, but that allow him to continue the life of excess that rule by the appetites entails.

> They do not want to hear that nothing can help them—not drugs, nor surgery, nor amulets, nor incantations, nor anything else—until they give up idling, gluttony, wenching, and drunkenness.[507]

The never-ending evasion of the true medicine of philosophy that occupies Cephalus and all of his heirs has as its corollary the evasion of death to which the soul ruled by the appetites directs all of its attention. Rather than living *well*—a possibility granted only if the Good illuminates and empowers the faculty of reason—the soul seeks to *live forever*. The healthy soul and the sick soul each long to escape from the world that comes into being and passes away; the just soul knows that the gift of illumination is the only manner in which mortal man may rest in Eternity, while the divided soul opines that surcease involves living in perpetuity. Mortal man will always search for immortality, it seems; and always in one of these two ways.

In the Cave, therefore, there will be ample opportunity for Herodicus and his heirs to assist those whose lives are lived out in the condition of lingering death and who seek to live in perpetuity. Unable to render each part of their soul its due, patients who are ruled by the appetites will squander the resources of the Cave in the hope that the mortal gold they are able to amass can be a credible substitute for the divine gold that yet slumbers in their soul and on which they do not know how to draw. All

[504] See Plato, *Republic*, Book IX, 576e (emphasis added).
[505] Plato, *Republic*, Book VII, 533b–d.
[506] Plato, *Republic*, Book III, 407e.
[507] Plato, *Republic*, Book IV, 426b.

the riches of Midas, however, will be exhausted rendering Herodicus his due. Even the oligarchic regime, the regime most capable of yielding such riches, cannot generate wealth enough to stave off death—try though it surely will. Wealth (money) that is not true wealth will be expended securing health that is not true health (lingering death). The bastard offspring of divine currency will be given to purchase the bastard offspring of true health.

The matter of the prevalence of lawsuits betrays the same pattern. Prisoners who are ruled by the appetites will be perpetually unable to grant each its due within their own souls, and for that reason will never be able to steer clear of the law courts, the concern of which is the provisional determination of "mine" and "thine" that is made necessary when the real site for this determination has been overlooked. *Legal* determinations of how each may be "rendered its due" bears the same relationship to justice as does mortal currency to divine currency, and as does the medicine of Herodicus to the medicine of the Asclepius: It is the bastard offspring of the real thing. At its best, "legal justice" is the interest on the principle—derived from justice but not equivalent to it. Whatever power it possesses to bind bears witness to the binding power of the original of justice of which it is imitation.

The prisoners in the Cave claim to be content with this arrangement by which they rely on the offspring of the Good, the interest on the principle. They are resolved to stay the course, in spite of their medical crises and legal gridlocks, and dare not consider the possibility that medicine and law cannot but bring harm unless comprehended within the larger context of justice, properly understood. Only the philosopher knows this standard of health, and so may administer medicine and law in such a way as to assist the patient in becoming healthy. In the philosopher's hands alone will the use of medicine and law not beget terminal illness. The prisoner rightly knows that human life requires supplementary arts in order for it to go well,[508] but rather than listen to the true doctor— and, we may add, to what is the same thing, the true lawyer—he prefers those whose medical and legal supplements promise to maintain him perpetually *as he is*: ruled by the appetites, frightened of death, and grasping for "his own," as if what he believes himself to want is durable and worth possessing. Philosophy is what he truly needs; yet he stumbles away from it as if from a plague. The pain to which he is unremittingly subject is the pain not of "death" endured by the reoriented soul, but rather the pain of *staying put*, surrounded by the apparent satisfactions of the Cave, all the while relying on medicine and law to maintain his life of lingering death.

[508] Plato, *Republic*, Book I, 342a–b.

Let us bring to a close this discussion of the prisoner's dilemma. In the Allegory of the Cave, we are told, a prisoner is "dragged"[509] up the steep slope that leads out to the Real World, suffering disorientation and pain as he goes. About the pain endured by those who remain we hear nothing, which leads us to conclude provisionally that they do not suffer at all. Yet there is ample evidence in the larger fable of the *Republic* that confutes that proposition. The unjust life against which Plato's rhetorical, poetic, and allegorical acumen is directed is shown, finally, to be no less at the mercy of forces that drag the soul around in the Cave than is the soul that is, at great cost to itself, dragged and turned toward the Good.

> Now let us turn back to the one who tells [the man whose soul is divided] that it pays to be unjust and that he will find justice inexpedient. Let us say that all his assertions amount to no more than a recommendation to gorge and exalt the many-colored beast and the lion and all that the lion symbolizes. They offer a recipe that will starve the human being within him to the point where *he can be dragged [helkesthai] wherever the other parts of the soul want to go.*[510]

Man will either be dragged *out of* the Cave or dragged around *in it*. The prisoners are in fact faced with a dilemma, whether or not they recognize it as such. Man ceases to be at the mercy of the beast within him only when he is at mercy of the Good, which illuminates his reason, and thereby bestows on it the power to "render each its due." Mortal man can "stand up and look around" only *after* he has been dragged upward toward the Good; absent this, he never acquires his footing, is perpetually bruised, and then dies.

That Plato does not explicitly express this dilemma is telling. Perhaps he thought that specifying it in terms of two "alternatives"—either staying put or leaving—would render the problem with which he is concerned in a deceptive light. Not one of the prisoners, after all, simply *chooses* to leave the Cave. This situation would not change even if the prisoners understood that the pain that they endure there is no laughing matter. Mortal man may choose to change *locations*, but not *dimensions*. To be drawn across that dimensional threshold beyond the "measure that fall short of the true measure"[511] involves a *turn* rather than a choice, a dying to lingering death, of which the soul that chooses among *available* alternatives knows nothing—for in *this* death, nothing is any longer "available" for man.

[509] Plato, *Republic*, Book VII, 515c–e.

[510] Plato, *Republic*, Book IX, 588e–589a (emphasis added). See also Plato, *Protagoras*, 352b–c.

[511] Plato, *Republic*, Book VI, 504b–c.

Attending to the prisoner's dilemma, then, cannot have the purpose of illuminating the *choices* available to the prisoners. It can, nevertheless, alert souls that are inebriated to the catalogue of pathologies to which they are prone unless they are turned toward the Good: envy that lurks under the pretense of community; sadomasochism that masquerades as pleasure; rights ever in search of a warrant to authorize them; the refusal to avow the full ethical implication of the relativity of all things, the ceaseless task of averting ruptures, the disquieting search for precise measures, and the respect in which the desire for power underwrites that search; knowledge that decays into trivia; burgeoning medical crises, along with legal gridlock, and so on. Here is a world poisoned by the very things on which the prisoners rely while they stay put.

A natural enough reaction to an indictment of this sort would be to rise to the defense—as Polemarchus did when Cephalus, his father, no longer could—and declare that the situation is indeed salvageable. Let us fall silent, however, and concede that the various charges are warranted and that the prisoners below are not healthy, as they claim to be, but rather ill in a terminal sort of way. Let us do so, however, in order that we may begin to explore the question of whether such an admission is, indeed, the requisite point of departure for wisdom to emerge, for man to play his part in ascending to—or, more modestly, *in receiving*—the divine measure. "Until they became ill they had no idea that health is the greatest of all pleasures,"[512] Plato says. Might it be the case that this terminal condition called lingering death contains within it that great compensation of pointing man *in the right direction*—through death rather than evasively around it?[513] Might philosophy actually be of some use after all to the sick soul, the soul in fever—let us add, the soul that is *more* divided and at war with itself rather than less? And if this is so, is it not the case that the democratic and tyrannical soul are, by virtue of the fact that their illness is *out in the open*, closer to health than are the timocratic and oligarchic souls, whose illness is yet concealed to them?

On this prospect, I suggest, hinges the *possibility* of ethics. Said other-

---

[512] Plato, *Republic*, Book IX, 583d.

[513] Theologically considered, might this be akin to St. Paul's formulation, "[W]hen sin abounded, grace did much more abound" (Romans 6:1)? See also Calvin, *Institutes*, vol. I, book II, ch. VII, secs. 3–9, pp. 351–58; and Martin Luther, "Heidelberg Disputations," in *Basic Theological Writings*, ed. Timothy F. Lull (Minneapolis, Minn.: Augsburg Fortress Press, 1989), sec. 17, p. 42: "A sick person seeks a physician when he recognizes the seriousness of his illness." See also ibid., sec. 24, p. 46: "[T]o be born anew, one must consequently die first and then be raised up with the Son of Man. To die, I say, *means to feel death at hand*" (emphasis added).

wise, inscribed into the last two defective forms of democracy and tyranny is the possibility (but not the assurance) that the son's break with the father—a break that noble Polemarchus could not possibly have made, since he wished to remain his father's "heir"⁵¹⁴—can be sanguine insofar as the sons begin to *look elsewhere* than to mortal patterns given by the fathers for guidance. This break, which democracy and tyranny for the first time provide, offers the possibility of ethics, about which more below.

Ethics as First Science

[Now Callicles], I think that I am one of the very few Athenians, not to say the only one, engaged in the true political art, and that of the men of today I alone practice statesmanship.⁵¹⁵

Parting in such a fashion, he would have left behind him no small achievement.⁵¹⁶

The scandalous suggestion in the *Republic* that ethics is the highest science is not yet a metaphysical claim, and hence it cannot properly be subject to the scrutiny of those who spend their time "polishing [their] intellect."⁵¹⁷ By virtue of its location in Plato's fable immediately after Socrates has warned Glaucon not to "falsely reckon the interest"⁵¹⁸ with the principal—a principal that neither he nor anyone else can utter—it is not immediately clear how Socrates' specification of the relationship between the Good and Being can be evaluated at all. He tells us here not what the Good *is*, but what it is *like*. So, too, with the relationship between the Good and Being: The "generative" power of the Good—the Being it begets—is said to correspond to a relationship with which we are familiar, namely, the sun's generative power in the world of things. But since the familiar world is the one that the *Republic* perennially disrupts, we are left to wonder how helpful this familiar example, reiterated below, really is.

I assume that you would agree that the sun not only confers visibility on all that can be seen but is equally the source of generation, nurture, and growth in all things, though not the same as generation. . . . The objects of

---

⁵¹⁴ Plato, *Republic*, Book I, 331d.
⁵¹⁵ Plato, *Gorgias*, 521d.
⁵¹⁶ Plato, *Republic*, Book VI, 496e.
⁵¹⁷ Ibid., 500d.
⁵¹⁸ Ibid., 507a.

knowledge are not only made manifest by the presence of goodness. Goodness makes them real. Still goodness is not itself being. It transcends being, exceeding all else in dignity and power.[519]

In the Allegory of the Cave, only a short while later, we are given further warrant for caution when Socrates tells us that we can confirm the relationship he has specified between the Good and the world of True Things only *after* we have emerged from the Cave, after our souls have been turned away from shadowy darkness, toward the Light that does not deceive.[520] Whatever we are being told about the relationship between the Good and Being, it cannot be properly understood as a metaphysical doctrine at all, since what Socrates provides is less a specification on the basis of which we can contentedly rest (or argue about, for that matter), than a *wager* to which we can either attend or ignore. *For us*, Socrates' suggestion is an invitation, which we can ponder and perhaps live toward, but not possess as an *object* of knowledge. When we are able to move beyond opinion, when reason has been wakened from its slumber, then and only then can we *know* whether Socrates' intimation is true. Until then, any measure we take of what he says will be no measure at all.[521]

If the relationship between the Good and Being *is* to be understood, Socrates suggests, it will be possible only by taking "the longer way [*makrotera . . . hodos*],"[522] namely, by living philosophically—that is, by *practicing death*.

We have already had occasion to refer briefly to this philosophical practice in the discussion of the timocratic soul ("Timocracy," above). There, however, the concern was merely to indicate in passing that the timocratic soul does not know how to practice death rightly. As the *Republic* unfolds, we discover that higher than the guardian-timocrat who does not fear dying is the philosopher who practices death rightly.[523]

---

[519] Ibid., 509b. Cf. Emerson, "Self-Reliance," in *Selected Essays*, p. 269: "In that deep force, the last fact behind which analysis cannot go, all things find their common origin."

[520] See Plato, *Republic*, Book VII, 516b–c.

[521] See Plato, *Republic*, Book VI, 504b–c.

[522] See Plato, *Republic*, Book IV, 435d; Book VI, 484a.

[523] The first differentiation of the guardian class occurs at Book III, 413e–414b. There, the true guardians are those who are best able to honor the music and gymnastics they have learned—both of which arts, we are told only a little while before this announcement, are gifts of the gods (411e). The second differentiation, in which philosophers are revealed to be the true guardians, occurs at Book VI, 503b—shortly after being informed that the city will be happy only if it relies on divine rather than human models (500e). It is probably not by accident that the two differentiations of the guardian class are heralded by the disclosure that what is offered (411e) or needed (500e), respectively, is divine rather than mortal in origin.

And since we are told that the philosopher has before him the spectacle of the Good, we must presume that such spectacle is disclosed through the practice of death, rightly understood. Ethics, or questioning concerning the Good, must involve death, rightly understood.

All who are *not* philosophers, however, evade death. That Plato should draw our attention to this evasion near the beginning of the *Republic*, in the character of Cephalus, is, in this light, understandable enough; but that he should also associate the attribute of "paying debts" with the evasion of death that Cephalus displays raises a question about whether debt sidesteps the death that is needed, and so stands in the way of ethics. To that question we now turn.

Beyond Debt

The fable of the *Republic*, as we know, begins in the Piraeus. Shortly thereafter, and not far away, we hear of Cephalus' definition of justice, according to which justice involves paying one's debt.[524] This coincidence should not be too surprising, of course, since in the Piraeus money—mortal gold, as I have called it elsewhere—is exchanged, and debt and credit are tallied. When we behold the city set up in the heavens at the end of Book IX, however, justice no longer pertains to debt. We have discovered along the way, moreover, that mortal gold is a cheap substitute for reason,[525] for the divine gold that costs nothing and renders its possessor infinitely richer than Midas. The appearance of debt at the outset of the discussion of justice, and its disappearance at the conclusion, warrants some attention. Here we are prompted to ask: If mortal gold is the currency by which debt can be measured, then must the currency of ethics be *beyond debt*? Is what is disclosed through ethics, in other words, beyond the possibility of payment?

The figure of Cephalus is helpful in elucidating the question. His understanding of justice, as we know, involves debt and payment. His hope is that by paying back his debts he may pass over the "threshold of old age"[526] and go to his death debt-free. Life's burden is debt, which must be discharged in order for death to be peaceful. And since he has the money to pay back what he owes, he is content. Nothing really

---

[524] Plato, *Republic*, Book I, 331b.

[525] Plato, *Republic*, Book III, 416e. See also *Republic*, Book I, 336e: "Had we been searching for gold [Thrasymachus], we surely would not have played games with each other and risked letting the treasure slip from our hands. But here we have been looking for justice, something far more precious than gold."

[526] Plato, *Republic*, Book I, 328e.

disturbs him. Money makes for deep sleep—and "the pleasures of good conversation." [527]

As he takes leave of the conversation, Cephalus observes that he must "attend to the sacrifices." [528] In light of what we know of him, we may conclude that his understanding of *atonement* in all likelihood corresponds to his understanding of debt, namely, that here, too, payment is necessary. In matters pertaining to men (debt) and in matters pertaining to the gods (atonement), mortal gold can pay the bill, or so he opines. Indeed, so opines the whole of ancient Greek religious practice to which Plato's fable is a cautious affront.

Before turning to the basis of Socrates' dissatisfaction with this account, and with a view to illuminating the extent to which Cephalus' rendition of the problem of atonement misses the mark, let us briefly consider that subsequent "ghastly" [529] understanding of atonement wrought by Christianity. The comparison will be helpful for understanding the gravity of the problem of debt in Plato's fable, which has not received the attention it warrants.

> We must recall first that atonement is something other than making good. Rather, atonement is made for that for which reparation cannot be made. Faith in atonement presupposes that there is such a thing as *irredeemable* transgression, that there is a kind of debt that is unlike other debts [that] can be calculated and paid. Such transgression or debt can in no way be repaid *from the side of the debtor*. It is not that the debtor must give something away, even if it were a great deal, but rather that he or she must give him- or herself, his or her life, in order to atone for the debt. [530]

Christianly speaking, *irredeemable* debt is the problem of man. By virtue of Adam's sin, all sin. And since "the wages of sin is death," [531] all would have been condemned to die had not Christ been sent by the Father. [532] Mortal currency can in no way compensate, *on man's side of the ledger sheet*, for the "wages of sin" that he is paid *ad infinitum* each

---

[527] Ibid., 328d.

[528] Ibid., 331d.

[529] See Nietzsche, *The Genealogy of Morals*, First Essay, sec. 8, p. 35: "And could spiritual subtlety imagine any *more dangerous* bait than [Christ]? Anything to equal the enticing, overwhelming, and undermining power of that symbol of the 'holy cross,' that ghastly paradox of a 'God on the cross,' that mystery of an unimaginable ultimate cruelty and self-crucifixion of God *for the salvation of man*?" (emphasis in original).

[530] Eberhard Jüngel, *Theological Essays II*, trans. Arnold Neufeldt-Fast and J. B. Webster (Edinburgh: T&T Clark, 1995), ch. 8, p. 176 (emphasis in original).

[531] Rom. 6:23

[532] See John 3:17: "For God sent not his Son into the world to condemn the world; but that the world through him might be saved."

moment he lives.[533] Not even Midas' wealth can pay off his debt; for mortal currency is of no account with respect to the death that man has "earned." Another *kind* of payment, a divine "ransom,"[534] is needed to settle the account. Only divine currency can pay the debt. Again from a Christian perspective, the problem of debt remains insoluble from the mortal point of view, try as man may (and does) to add to his own side of the ledger sheet by increasing his "wealth."[535]

The Christian account of debt differs in many important respects, of course, from the account offered in Plato's fable. The divine irruption of God into time is, for Christians, made necessary because of the radical problem of sin.[536] In the *Republic*, however, there is a "flaw"

---

[533] Cf. Hegel, "The Spirit of Christianity and Its Fate," in *Early Theological Writings*, sec. iii, p. 241: "The Jew . . . in paying his debt had simply readopted the service he wanted to escape, and he left the Alter with the feeling of an abortive quest and the re-recognition of his subjection to bondage." Hegel's reconciliation of this predicament of Old Testament man is love, made possible by the God-man, Christ. Hegel's treatment of Judaism in his later works accords to Judaism the "interiority" of soul that he here accords only to Christianity. See note 36.

[534] See Matt. 20:28: "Even as the Son of man came not to be ministered unto, but to minister, and to give his life as a ransom for many."

[535] Weber's assessment of the origins of capitalism does not systematically address the problem of debt in quite the sense being explored here, yet this account is consonant with his explanation. Of all the sects of Christianity, the followers of Calvin were perhaps the most systematic and clear about the radical problem of debt. Where Weber suggests that the key to understanding the origin of the worldly asceticism that was necessary for capitalist accumulation to get started could be found in the unbearable psychological tension Calvinists endured because of the mystery of predestination, it is worth considering whether the cause has as much to do with the insoluble problem of debt. Attentive to the problem of debt, Calvinists who could not endure the agony of unpayable debt sought to pay it back by increasing the mortal currency in their own account! In this respect Hobbes is also informative. In *Leviathan*, Hobbes is no less stark than Calvin with respect to the problem of unpayable debt (See *Leviathan*, part I, ch. xii, para. 7, p. 59; part II, ch. xxxviii, para. 25, pp. 313–14). Concomitant with this awesome and unbearable formulation of the mortal dilemma, Hobbes also humanizes it, so to speak, by transposing sin into pride and vainglory. For the former, Christ is of course necessary; for the latter, a Leviathan, an artifice of man, will do. Under the rulership of a Leviathan, commodious living—that is, contracting, buying, and selling of mortal gold—becomes possible. C. B. Macpherson is not entirely wrong, then, in *The Theory of Possessive Individualism* (Oxford: Clarendon, 1962), in suggesting that Hobbes offers a justification for the emergence of capitalism; though this justification is best understood not in terms of a Marxist theory of history, but rather in terms of mortal man's incapacity to accommodate himself to the radical problem of debt highlighted by the Reformers. Weber notes the fixation on debt among Calvin's heirs (see *Protestant Ethic*, part II, ch. V, p. 176), but understands the cause of the changing locus of debt—from the transcendent to the mortal domain—in terms of his general historical theory of the disenchantment of the world.

[536] See I Cor. 15:21–22: "For since by man came death, by man came also the resurrection of the dead. For as in Adam all die, even so in Christ all shall be made alive." See also

[*pathēmati*][537] in human nature, but there is no sin. Where no radical problem exists, no drastic and scandalous solution is made necessary.

Nevertheless, we would be wise not to overemphasize the differences between the problem of debt in the Greek and Christian idioms. This mortal problem suffuses the writings of the ancient Near East, from the Code of Hammurabi onward. It held a prominent place during the age of Homeric Greece, in the Hebrew Bible, in the New Testament, and, yes, in Plato's fable as well. Discovering apt comparisons between the problem of debt in Plato's fable and in Christianity less makes them related to each other, than makes the two of them together nearby chapters in a longer book that contains articulation after articulation of this problem with which man alone, throughout history, seems concerned.

In Plato's fable, justice is *initially* comprehended under the rubric of "rendering each its due," as if to suggest that the first narrative formulation offered, that justice equals paying debts, corresponds to the primeval formulation that the historical record discloses. "In the beginning was debt." Yet at the end of Plato's fable, as we have noted, justice does not involve debt at all. Might this mean that while man's initial impulse is to believe that he can live well by freeing himself from debt by his own means, in fact he cannot achieve what he needs to achieve without justice, which is possible only if divine reason has been awakened? That is the suggestion being made here.

In Plato's fable, while reason slumbers, while man lives a life of lingering death, he is neither free from the haunting specter of debt nor able to move *beyond* debt to ethics—as Cephalus' troubled confession attests.[538] *Man stands between.* Just as when reason yet slumbers man is situated between Nothingness and Being, between ignorance and knowledge, and between death and life, so, too, when reason yet slumbers man is situated between ignorance of debt and knowledge of ethics. There, he is lost in payment.[539]

Rom. 5:18–19: "Therefore as by the offense of one judgment came upon all men to condemnation; even so by the righteousness of the one the free gift came upon all men into justification of life. For as by one man's disobedience many were made sinners, so by the obedience of one shall many be made righteous."

[537] Plato, *Republic*, Book X, 602d. Instead of "flaw," "misfortune" might be substituted.

[538] See Plato, *Republic*, Book I, 330d–e: "Let me tell you, Socrates, when death comes near, a man begins to fear and worry about things that before seemed innocuous. If once he laughed at stories of the netherworld and the punishments said to be in store for earthly misdeeds, his unbelief now retreats before his fears that the stories may be true."

[539] It is not mere coincidence that oligarchy—that type where the problem of payment predominates—is situated directly between the philosophy and tyranny. The philosopher is

In Plato's fable, being lost in payment, in debt, is a mortal dilemma no less grave than it is on the Christian account. Moreover, as has been already indicated, this dilemma cannot be resolved by mortal means, strictly understood. Reason, itself divine, must be awakened for man to be extricated from this dilemma.[540] To put the matter succinctly: Merely mortal man would wish that the burden of life be discharged through the payment of debt; payment of debt by mortal means leaves the predicament of man essentially unaltered; a divine resolution of the predicament is made necessary by man's inability to move beyond lingering death; and, finally, the disclosure of the divine resolution occurs on the occasion of death, rightly understood—which moves the soul beyond the contradictions of hypothetical thinking, to unpremised knowledge.

Where Christianity comprehends this necessary death in terms of the self-sacrifice of *God Himself*, so that man may finally be released from the bondage of debt and be "reborn" unto new life,[541] Socrates intimates a somewhat different resolution: Philosophical death discloses an understanding of justice according to which 'rendering each its due' has superceded the exigencies of debt.[542] Philosophy draws man beyond the predicament in which he initially finds himself; short of that, man is lost in payment.[543] Whatever may be the explicit political resonances of the

---

beyond debt; the tyrant is wishes to deny even the mortal problem of debt, and so "cancels debts" as one of his first acts in office. See Plato, *Republic*, Book IX, 566a. The tyrant, like the philosopher, knows that life must be lived "beyond debt," though the tyrant does not really know how this can be rightly done.

[540] See Plato, *Theaetetus*, 176b: "[To escape the evils] that prowl about this earth . . . a man should make all haste to escape from earth to heaven; and escape means becoming as like a God as possible; and a man becomes like God when he becomes just and pure, with understanding." The curious prayer at the end of *Phaedrus* illuminates the problem with which we are considering here. Socrates prays that the gods will grant him the understanding that wisdom is more precious than mortal gold (*Phaedrus*, 279b–c). The capacity to know that the divine currency of wisdom is greater than mortal gold can be given only by the divine, it would seem. On *this side* of such knowledge we are drawn to fool's gold.

[541] See John 3:3. It is not without significance that in John 12:5, Judas is shown to think only in terms of mortal coin. There he reprimands Mary for pouring out oil on Jesus' feet, which could have paid for food for the poor, and shows no comprehension of a sacrifice that cannot be rendered in terms of equivalents. Mary's "sacrifice" there foreshadows Christ's sacrifice.

[542] Cf. Plato, *Phaedo*, 69a–b: "My good Simmias, I fear this is not the right exchange to attain virtue, to exchange pleasures for pleasures, pains for pains and fears for fears, the greater for the less like coins, but that *the only valid currency for which all these things should be exchanged is wisdom*" (emphasis added).

[543] Aristotle, too, seems to recognize that things divine are "beyond debt," though he does not work through this idea in a systematic way. See *Nicomachean Ethics*, book X, ch. 8, 1178b8–15.

well-known declaration by Socrates that "there can be no end to troubles . . . in our cities or for all mankind [without philosophy],"[544] another resonance, perhaps deeper still, which is not without political ramification, pertains to this predicament of debt—beyond which lies ethics. Only philosophy can save man.

Philosophy saves man, however, by gently dislodging the hypotheses about the nature of the Good that *adhere* to the life he lives. This formulation is apt because hypotheses about the Good are not akin to the knowingly held "lies of words" about which Socrates speaks earlier in the *Republic*, but rather akin to "lived lies" that adhere to man unknowingly.[545] Philosophical death pertains to these latter, more ensconced lies that are resistant to being exposed in the light of day as the deceptions that they are.

The seemingly innocuous characterization elsewhere that hypothetical thinking "operates with the kind of assumptions that lead to conclusions and not to first principles"[546] is not without significance here; for the apparently easier course available to man—the course that fortifies "lived lies" rather than exposes them—involves precisely this evasion of death that forecloses ethics. "Lived lies" are the source of hypothetical thinking; only philosophical death frees man from both, frees man from a life of lingering death, draws him beyond debt, "[leads him upward] from Hades to the halls of the Gods."[547] The science of ethics involves that practice of death by which man moves beyond the merely hypothetical knowledge whose security is vouchsafed by the calculus of debt. The impasse in which the science of ethics perennially finds itself stems from this refusal to practice death rightly, to move beyond hypothetical knowledge, and to linger amidst debt.

Such lingering amidst debt does not evince itself only as disquiet of the sort that Cephalus displays, for the larger problem here is a mistaken judgment concerning reality itself. This mistake appears in one of its guises as disquiet, apprehension, and so on—in short, as a *mood* that man exhibits. But if this guise is to be more than merely a "bad mood" that is incidental to Cephalus' character, then the problem must also make an appearance in man's judgment concerning the whole of the world in which he dwells. The problem must show up, in other words, in man's understanding of the very world where such moods are given place. Does debt have more than a "merely" existential component?

[544] Plato, *Republic*, Book VI, 473d.
[545] Plato, *Republic*, Book II, 382a–b.
[546] Plato, *Republic*, Book VI, 510d.
[547] Plato, *Republic*, Book VII, 521c.

It may be argued, of course, that this disquieting mood circumscribed by the experience of debt has no place in any cosmological scheme. Yet if debt *really is* the primordial condition of man, then debt cannot so much be eradicated as relocated. Modern science does just this.

However more sophisticated modern science may be than the understanding of the mortal condition in shadowy times set forth in Plato's fable, it cannot claim to have absolved man from the problem of debt in its entirety. True, modern science dispenses with that mortal embarrassment of requiring a divine rescue from the calculus of debt in order that man may be saved from death. That a divine intervention, of sorts, is needed to resolve the irresolvable dilemma of mortal life strikes the scientific mind as a childish sentiment[548] or, more pathetically, as a projection of a wounded animal.[549] But while debt loses its, as it were, existential aspect in modern science, the ontological aspect is the foundation stone of its entire enterprise. In modern science there is no possibility of a domain beyond debt: The whole of the cosmos is constituted by it. Do not the laws of conservation by which modern physics understands the world presuppose the centrality of payment, of balance sheets on which there is no unpaid debt?[550] As such, modern science—quantum physics perhaps aside—shares the fate suffered by Cephalus: It is lost in payment.

It is not a coincidence, in this light, that the scientific edifice of the modern world can find no place for the science of ethics. Absent the specter of unpayable debt, ethics cannot emerge.

Modern science is not alone in ruling out ethics. So, too, is it ruled out by the oligarchic presumptions by which we are predominantly oriented in the social sciences. Here, what appears in the place of ethics, as the bastard offspring,[551] is a calculus of preferences, where "units" of desire and aversion are weighed and measured, one against another, by crouching reason.[552] Here, all of man's deliberations and acts are purportedly capable of being placed on the balance beam of costs and benefits.[553]

---

[548] See Freud, *Civilization and Its Discontents*, ch. II, p. 22.

[549] See Nietzsche, *Genealogy of Morals*, Second Essay, sec. 22, pp. 92–93.

[550] Cf. Ralph Waldo Emerson, "Compensation," in *Selected Essays*, pp. 285–302.

[551] Just as sophistry emerges as the illegitimate offspring of philosophy (see Plato, *Republic*, Book VI, 496a), so, too, does a calculus of preferences emerge in the absence of ethics, when the world is lost in payment.

[552] See Hobbes, *Leviathan*, part I, ch. vi, para. 2, p. 28, on appetite and aversion. See also ibid., ch. viii, para. 25, p. 44: "[T]he burden of the Lord [is] not possession, but command." By this Hobbes meant to answer the Reformers, for whom the unpayable debt of sinful man pointed to the need for the indwelling "possession" by the Holy Spirit. For Hobbes, life can be understood wholly in terms of payments that can be rendered.

[553] Consider, in this context, Euthyphro's reluctant assent to Socrates that the sort of piety he (Euthyphro) has in mind "would then be a sort of trading skill between gods and

While we might be tempted to locate the advent of this assessment with Utilitarianism, and therefore provocatively near the time of the emergence of modern science, it should not be forgotten that Socrates had already treated this possibility—replete with a subtle understanding of the principle of marginal utility—in Book IX of the *Republic*.[554] I speculate here, but it is worth wondering whether this calculus took as long as it did to emerge as the unrivaled victor in the West because of the *receding* preeminence of Athens and Jerusalem—the former of which emphasized magnanimity, the latter of which emphasized the unpayable debt man owes to God. Athens and Jerusalem each represent distinct human types.[555] The world constituted in and around payment is foreign to both, and may have emerged against the backdrop of their decline.

Taken together, the underlying assumptions in modern natural science about the balance of payments, and the underlying oligarchic assumptions in the social science, preclude ethics. If there is to be ethics, it must begin in that place where natural science and social sceince are mute; it must begin with the possibility—confirmed by the nearness of death—of unpayable debt.

The Misplaced Search for Origins

Let us continue to consider the shadowy paths down which mortal man travels, where ethics is needed but cannot be found. The relationship of

---

men" (*Euthyphro*, 14e). Euthyphro seeks to understand the gods not in terms of gifts but in terms of payment.

[554] Plato, *Republic*, Book IX, 586b–c: "It is this *juxtaposition* of sensations that gives to each [pleasure] its color and intensity" (emphasis added). See also Plato, *Philebus*, trans. Dorothea Frede, in *Plato: Complete Works*, 47c.

[555] Cf. Leo Strauss, "Jerusalem and Athens: Some Preliminary Reflections," in *Studies in Platonic Political Philosophy*, pp. 147–73; and Nietzsche, *Genealogy of Morals*, First Essay, sec. 10, pp. 36–39. Alternatively, it might be the case that the categories of honor and unrepayable debt correspond, sociologically, to the absence of a middle class, which emerges only in the modern age. Prior to that, the ruling class was animated by honor, and the class that is ruled was oriented by unrepayable debt. With the rise of the middle class the idea of the possibility of payment predominates. The emergence of this novel class renders obsolete the "types" about which Strauss and Nietzsche write. See Tocqueville, *Democracy in America*, vol. II, part III, ch. 10, p. 531: "In nations where an aristocracy dominates society, the people finally get used to their poverty just as the rich do their opulence. The latter are not preoccupied with physical comfort, enjoying it without trouble; the former do not think about it at all because they . . . are driven to dwell in imagination on the next world. . . . But when distinctions of rank are blurred . . . a lot of middling fortunes are established. Their owners have enough physical enjoyments to get a taste for them, but not enough to content them. . . . The passion for physical comfort is essentially a middle class affair; it grows and spreads with that class and becomes preponderant with it."

Polemarchus to Cephalus, of which much has been made already, introduces the issue to be addressed here as well.

As we know, Polemarchus wishes to honor his father. Yet throughout the *Republic*, the looming question is whether the sons can receive from their fathers what they truly need. The argument Polemarchus inherits[556] from his father proves to be inadequate, thus casting doubt about whether the home into which we are born, the *mortal* basis of our origin, so to speak, is the one in which we may contentedly rest—with all that this insight may imply about the adequacy of the conventions of mortal life that we inherit. No, the son's home is not, finally, the home he inherits from his "father." The source of his generation is to be found elsewhere. That source is the Good, his true Home. The art of dialectic leads the son to discover that "he is not the child of those who call themselves his parents."[557] The dialectic leads children "to turn upward the vision of their souls and fix their gaze on that which sheds light on all."[558] The son who has grown out of his childhood discovers that his father's home has been a proxy, which he must continue to honor even though he has outgrown it.

If the source of man's generation is the Good, then the question "From whence does *man* arise?" cannot be answered by tracing the lineage and development of mortal patterns. That is, a *chronological* account cannot provide a true account of the emergence of *man*—by which is meant here a being oriented, in small part, contradictorily, or nearly in full, by the Good. The cause of such an orientation cannot be found in the world of coming-into-being-and-passing-away, since such a world cannot offer any stable instance in which the Good may dwell. In a world forever in transition, goodness is transient and relative—now "this," now "that." Opinion, the faculty available to man in the world of coming-into-being-and-passing-away, is dimly illuminated by the traces of the Good, but nothing more. Goodness emerges not chronologically, but rather irruptively. Goodness hovers over a world that "comprehends it not."[559]

The sons—and the defective fathers, for that matter—do not wish to be beholden to such gifts, however; and they prefer to attribute the origin of all good things to the world with which they seem to be already familiar. In such a world, goodness is purported to be *emergent*. Lying in wait, immanent in the world man already knows, goodness shows itself in good time. Here, goodness does not descend *into* time, but rather emerges with the passage *of* time; and the project of finding man's origin consists in providing an account of how, over the course of prehistory

---

[556] Plato, *Republic*, Book I, 331d.
[557] Plato, *Republic*, Book VII, 538a.
[558] Ibid., 540a.
[559] John 1:5.

and history, the "good things" of life—music, play, spoken words, fire, civilization, law, writing, and so on—could have emerged from the rudiments of matter.[560]

Neither wishing to attribute the entirety of this development to a single author nor being warranted in doing so, I note that Kant's thinking is nevertheless paradigmatic of the configuration I am considering here. While he may have wished to have saved a place for God by putting Him beyond the reach of reason,[561] the scheme of development that he traces in his "Idea for a Universal History with Cosmopolitan Intent" requires only that Nature contain within itself the possibility of an unfolding for which alone is needed the leaven of man's "unsocial sociability."[562] Out of what is base emerges what is highest—this is the credo on which the edifice of any number of the sciences of man—psychology, anthropology, economics, and political science, prominent among them—are built.

We would be remiss not to note here that Plato's fable, too, sets forth a variant of this idea, though with a decisive difference. I have indicated above in the section on "The Origin of the City" that appetitive transgression is necessary for the emergence of the differentiation of the soul into its component parts. Without that having occurred, reason remains nascent, and what is highest in man fails to emerge.[563] So stated, this sounds remarkably like Kant's formulation. Kant, however, would never be so bold to say that this ascension discloses what is god-like *in* man. Rather, with Kant's formulation the height to which we ascend amounts to a progressive enhancement, "wherein all the original capacities of the human race can develop,"[564] the collective fruit of which is the achievement of culture,[565] in all of its multiplex expressions. Culture is an ac-

---

[560] Cf. Plato, *Statesman*, trans. C. J. Rowe, in *Plato: Complete Works*, 274c–d, where all the rudiments of civilization are gifts of the gods. See also Plato's *Laws*, 624a–b, where all beginnings are said to be divine beginnings.

[561] See Immanuel Kant, "Perpetual Peace," in *On History*, ed. Lewis White Beck (New York: Macmillan, 1963), First Supplement, p. 108: "[T]he use of the word 'nature' is more fitting to the limits of human reason and more modest than an expression indicating a providence unknown to us."

[562] See Kant, "Idea for a Universal History from a Cosmopolitan Point of View," in *On History*, "Fourth Thesis," p. 15.

[563] See also Plato, *Phaedrus*, 253d–54e, on how the bad steed takes the lead even though ultimately bridled by the charioteer.

[564] Kant, "Idea for a Universal History," in *On History*, "Eighth Thesis," p. 23.

[565] See ibid., "Seventh Thesis," p. 21. The achievement of culture is not yet the achievement of morality. Morality, an accomplishment more noble than culture, is a promise held out for the more distant future. In contradistinction to Kant, see Nietzsche, *Genealogy*, First Essay, sec. 12, pp. 42–43: "Supposing that what is at any rate believed to be the 'truth' really is true, and the *meaning of all culture* is the reduction of the beast of prey

complishment *in time*, the labor of generation upon generation,[566] requiring no divine gift from above. The *refinement* of man is quite enough—and to push matters only a little further, God himself is such a refinement, a dubious projection of a being imperiled by the civilizational need to rein in the appetites so that weakened reason may prevail.[567]

Socrates does not, however, end his ascent in the *Republic* with culture, with that refinement of man accomplished at the cost of the sublimation or repression of his appetites. Rather, the ascent from the appetites culminates in the irruption and revelation of the divine pattern that was unknown and unanticipated at the outset.

There is more: Knowledge of the divine pattern, secured as it is by the awakening of reason, entails not the repression and redirection of the appetites so that the costly accomplishments of culture may emerge,[568] but rather their being *befriended* by reason. In Plato's fable, moreover, the formulation that culture is *emergent* is the projection of the soul enthralled by the irresolvable tension that manifests itself under oligarchy—that first of the defective types wherein reason attempts, albeit unsuccessfully, to *repress* the appetites.[569] It is no mere coincidence, on this reading, that culture is "discovered" in the modern age at the moment when the oligarchic "type" is in ascendancy. Ethics, however, cannot be comprehended under the auspice of this oligarchic schema, which knows nothing of divine gold.

Our concern here, let us recall, is with the manner in which the science of ethics is derailed by the misplaced search for origins. The Kantian view (and not only the Kantian view)[570] would have goodness

---

'man' to a tame and civilized animal, a *domestic animal*, [we would then be justified in the judgment that these] 'instruments of culture' are a disgrace to man and rather an accusation and counterargument against 'culture' in general" (emphasis in original).

[566] Kant, "Idea for a Universal History," in *On History*, "Third Thesis," p. 14.

[567] See Nietzsche, *Genealogy*, Second Essay, sec. 22, pp. 92–93; Freud, *Civilization and Its Discontents*, chs. III and IV, pp. 37–63.

[568] Cf. Rousseau, *First Discourse*, part I, para. 13, p. 8 *passim*.

[569] It is somewhat misleading to suggest, as Taylor does, that Plato is concerned with "self-mastery" (*Sources of the Self*, ch. 6, p. 115). To the contrary, when reason rules, the appetites are befriended.

[570] The origin of this seemingly pure secular view may well be traceable to the Hebrew Bible. The God who creates Adam does not send him forth equipped with all the accouterments of civilization. Rather, the history into which Adam and his descendants fall is the resume of an unfolding articulation of the mortal situation, which while "already" present in the creation account, was nevertheless also "not yet." History is the unfolding of that "not yet," which could not have been known had Adam not defected from God. Kant doesn't use this language, but his claim that without disharmony "all talents would remain hidden, unborn in an Arcadian shepherd's life" (Kant, "Idea for a Cosmopolitan History,"

emerge from within the world of coming-into-being-and-passing-away gradually, as a consequence of agonistic refinement. Goodness need not be a gift from above, since the narrative of history, properly understood, tells the tale of its advent. Culture is the resume of man's ascent in time.[571]

We would be remiss not to mention that the kindred account of man's *prehistory* is no less a projection of this appetitive schema. Under the rubric of "evolutionary advantage," man is said to have emerged in the crucible of adversity, by which is meant a never-ending condition of constraint and shortage—in short, of the impossibility of gratifying the appetites that would wish to express themselves if only material conditions were more forthcoming. Prehistory is the story of simple human need and the long-suffering patience of the appetites, which above all want to put an end to "scarcity."[572]

Socrates had already dealt with the question of whether the Good can be understood in terms of this primitive austerity when he considered whether justice could emerge from a city constituted by human need.[573] Other animals may have "needs," but man's "flaw" renders him too anomalous to be characterized simply in terms of animal need. The moderate city that Socrates constructs is the city constituted by such animal need. Justice, however, cannot be found there. And let us be clear why this is so: Without the soul in fever—without man being ill in the way that animals can never be—the soul would remain in its original compact and undifferentiated form.[574] Man's *illness*, not his "need," engen-

---

Fourth Thesis, p. 15) closely accords with this account. See also Hegel, *Philosophy of History*, part III, sec. III, ch. 2, p. 321: "[T]he Fall is the eternal Mythus of Man." By this he meant that historical unfolding is the very condition of human knowing.

[571] Cf. Plato, *Republic*, Book III, 411e, where music and gymnastics—let us call the former "culture"—are said to be a gift of the gods. See also Plato, *Protagoras*, 320d–322d, for an account of the orgin of civilization that is a gift of the gods rather than the consequence of cultural development.

[572] In this sense, Marx should be viewed as an appetitive soul. The original opposition between man and nature is brought to an end on the advent of late capitalism, after which—under communism—"[man may] hunt in the morning, fish in the afternoon, rear cattle in the evening, criticize after dinner . . . without ever becoming a hunter, fisherman, shepherd or critic" (Karl Marx, "The German Ideology," in *The Marx-Engels Reader*, p. 160). After the problem of scarcity has been overcome, the need for division of labor will no longer be necessary, since the long suffering of man in history will finally have yielded true, not alienated, freedom.

[573] Plato, *Republic*, Book II, 369c–372c.

[574] For Voegelin, "Plato's philosophizing remains bound by the compactness of the Dionysiac soul" (Eric Voegelin, *Plato* [Baton Rouge: Louisiana State University Press, 1957], ch. 3, sec. 2, p. 62). By this Voegelin meant to distinguish the "depth" achieved by the Greek soul from that achieved by the Christian soul (see ibid., sec. 3, p. 70; sec. 4, pp. 92, 115). Notwithstanding the extraordinary subtlety of his analysis of the *Republic* and

ders the articulation of the soul into its parts; and it is only as a consequence of such an articulation that the faculty of divine reason is awakened, illuminated by the Good, and thereby empowered to render each its due. Justice, which is the achievement of precisely this arrangement, is the condition of health that man's illness at once imperils and makes possible. "Need" knows nothing of justice.[575]

There is, therefore, no ascendant narrative of history configured in accordance with the oligarchic pretense that can reveal man's true origin nor his plight.[576] Such narratives, and others that even purport to be critical of them,[577] are the poetry of spectators, beholden to any number of tropes. They are, however, incapable of illuminating the science of ethics. Man can know nothing of his origin, of the Good, except across the barrier of philosophical death. Historical narratives may indeed be edifying tales; but they have little to do with ethics. At their best, such narratives are a beginning—akin to fables appropriate for the education of children. At their worst, such narratives reinforce and project backward and forward, from the Alpha to the Omega, the secret confessions of those who

---

the seriousness with which he treats the idea of transcendence (see esp. ibid., sec. 4, pp. 112–13), Voegelin often seems rather beholden to Heidegger's categories. It seems strangely out of place, for example, to suggest that for Plato, "the anxiety of the fall from being" constitutes the experiential dilemma of man (ibid., sec. 2, p. 62; see also p. 70). Being is not the highest concern for Plato; the Good is. In this regard, both Voegelin and Heidegger miss the mark.

[575] Nature cannot disclose what is highest in man, but neither does nature disclose the depravity to which man may descend. See Plato, *Republic*, Book VI, 488a: "[N]othing in all of nature can be found to match the cruelty with which society treats its best men."

[576] See Søren Kierkegaard, *Philosophical Fragments*, ed. Howard V. Hong and Edna H. Hong (Princeton: Princeton University Press, 1985), vol. I, p. 11: "Viewed Socratically, any point of departure in time is *eo ipso* something accidental, a vanishing point, an occasion."

[577] For Strauss, the history of political thought is comprehended *religiously*; here, the Old Testament themes of repentance and submission are transposed in such way that the sickness of modernity can be healed only through "return" and "textual deference," respectively. For Voegelin, the history of political thought is comprehended *heroically*; here, the sickness of the modern soul can be healed only by a heroic journey back to the foundation of civilization itself, in an attempt to gather pre-modern insights that can be brought back to modern man, that he may become healthy again. For Arendt, the history of political thought is comprehended *politically*; here, the illness of modern man is attributed to the fact that he has lost sight of the purely political dimension where immortality—leaving one's name behind in word and deed—is possible, a loss that condemns him to die and be forgotten. For Taylor, the history of political thought is comprehended *aesthetically*; here, the beautiful and productive tension of the pre-modern world was destroyed, leaving modern man to wander numbly through a world where instrumentality is sovereign, still dimly aware of a sublime dimension that has been silenced, about which he no longer knows how to speak. For Manent, the history of political thought is comprehended *aristocratically*; here, the illness of modern man stems from his defection from Rome and his groundless choice to embrace things Protestant, German, and democratic.

purport dispassionately to convey them;[578] they divide prospective interlocutors into different and incommensurable confessional communities
that "refuse to listen"[579] to each other; and they keep philosophical death
at bay. Without philosophical death the search for origins can yield no
univocal account to which all could, in principle, accede. And if the Good
is not taken to be man's true origin, revision must necessarily follow revision,[580] as one shadow is followed by another. The Good alone gives the
light by which the sons may see clearly rather than see double.

The Opinings of the Divided Soul

Let us continue working through the proposition that the Good can be
known only across the barrier of philosophical death, only this time, let
us do so with reference to the question of the relationship between what
is opined and what rules in the defective, divided soul. Let us, in other
words, consider the opining that occurs *on this side of that barrier*. If the
soul ruled by reason and illuminated by the Good can see the world as
it really is, then souls ruled by the love of honor, wealth, freedom, and
power must be understood to possess a visual defect of sorts, an aperture through which light of only a certain hue and intensity passes,[581]
so that whatever *is* seen as a result of the light that is available accords,
self-evidently, with the principle that rules.[582] Any and all disclosures
about the nature of the "world" within which the timocrat, oligarch,
democrat, or tyrant finds himself will invariably be self-confirming,[583]

---

[578] See Nietzsche, *Beyond Good and Evil*, Part 1, sec. 6, p. 13: "Gradually it has become
clear to me what every philosophy so far has been, namely a personal confession of its author and a kind of involuntary and unconscious memoir; also that the moral (and im-
moral) intentions in every philosophy constituted the real germ of life from which the
whole plant has grown."

[579] Plato, *Republic*, Book I, 327b.

[580] See Nietzsche, *Genealogy of Morals*, Second Essay, sec. 13, p. 80: "[O]nly that which
has no history is definable."

[581] See Plato, *Republic*, Book V, 478c: "[Let us] deem opinion as something whose light
is less than knowledge but brighter than ignorance."

[582] See Plato, *Republic*, Book IX, 580d–583a, where the man who loves wealth, Socrates
says, cannot understand the happiness of the man who loves honor; and the man who loves
honor cannot understand the happiness of the man who loves wisdom. The man who loves
wisdom, on the other hand, can understand the happiness of both wealth and honor. Nietzsche's typology, though different in important respects from Plato's, also exposits the misunderstanding that occurs between "noble man" and "rational man" (*Genealogy*, part I, secs.
2–4, pp. 25–28 *passim*); as does Tocqueville's (*Democracy in America*, vol. II, part IV, ch. 8,
p. 704). See also Manent, *The City of Man*, ch. III, pp. 93–97, on Adam Smith's nearly irre-
sponsible misconstrual of the aristocratic ethos. Wealth cannot comprehend honor.

[583] Karl Marx's letter to Friedrich Engels of August 2, 1862, cited above in note 91,
bears repeating here: "[I]t is remarkable how Darwin recognizes among beasts and plants

since the aperture through which the illuminating light passes remains unaltered by the inquiry that is undertaken—as it must unless a *turn* toward the Good mysteriously occurs, and the aperture is enlarged.

The *closure*, if you will, by which man's understanding of the world perennially conforms to the ruling principle set up in his soul[584] is the occasion of Socrates' reluctance to attend to any question other than the (at once human and divine) question of how to live well. All other questions merely "polish the intellect,"[585] leave man unaware of his drowsy, unenlightened, opinion concerning the Good, and direct his attention toward those places that his chains and blinders already make available to him.[586]

This situation is not, however, without its provocations, discoveries, and wonder. Let us not forget that the typological decline from timocracy to tyranny is not a continuous slide, but rather has distinct nodal points of rest, each of which seems to be a coherent whole, whose fecundity purports to sustain man. And this is as it should be, since life "here below" draws its nourishment from "there above." The warmth of the fire may not sustain man well, but that it does so at all, even in some small measure, can be attributed to that fact that the wood that burns— the light that illuminates—originates from the living trees outside the Cave, whose source of generation is the sun.[587] "Here below" man lives off of the interest on the principal.[588] That there are provocations, dis-

---

his English society" (in *Marx-Engels Correspondence*, p. 120). Consider, in this light, Plato, *Phaedo*, 85a: "But men, because of their own fear of death, tell lies about the swans and say that they lament their death and sing in sorrow." See also Hobbes, *Leviathan*, part I, ch. ii, p. 8: "For men measure, not only other men, but all other things, by themselves." Man projects outward into the cosmos an understanding whose light is only as bright as his soul admits.

[584] Worth considering is whether the categories that inform Thomas Kuhn's *The Structure of Scientific Revolutions* (Chicago: University of Chicago Press, 1962) correspond to several of the distinctions being made here. "Normal science" may correspond to the nodal points of stability (timocracy, oligarchy, democracy) within which it appears that the world can be rendered as a coherent whole in accordance with what rules. "Anomalies" would appear when, say, timocracy is supplanted by oligarchy, etc. "Paradigm shifts" correspond to the ascension into dominance of a new type. Since the period about which Kuhn is writing can be said to correspond to the rejection of honor as a sufficient ruling principle and the emergence of wealth, followed by freedom, it might be possible to link the seminal scientific events he identifies with these transformations. See especially *Structure*, ch. IX, pp. 92–94, for the linkage between paradigm shifts in science and political transformations. For a kindred explanation, see Michael Oakeshott, "Political Philosophy," in *Religion, Politics and the Moral Life*, ed. Timothy Fuller (New Haven: Yale University Press, 1993), sec. 3, pp. 140–42.

[585] See Plato, *Republic*, Book VI, 500d.

[586] Plato, *Republic*, Book VII, 514b.

[587] See Plato, *Republic*, Book VI, 509b.

[588] Ibid., 507a.

coveries, and wonder "here below" indicates less that the nodal points of timocracy, oligarchy, and democracy are self-sustaining than that the Source from which they originate has a fecundity whose boundlessness is such that even by its derivative manifestations the sons may be awed and enticed.[589]

In this summons to pause absentmindedly, to attend to what the limited aperture of the divided soul illuminates, the vista before man invites a certain dubiety about the bearing of the Good on the world it authors. This dubiety—in the modern period expressed, say, as Hume's skepticism about the connection between "is" and "ought"[590] or as Heidegger's purported recovery of the primacy of the question of Being[591]—is perennially inscribed into the initial condition in which man finds himself. In the Cave, all evidence suggests that the Good has no bearing on the world of coming-into-being-and-passing-away. Just as the shadows beheld in the Cave bear witness to the flickering light of the fire, but not advertently to the Good that is the generative source of the wood that gently burns, so, too, the cosmos beheld by man bears witness to the soul's constricted aperture, but not to the Good that is the source of the light that dimly illuminates it. Man lives in this interstice: In wonder he gazes on a world to which the Good does not declare itself, but which can neither exist nor be known without such divine authorship. The cosmos set before man in this interstice is a testament of the soul writ

---

[589] In our own day, we might ask how Socrates would account for the *accumulation* of capital—of mortal gold—that oligarchy seems to make possible. If accumulation is possible, then how can it be that oligarchy, like every other defective type, lives only on the interest of the principal and that it is but a resting place on the way to tyranny, which is such an impoverished condition that the tyrant is finally forced to "sell the city's sacred treasure" (Plato, *Republic*, Book VIII, 568d)? Socrates would perhaps respond by saying that oligarchic accumulation must nevertheless privilege justice *in some measure* (and the divine gold on which it is based) if wealth is to be generated at all. Transposed into slightly different terms, "social capital" is the necessary ingredient even of commercial success, as a growing number of economists have realized. The "principal" of social capital cannot be eroded without diminishing the "interest" that capital is capable of accumulating. The manner in which it shows itself is variable, but this principal cannot be eroded without "cost." In Platonic terms, the "city's sacred treasure" of divine gold is still the basis of what can be bought and sold.

[590] See David Hume, *A Treatise of Human Nature* (Oxford: Oxford University Press, 1978), book III, part I, sec. I, p. 458 *passim*.

[591] See Martin Heidegger, "Plato's Doctrine of Truth," in *Philosophy in the Twentieth Century*, ed. William Barrett and Henry Aiken (New York: Random House, 1962), vol. 3, pp. 251–70. Heidegger's suggestion that Plato shifts the meaning of truth from unconcealment to "correctness" of vision, and therefore that Plato inaugurates man's closure to Being, is unwarranted. Correctness of vision, if such a term is apt at all, is a consequence of the turn toward the light of the Good, which is not in the purview of man to control.

large,[592] a dream projected by the divided soul, a resume and a comfort on *this side* of the barrier of philosophic death.

How, then, is this barrier traversed, this predicament of closure averted? Confined to his enshackled place, unmoved and unmindful, the mortal dilemma cannot be resolved by speech as such. Man is not saved by "conversation and its pleasures."[593] "Here below" speech is garbled[594] and falls on ears that can listen only to the frequency to which they are already attuned. The philosopher, consequently, must be attentive, not to the purported verities of the world that come-into-being-and-pass-away, to "science," but rather to the sorts of souls with which conversation occurs.

> Since the nature of speech is in fact to direct the soul, whoever intends to be a rhetorician must know how many kinds of souls there are. Their number

---

[592] Polanyi, whose work I mentioned above (in note 25), sought to develop a post-critical theory of knowledge that moved beyond the two seemingly nodal alternatives of objectivism and subjectivism. His term "personal knowledge" was meant to offer a third alternative. In his words, "[The personal] is neither subjective nor objective. Insofar as the personal submits to requirements acknowledged by itself as independent of itself, it is not subjective; but insofar as it is an action guided by individual passions, it is not objective either. It transcends the disjunction between subjective and objective" (*Personal Knowledge*, ch. 10, sec. 2, p. 300). The linchpin of Polanyi's theory is the fiduciary relationship among the various practitioners in a given field of knowledge. Even were this post-critical approach able to meet the epistemological objections it purports to, however, the broader ramifications of the category of "personal knowledge" are exposed to doubts of the sort that Socrates raises in the *Republic*. If knowledge is ultimately rooted in a fiduciary relationship, then tradition is certainly provided a justification of the sort that positivism cannot. Within the terms of Plato's fable, however, this does no more than privilege the sort of noble education (which hands down patterns from fathers to sons) that is superceded by that education alluded to in the Allegory of the Cave (Book VII, 514a–517a). In this regard, Polanyi sounds remarkably like Aristotle: "All knowing depends on a fiduciary framework, and moral knowledge is no exception. We come to accept moral teachings, like any other body of skillful knowing, by entrusting ourselves to a moral tradition or teacher in a process often referred to as interiorization" (*The Study of Man* [Chicago: University of Chicago Press, 1958], p. 28). (Interestingly, Aristotle cites Plato as confirming this idea in *Nicomachean Ethics*, book II, Ch. 3, 1104b11–13 ["[H]ence we ought to have been brought up in a particular way from our very youth, as Plato says, so as both to delight in and to be pained by the things that we ought, for this is the right education"], but he did not seem to understand that Plato was not finally satisfied with this sort of education.) In short, what Polanyi does not account for is the relationship between "personal knowledge" and the Good, in the same way that abiding questions must be raised about the relationship between "excellence" and the Good in Aristotle's thought.

[593] These are Cephalus' words, at the outset of the *Republic* (Book I, 328d).

[594] See Plato, *Republic*, Book VII, 515b: "*And if they could talk with one another*, don't you think they'd suppose that the names they used applied to the things they see passing before them?" (emphasis added).

is so-and-so many; each is of such-and-such a sort; hence some people have such-and-such a character and others have such-and-such. Those distinctions established, there are, in turn, so-and-so many kinds of speech, each of such-and-such a sort. People of such-and-such a character are easy to persuade by speeches of such-and-such a sort in connection with such-and-such an issue for this particular reason, which people with such-and-such another sort are difficult to persuade for those particular reasons.[595]

In this way, the philosopher-midwife may assist the soul. Only when speech is synchronized with the aperture of this or that sort of soul can it be heard. The science of ethics begins not from the presumption of a ubiquitous capacity for speech in man, but rather from the grave prospect for misunderstanding that can be obviated only by teachers who know what sorts of souls their interlocutors have.[596] The science of ethics has neither dogma nor doctrine; it advances singularly, one soul at a time—not by treatise,[597] but by patient entreaty, with a view to assisting in the supersession of the opinings of the divided soul.

The Inaction of the Divided Soul

Only the philosopher "does." The divided soul cannot *itself* act, because the animus behind the events that unfold before it are perennially *observed* to originate now from "this" place in the soul, now from "that." From a distance one part of the soul always witnesses what another part seemingly directs. Authorship is now vaguely familiar, now alien. One part always *stands by*, sometimes passively, sometimes encouragingly, sometimes with incredulity and outrage. The divided soul watches.[598] Chained to its place in the Cave, the divided soul is a specta-

---

[595] Plato, *Phaedrus*, 271d.

[596] Again, see Plato, *Laws*, Book I, 650b: "So this insight into the nature and disposition of a man's soul [that drinking parties reveal] will rank as one of the most useful aids available to the art with is concerned to foster a good character—the art of statesmanship, I take it?"

[597] See Plato, *Phaedrus*, 275d–e: "When it has once been written down, every discourse rolls about everywhere, reaching indiscriminately those with understanding no less than those who have no business with it, and it doesn't know to whom it should speak and to whom it should not. And when it's faulted and attached unfairly, it always needs its father's support; alone, it can neither defend itself nor come to its own support."

[598] Augustine's ruminations on the brokenness of man contain a kindred observation about watching. On his account, sin is the occasion for the errancy of man's body, the erotic sites of which he watches, without being able to control. See Augustine, *City of God*, in *Writings*, vol. 7, book XIV, ch. 23, p. 399: "Why, then, should we refuse to believe that the organs of generation, in the absence of that lust which is a just penalty imposed because of the sin of rebellion, could have obeyed man's will as obediently as other organs do?" (*CG*, p. 585). Cf. Rom. 7:23.

tor of passing shadows. Try as it may to act, for the divided soul life *happens*.

Let us disentangle this provocation by considering each of the defective types, in reverse order, from tyranny to timocracy. By proceeding in this way, we will take account of the less difficult cases first and conclude with the more difficult and audacious claim that the timocratic soul—the warrior, oriented by honor—does not act.

On this side of the glittering façade that the tyrant conveys, all evidence indicates that he is a man of action. Indeed, the case for justice is so difficult for Socrates to make because the tyrant appears to be the consummate man of action, while the philosopher appears to be the impotent "loser."[599] The philosopher, however, "probes into every corner and at all levels,"[600] and so is able to see past the tyrant's glittering façade. From this penetrating vantage, what matters is not the shifting shadows, but rather justice or injustice—whether what is "done" is *authored* by a unified soul or emanates incoherently now from this part of the soul, now from that. *On this side* of the glittering façade, the only thing that seems to matter is the *power* that alters the shadows that come into being and pass away. Power is taken to be the proxy for authorship. *On the other side*, this proxy is revealed to be an imperfect measure, for unless power is linked to justice, there can be no authorship, no real "doing." Without justice, what is "done" occurs as in a dream that man witnesses—a fitting image in light of Socrates' claim that the tyrant is ruled by those appetites that emerge when man sleeps. Power he may have, but authorship forever slips from his grasp, as do all things when man dreams.

> Then the tyrannical soul—I'm taking about the whole soul—will also be least likely to do what it wants and, forcibly driven by the stings of a dronish gadfly [*oistrou*], will be full of disorder and regret.[601]

On this side of the tyrant's glittering façade man opines that his real interest—the manner in which he may "be political"—involves the use of power to alter appearances; *on the other side*, man knows that his real interest is how to live justly amidst such appearances. Without justice, power is useless. The actions of the tyrant are not efficient, but rather deficient.[602]

---

[599] See Plato, *Republic*, Book I, 343d.

[600] Plato, *Republic*, Book IX, 576e.

[601] Ibid., 577d–e.

[602] See Augustine, *City of God*, vol. 7, book XII, ch. 7, pp. 257–58 (CG, pp. 479–80). For Augustine, God created the world *ex nihilo* with the foreknowledge that Satan—and subsequently man—would turn away toward darkness. Why this happened we will never know, for it is an inscrutable mystery of creation and of Providence. The man who, *with God's help*, turns toward God has an efficient will; the man who turns away from God has a

The tyrant, then, watches as the appetites that appear in his dreams demand indulgence. The democratic soul, while ruled by the appetites, is not yet ruled by appetites that appear when man is asleep, and so "watches" under less duress than does the tyrant. The democratic soul is, recall, proud of its "spontaneity"—by which is really meant: confident that the rate at which the appetites "come at him" is manageable. The democratic soul, the kaleidoscopic soul, responds as needs are felt and calls this a life of action. There is, to be sure, constant motion in democracy. Motion, however, is not to be confused with action. A "stirring without precise aim"[603] reveals the deep dissatisfaction that lurks in all the democratic soul does.[604] The democratic soul seems to be free to do as it pleases, yet because what is done is "a matter of random choice,"[605] such a soul is haunted by the *lack* of power to accomplish what it cannot even coherently want, and so is apt to be perennially disheartened.[606] The democratic soul clamors for "opportunity," spends mortal coin to secure it, perhaps asks government to increase it, and does not recognize that the *real* opportunity to act has little to do with the occasional heroic dreams that are beyond its reach,[607] but with philosophy, which is available without cost.

> Only in [a well-governed state] will those who rule be really rich, not in gold but in the wealth that yields happiness: a life of goodness and wisdom.

---

deficient will. From God, only goodness can come—which raises a profound problem about the source of evil. The Christian doctrine of sin is an attempt to address that problem, though it gives rise to any number of additional questions. Socrates, too, says that God is the source of all goodness and that "for the causes of evil we must look elsewhere" (*Republic*, Book II, 379c). What is notable here is the absence of any account of the origin of evil, though it can be argued that the *Republic* itself is a myth on the basis of which further reflection on the cause of evil becomes possible. For both Plato and Augustine, evil is a privation of being. In many of his writings, Augustine expressed this in philosophical language (see Augustine, *City of God*, vol. 7, book XI, ch. 22, pp. 219–21 [*CG*, pp. 453–54 *passim*]); perhaps more wisely, Plato conveys this through the Allegory of the Cave (*Republic*, Book VII, 514a–517a).

[603] Tocqueville, *Democracy in America*, vol. I, part II, ch. 5, p. 211.

[604] See ibid., vol. II, part II, ch. 13, p. 536: "Americans cleave to the things of this world as if assured that they will never die, and yet are in such a rush to snatch any that come within their reach, as if expecting to stop living before they have relished them. They clutch everything but hold nothing fast, and so lose grip as they hurry after some new delight."

[605] Plato, *Republic*, Book VIII, 561b. See also Tocqueville, *Democracy in America*, vol. II, part III, ch. 15, p. 611: "Habitual inattention must be reckoned the great vice of the democratic spirit."

[606] See Tocqueville, *Democracy in America*, vol. II, part III, ch. 19, p. 632. Tocqueville's analysis of this democratic phenomenon was sociological, not philosophical. By restricting the scope beyond which wealth could not be amassed and by encouraging the pride of the middle class, he thought that the sense of impotence among democratic citizens could be ameliorated.

[607] See Arendt, *The Human Condition*, ch. II, sec. 6, pp. 38–49, for a discussion of the rise of the "social" and the eclipse of the "political."

But such a government is impossible if men behave like beggars, turning to politics because of what is lacking in their private lives.[608]

The oligarchic soul, unlike the democratic soul, is only under the sway of necessary appetites, and so seems to be the first of the defective types for whom action is not mistakenly understood as spontaneity (democracy) or caprice (tyranny). Here, perhaps, is a soul for which the case can be made that action is possible. Having repressed most of its appetites in the service of making money, is not the oligarch hardheaded and capable of getting things done?

The oligarch does not "watch" as his appetites appear, for they are not allowed to do so. He is animated by the nearly palpable fear that his appetites will exceed his capacity to fulfill them.[609] The oligarch accumulates because he is haunted by the specter of depletion that his repressed appetites portend.[610] He does not "watch" because he has no time; he has no time because he is busy repressing the appetites he does not want to see. All that the oligarch does corresponds to this vanishing point of invisible threat. Where the tyrant shows himself under the guise of frenetic motion, and the democrat under the guise of random motion, the oligarch shows himself under the guise of urgent motion. Bold in one sense, the scope of what the oligarch does and understands is nevertheless confined and narrow.[611]

---

[608] Plato, *Republic*, Book VII, 521a.

[609] This was Rousseau's formulation. See *Emile*, book II, p. 81: "He whose strength surpasses his needs, be he an insect or a worm, is a strong being. He whose needs surpass his strength, be he an elephant or a lion, be he a conqueror or a hero, be he a god, is a weak being. . . . Man is very strong when he is contented with being who he is; he is very weak when he wants to raise himself above humanity. Therefore do not fancy that in extending your faculties you extend your strength. On the contrary, you diminish your strength if your pride is extended farther than it."

[610] Tocqueville's understanding was perhaps different. In one respect he would concur with the analysis so far offered here: Man is drawn toward wealth because of the gnawing fear that he will never have enough (see *Democracy in America*, vol. II, ch. 13, p. 536). Elsewhere, however, he seems to suggest that the source of the desire for wealth comes not from appetites that are unbridled, but rather from a transcendent dimension that is the basis both of man's dignity and of his despair. "In man an angel teaches a brute how to satisfy his desires," he says (ibid., ch. 16, p. 546). Unlike Marx, for whom man produces because he is a "species being" ("Economic and Philosophic Manuscripts of 1844," in *The Marx-Engels Reader*, pp. 75–76 *passim*), for Tocqueville man produces because he transcends the world in a way that other animals simply cannot—because they have no foothold in a world beyond what materialism of one sort or another discloses. Transposing Tocqueville only slightly: Man is drawn to mortal coin, and can use it to good effect, only because he has within him a divine currency. Expressed this way, Tocqueville and Plato are in accordance.

[611] See Tocqueville, *Democracy in America*, vol. II, part I, ch. 3, p. 440: "The English have long been a very cultivated people and a very aristocratic one. While their culture continually drew them toward generalizations, their aristocratic habits confined them to

Moreover, noble countenance, valor, magnanimity, heroic aspiration—all those attributes of which the timocratic soul who is unafraid of death may boast—exceed his grasp. He "acts," therefore, with a two-fold blindness: Democratic freedom he dare not look at; timocratic honor he cannot see. Enshackled to a midpoint between the two, he is repulsed by the one and insentient to the other. Living between freedom and honor, the oligarch is fearful both of the appetites that democratic man legitimates and the death that timocratic man endures. Mortal gold is his only measure, and as this is "no measure at all,"[612] what is "done" in its name is, likewise, nothing at all.

The conceit of the oligarch and democrat is that each purports to act, while the defective type below it does not: The democrat boasts of his spontaneous action over and against the tyrant, who is exhausted in spite of his success; and the oligarch boasts of his single-mindedness over and against the democrat, who turns out to be no more capable of action than is the tyrant. No less is true for the timocrat, who boasts of the scope of his endeavors, next to which the oligarch is but a shadowy figure that seems incapable of genuine action.[613]

And from a mortal vantage point, this is surely true. The timocrat is the highest type *visible to mortal eyes*.[614] He "acts" with a view not to saving himself from death with his "savings" but to expending himself, to discharging the excess of energy that distinguishes him from the common man.[615] His magnanimity grants to him that form of mortal-immortality that the remembrance of heroic deeds confers. The oligarch measures success according to the temporal horizon of his own life and

---

the particular. From this arose that brand of philosophy, *at once bold and timid*, broad and narrow, which still dominates English thought up to our time and still hampers so many minds" (emphasis added). While Tocqueville does not say explicitly, there is reason to believe that he was thinking of the utilitarianism here. This philosophy is bold because it purports to comprehend the wellspring of action entirely in terms of the calculus of pleasure and pain; it is timid because it does not recognize that there are nobler ways of understanding what animates man.

[612] Plato, *Republic*, Book VI, 504b–c.

[613] Rousseau's critique of bourgeois man authorizes this view. "Two famed Republics contended for the Empire of the World; the one was very rich, and the other had nothing, and it was the latter which destroyed the first. The Roman Empire, having swallowed the riches of the Universe, in turn fell prey to men who did not so much as know what riches were" (*First Discourse*, part II, para. 42, p. 18). The warrior "does," while the man of commerce is incapable of action.

[614] I have in mind here the distinction Aristotle makes in his *Nicomachean Ethics*, between the highest life man may lead qua man and the sort of life that is beyond mortal comprehension—namely, philosophy. The highest that man can attain qua man is political excellence (see *Nicomachean Ethics*, book I, ch. 13, 1102a14–15 *passim*).

[615] See also Nietzsche, *Genealogy of Morals*, First Essay, sec. 2, p. 26.

death; the timocrat measures victory according to the historical horizon
of the city that honors him. The warrant for the claim that the timocrat
alone "does" arises out of this prospect that he will not be forgotten.
Compared with the others with whom he competes for remembrance,[616]
the timocrat is unmatched; like an Olympian, he is *better* than the rest
and, so distinguished, leaves his mark, so long as the city that honors
him endures in this world that comes-into-being-and-passes-away.

What, then, shall we make of Socrates' suggestion that "[the philoso-
pher] will live a life happier than the most blessed lives of the Olympic
victors"?[617] Might it be the case that the endeavor of the timocrat appears to meet the criteria for acting only when juxtaposed to the more
defective types below him, that from the divine vantage point of philosophy, which those whose reason slumbers cannot know, *the timocrat does
not really act at all*?
Already in Book I, we had been alerted to the distinction that renders
this provocation plausible.

> Now, when a musician tunes his lyre by tightening and loosening the
> strings, is he trying to outdo other musicians or is he trying to meet the re-
> quirements for correct tuning?[618]

If the musician were trying to be *better* than the rest, then all that he did
would be directed toward "outdoing" others; if, on the other hand, he
were trying to be *good*, then comparisons with others would be to no
avail. Higher than "better" is "good."
In this light, the meaning of Socrates' suggestion about Olympic
victors is clear: Just as it would be folly to attribute musicianship to
the musician who plays his instrument "better" than do others, without
reference to a "goodness" that outstrips such comparisons, so, too, it
would be folly to attribute action to the timocrat whose Olympian accomplishments distinguish him from the rest,[619] without reference to

---

[616] Tocqueville thought of honor in sociological rather than psychological terms. That is,
honor arose in the aristocratic age because of the comparisons that social class made possible.
As the democratic age dawns, social distance collapses, and with it the viability of the idea of
honor and the possibility of being remembered. The timocratic soul about which Socrates
speaks will disappear—and be forgotten—with the final victory of the democratic age.

[617] Plato, *Republic*, Book V, 466d.

[618] Plato, *Republic*, Book I, 349e.

[619] Cf. Aristotle, *Nicomachean Ethics*, book I, ch. 8, 1099a3–5: "And as in the Olympic
Games it is not the most beautiful and the strongest that are crowned *but those who com-
pete* (for it is some of these that are victorious), so those who act rightly win the noble and
good things in life" (emphasis added). Within the terms of Plato's fable, Aristotle conceives
of human excellence as would a timocrat: Suspicious of both wealth and pleasure as a ruling principle, he holds honor in highest esteem.

a "goodness" that honor cannot comprehend. Honor knows "better," but not "goodness."[620] Philosophically speaking, the "doing" that the timocratic man does is akin to a sports event. His deeds are remembered, *but for those who can truly see*, they have an unreal character about them because they occur within the confines of a game: His deeds amount to an exposition of a hypothetical good, specified by the rules of the game, which is taken for granted rather than itself questioned.

The questioning that the timocratic soul avoids, as we well know, involves death of the sort that the philosopher endures. While the timocrat is surely willing to die, the death that he would proudly endure amounts to death practiced wrongly, for it evades the higher practice that alone turns man toward unmediated knowledge and toward the Good. The timocratic soul is in many respects superior to the soul ruled by the appetites, for unlike the latter, it knows that death is not to be feared.[621] Therein lays its great "advance." But unless this advance is properly understood, the timocratic soul remains insufferably proud of the chasm that separates him from those who fear death—without knowing that the very mark of his distinction presupposes, exactly as it does for the soul ruled by the appetites, that death is a *literal* affair. The distinction the timocrat makes turns out to be no distinction at all. The real chasm,

---

[620] Aristotle, too, makes this distinction, though in terms of the difference between things "praised" and things "blessed" (*Nicomachean Ethics*, book I, ch. 12, 1101b20–26 *passim*). While he notes that things blessed are divine, it is not clear what relationship obtains between things praised and things blessed, between things that receive mortal esteem by virtue of the *comparisons* men make and things for which no comparative reference can be made (because they are divine). This same tension afflicts Aristotle's analysis of relationship between political man and philosophical man in book X, chs. 7 and 8, 1177b27–1179a16 of the *Nicomachean Ethics*. The difficulty stems from his invocation of the category of activity, which well illuminates political man but casts little light on philosophical man, whose activity of contemplation seems oddly out of step with the excellence of man that Aristotle has, up to that point, set forth. ("The excellence of the intellect," he says, "is a thing apart" [ibid., 1178a22].) Plato, on the other hand, distinguishes the timocratic and philosophical man in terms of what rules in his soul, and therefore need not suggest that the timocratic man "acts" while the philosophical man "contemplates," as Aristotle does. It seems to be one of Plato's central intentions, moreover, to indicate that the philosophical life is, properly understood, a life of action.

[621] See Friedrich Nietzsche, "Homer's Contest," in *The Portable Nietzsche*, trans. Walter Kaufmann (New York: Viking Penguin, 1968), p. 38: "[W]hen we remove the contest from Greek life we immediately look into that pre-Homeric abyss of a terrifying savagery of hatred and the lust of annihilation." From Nietzsche's perspective, prior to *competition*, the Greeks were mired in pre-Homeric savagery. Within the terms of Plato's fable, the accomplishment of timocracy marks a victory of sorts over the appetites, those that emerge both when man is awake and when he is asleep. Yet it is also necessary, even if not possible by mortal means, to supplant timocracy with philosophy, for there to be justice.

the one only the philosopher can truly see, lies not between the timocrat and the soul ruled by the appetites, but between the philosopher and all the rest.

From the vantage point of the philosopher, who dies this death that the honor-loving timocrat can scarcely imagine, all that the timocrat (this highest form of merely mortal man) does is akin to a sporting event. Bring him fame though it may, the doing that the timocrat does amounts to the heroics of a well-trained sportsman, who for a time leaves his mark *in time*. As an image, of course, the sportsman is surely captivating; but anyone who knows the difference between games and real life— anyone, that is, in whom philosophy stirs—would not confuse the former with the realm of action. The connoisseurship associated with the excellence and virtue of the timocratic man is no doubt an extraordinary mortal achievement, but the habituation unto such character,[622] noble though it may be, is still one unbridgeable step away from philosophy. The Good by which the philosopher is oriented is beyond the mimetic achievement and happy fortune that the timocratic man comprehends. The timocratic man, *formed* as he is by shame and the specter of being watched,[623] knows nothing of the spectacle to which the philosopher is privy. What the timocrat "does" is not yet action, notwithstanding our hopeful declaration that of all the merely mortal types—tyrannical, democratic, oligarchic, and timocratic—the latter alone appears to have the requisite for which we are searching, and achieves the immortality for which we hunger.

We arrive now, unwittingly, at a rather scandalous conclusion, which is confirmable only with the divine knowledge that philosophy confers: *For the merely mortal man*, no action is possible.

Socrates' allegorical depiction of the situation of man in the Cave intimates this conclusion already, though he cautions us to remember that proof can be obtained only *after* the prisoner is liberated from his shackles.[624] *Bearing this admonition in mind*, let us ask what sort of thing action is, if being any one of the defective types forecloses it as a possibility. What can it mean to say that action in the Cave—action, that is, for the man in whom the divine faculty of reason slumbers—is beyond his

---

[622] See Aristotle, *Nicomachean Ethics*, book II, ch. 1, 1103b24–25: "It makes no small difference, then, whether we form habits of one kind or another from our very youth; it makes a very great differences, or rather it makes *all* the difference" (emphasis in original).

[623] Arendt understands human thriving in this way. See Arendt, *The Human Condition*, ch. II, sec. 6, p. 49: "Every activity performed in public can attain an excellence never matched in privacy; for excellence, by definition, the presence of others is always required, and this presence needs the formality of the public, constituted by one's peers."

[624] Plato, *Republic*, Book VII, 514b.

acquaintance? To indicate a provisional answer to this question, it may be helpful to recite the passage that began this section's inquiry into the primacy of ethics:

> [Now Callicles], I think that I am one of the very few Athenians, not to say the only one, engaged in the true political art, and that of the men of today I alone practice statesmanship.[625]

Socrates, the philosopher, is the consummate political actor. He alone does. And he *is* able to act because his soul is ruled by divine reason, which allows him to "render each its due." Thus enabled, he is not condemned to watch, with blinders on, the spectacle of one or another part of his soul animate him toward what appears, *from the outside*, to be an action that is his. Justice alone is the basis of doing; without justice there is as yet no unity of soul capable of authorial action. To do, to act, requires that there be justice.

> Justice is nothing else than the power that brings forth well-governed men and well-governed cities. *Our dream has come true.* We have made real what we only surmised at the outset of our inquiry when we suspected that some divine power was drawing our attention to a basic pattern of justice.[626]

The random play of faction, which is everywhere in evidence, need not involve justice, but political action does.

To the ambitious members of the crew who would wish to pilot the ship of state, a claim such as this one will seem fanciful, akin to a useless dream.[627] In this mortal "city of our birth"[628] into which we (and they) are thrown, where the appetites rule and reason slumbers, what need is there to attend to this "divine power" at all? What has this to do with the world of coming-into-being-and-passing-away in which we find ourselves?

Socrates' answer, of course, is that we do not *find ourselves* in such a world at all. "The life of man . . . from childhood to old age, is only an instant compared with all of time,"[629] he says. In that fleeting "instant" we watch as Aphrodite makes her demands; we are haunted by the specter of debt; are terrified by the prospect of death; and finally die to

---

[625] Plato, *Gorgias*, 521d.

[626] Plato, *Republic*, Book IV, 443b–c (emphasis added). Sterling and Scott here combine several slightly longer passages and leave out Glaucon's usual, and unknowing, assent. The sense of the original is unaltered.

[627] Plato, *Republic*, Book VI, 489a.

[628] Plato, *Republic*, Book IX, 592b.

[629] Plato, *Republic*, Book X, 608c–d.

the life of lingering death that we have lived. In short, we live out that first existential possibility presented in the *Republic*, namely, the life of Cephalus, who refuses philosophical death and, so, is unable to ascend from the underworld to the world of light and life. Only in the ascent from the underworld does man find himself; only through such ascension is action possible. Appearances notwithstanding, and from the point of view of authorship, all else is watching.

From the mortal perspective, to be sure, this seems rather silly. Yet if we strain our imaginations, we may yet catch a glimpse of what Socrates is directing our attention toward. To act rather than to watch requires justice. If the images Socrates has invoked throughout his discussion can be trusted, then "rendering each its due" is made possible by a gift, of sorts, that irrupts into the world of shadows but that cannot be rendered in terms of that world. Only the light of the Good grants man the ability to be just; without it, reason cannot rule and there can be no surcease from the life of chains. Justice is a gift—for those who are capable of seeing it.

> [Justice] has already proved that her gifts are real gifts; they are gifts that do not deceive those who are true to her.[630]

On the basis of this gift, man may act. The just man acts, let us say, with Eternity in view. This is, perhaps, why Socrates says that only justice "brings forth well-governed men and well-governed cities."[631] Faction is the currency of the divided soul, still under the sway of mortal mimesis, as we have called it throughout. And faction reproduces itself in its own image. Justice, however, is of a different order, requiring a communion of sorts with the very Source of the mimetic world to which we are otherwise enchained. Only by a communion with the Eternal can the links of these chains be broken and action undertaken. Action, as the timocrat will proudly point out, involves doing with a view to immortality. Let us correct our timocratic friend's opinion, however, and recognize that the task is not to leave a mark *in time*, but rather to enter into communion with what is *beyond time*. This, only the philosopher understands; this, only the philosopher does. Action involves doing of the sort that has the Eternal as its ineffable reference. Through such action, whose wellspring the divided soul cannot know, man does not so much supersede his destiny, which is forever to be a mimetic being, as he does discover his dignity, which is to pattern his life on the divine pattern that makes justice possible. Philosophy, then, *saves man* from the lifelessness of mortal mimesis—within the confines of which justice

---

[630] Ibid., 612d.
[631] Plato, *Republic*, Book IV, 443b–c.

is understood as debt and retribution, and law and custom as the out-works of power.[632]

[632] See Buber, *I and Thou*, part 3, p. 115: "It is not the periphery, the community that comes first, but the radii, the common quality of relation with the Center. This alone guarantees the authentic existence of the community." Socrates' statement that "there is some reason in the distinctions law and custom have made between fair and foul" (*Republic*, Book IX, 589c–d), appears, not incidentally, after justice has been acclaimed to be superior to injustice. Only *after* the divine pattern has been shown to be the basis of justice does Socrates suggest that law and custom may have emanated from the Good—in Buber's language, from "the Center."

Chapter 3

CONCLUSION

In the wish [for Eternity], the wound is kept open, in order that the Eternal may heal it. If the wound grows together, the wish is wiped out and then eternity cannot heal it, then temporal illness has in truth bungled the illness.[1]

My dear Glaucon, we are engaged in a great struggle, a struggle greater than it seems. The issue is whether we shall become good or bad. And not money, office, honor, nor poetry itself must be allowed to persuade us to neglect justice or any other virtue.[2]

The Fable of Liberalism

IN ORDER TO begin educating our young, Socrates informs us, we must "tell tales and recount fables."[3] Let us rehearse, here, the fable of liberalism, or at least the more generous rendition of its ascent that began to emerge in the eighteenth century and that was brought to completion in the nineteenth century by Tocqueville.[4] We do so not with a view to corroborating it as factually accurate—for the facts bear only a shadowy resemblance to Truth[5]—but rather with a view to establishing *what* rules in the souls that are depicted by this fable and whether the

---

[1] Søren Kierkegaard, *Purity of Heart Is to Will One Thing*, trans. Douglas V. Streere (New York: Harper & Row, 1956), ch. 10, p. 149.

[2] Plato, *Republic*, Book X 608b.

[3] Plato, *Republic*, Book II 376d.

[4] I leave aside, in this account, the superb twentieth-century retelling of this fable given a generation ago by Albert Hirschman, and more recently by Pierre Manent. While it would be difficult to find two books more diametrically opposed in their assessment of this fable than Hirschman's *The Passions and the Interests* and Manent's *The City of Man*, both authors reiterate its typology.

[5] In Plato's fable, facts would correspond to the domain of opinion, whereas truth corresponds to the domain of knowledge. Truth avails itself to the philosopher only; facts appear in that world that is between light and darkness, and therefore shift to and fro. See Oakeshott, "Political Philosophy," in *Religion, Politics and the Moral Life*, ch. 10, p. 141: "[Facts] are not another world from the world of opinions; they are merely relatively unshakable opinions."

typography of defective souls to which we are introduced in the *Republic* helps us to understand this fable in a new light. Let us, in other words, consider the fable of liberalism not as an account of the facts, but rather as a profession, a resume, a disclosure of, and coordinated reflection on, a type of soul that emerges into the light of day and seeks to understand the world in which it has suddenly found itself.

So let us recite, then, this fable that is appropriate for the young, which we have inherited from our liberal fathers. Our genealogy, so it begins, is marked by two distinct epochs. The first corresponds to a past that is either rapidly receding from view or irretrievably lost and that is known to us through the recorded deeds of men who evinced grandeur of soul that can no longer be fancied, let alone produced. Here loyalty, honor, virtue, manliness, and above all great longings held sway in the souls of a few. Here, too, pettiness, destitution, and squalor overwhelmed the lives of those countless many whose names have been forgotten. In this first epoch, society was a relatively well-understood hierarchy, even if not a well-ordered one, purportedly corresponding to nature itself, in which the bonds of affection where prescribed by the rank into which one was born. Authority was vested in men and not in abstract principles, and formality and protocol were, for the nobility (and not only for them), the "decent drapery of life."[6] Landed property was the basis of wealth, the consequence of which was the curious elevation of both prudential knowledge and military valor: the former, because the leisure alone afforded to a landed class could give rise to it; the latter, because there was no overarching power to secure the boundaries of landed property itself. The privileged knowledge of the aristocracy, and its incessant warfare, constituted the defining features of the epoch.

Where the warrant for the first epoch was the legacy of the past, the warrant for the second epoch is the promise of the future, a future not under the guardianship of a few great men, but rather the possession of

---

[6] This was Samuel Johnson's phrase, which Burke adopted to describe the caustic assault on aristocratic sensibilities wrought by the French Revolution. In his words, "But now all is to be changed. All the pleasing illusions, which made power gentle and obedience liberal, which harmonized the different shades of life, and which, by a bland assimilation, incorporated into politics the sentiments that beautify and soften private society, are to be dissolved by this new conquering empire of light and reason. All the decent drapery of life is to be rudely torn off. All the superadded ideas, furnished from the wardrobe of a moral imagination, which the heart owns, and the under-standing ratifies, as necessary to cover the defects of our naked, shivering nature, and to raise it to dignity in our own estimation, are to be exploded as a ridiculous, absurd, and antiquated fashion" (Edmund Burke, *Reflections on the Revolution in France*, ed. J.C.D. Clarke [Stanford, Calif.: Stanford University Press, 2001], p. 239).

nations, or even of humanity as a whole. The aristocrat was a steward who vouchsafed the mortal patterns inherited from his fathers; the human being of the present moment, however, labors alone—or is perhaps guided by the beneficent hand of a now invisible God—not in order to *imitate* the fathers but rather to innovate.[7]

Let us add that nature itself offers no guide to human beings in this second epoch, for it, too, arose out of a series of contingent events that could have been otherwise, whether by God's hand or not, we cannot say.[8] Gone, therefore, is nature's familiarity and humanity's easy confidence about a natural order into which it has been placed and to which its faculties correspond. Here loyalty can mean little, for it depends on organic union, which is illusory; honor can mean little, for it depends on rank, which affronts modern sensibilities; virtue can mean little, for it depends on character, which takes too much time and effort to develop; manliness can mean little, for it depends on the prospect for violence, which has been eliminated; great longing can mean little, for it depends on an emptiness of soul, the awareness of which has been buried by a glut of goods or made the object of therapy.

Where nature offers no comprehensive guide, humanity is thrown

---

[7] See Bernard Mandeville, *The Fable of the Bees* (Indianapolis, Ind.: Liberty Classics, 1988), part II, dialogue vi, p. 284 [335]: Cleo). "Man, as I have hinted before, *naturally loves to imitate* what he sees others do, which is the reason that savage people all do the same thing: this hinders them from meliorating their condition" (emphasis added). The editor of Smith's *Wealth of Nations* cites the passage immediately before this one in Mandeville's *Fable* as the possible basis for Smith's locution "the division of labor" (see Smith, *Wealth*, vol. I, book I, ch. I, p. 7). Marx's response to Smith is that bourgeois civilization reproduces itself in its "own image" ("Communist Manifesto," in *Marx-Engels Reader*, p. 477). Bourgeois civilization destroys one form of imitation, only to introduce another.

[8] Adam Smith, whom I allude to again shortly, was not prepared to go this far. See Adam Smith, *The Theory of Moral Sentiments*, ed. D. D. Raphael and A. L. Macfie (Indianapolis, Ind.: Liberty Classics, 1982), part VI, sec. II, ch. III, p. 235: "This universal benevolence, how noble and generous soever, can be the source of no solid happiness to any man who is not thoroughly convinced that all the inhabitants of the universe, the meanest as well as the greatest, are under the immediate care and protection of that great, benevolent, and all-wise Being, who directs all the movements of nature; and who is determined, by his own unalterable perfections, to maintain in it, at all times, the greatest possible quantity of happiness. To this universal benevolence, on the contrary, *the very suspicion of a fatherless world, must be the most melancholy of all reflections*; from the thought that all the unknown regions of infinite and incomprehensible space may be filled with nothing but endless misery and wretchedness. All the splendour of the highest prosperity can never enlighten the gloom with which so dreadful an idea must necessarily overshadow the imagination; nor, in a wise and virtuous man, can all the sorrow of the most afflicting adversity ever dry up the joy which necessarily springs from the habitual and thorough conviction of the truth of the contrary system" (emphasis added).

back on its own resources, on its "reason," which is now understood not in its unity as *communion* with God or with nature but in its dissevered, disenchanted aspects: *subjectively*, as self-interest; *objectively*, as science. The multiple and nuanced possibilities of human excellence that emerged in the first, enchanted epoch have here receded and been replaced by the monolith of reason—not incidentally, at the very moment that multiple social ranks collapse and give way to the univocal aspiration for "well-being," which is the very hallmark of social equality.[9]

Yet this forlorn situation of humanity without aristocratic bearings is not without recompense. Reason so delimited attains its proper object. In its subjective, self-interested aspect, the self-referentiality of reason invites the development of reflective judgment, private conscience, and, above all, individual responsibility. In its objective, scientific aspect, it invites the development of a generalized method of inquiry for the purpose of understanding and transforming the natural world, so that well-being may be secured for humanity as a whole.

Not only does reason attain its proper object in this second epoch, but also, in finally arriving at it, humanity need no longer indulge and exhaust itself endlessly in the passions of war. The calmer and tamer disposition of reason that is both cause and consequence of commerce triumphs as humanity is finally able to make a *productive* purchase on the natural world.

> Commerce cures destructive prejudices, and it is an almost general rule that everywhere there are gentle mores, there is commerce and everywhere there is commerce, there are gentle mores.[10]

The height to which humanity may ascend through reason is lower than the height to which the aristocratic man may ascend through glory, but reason's general availability and advantage to all constitutes its superiority. Glory was the purview of a few aristocratic men; reason is the purview of humanity as a whole. On the battlefields, a few great men emerged; in the marketplace, humanity as a whole benefits. The taming of man, and the advent of universal commerce for humanity, is the achievement of the second epoch. Here, money-making supplants the

---

[9] See chapter 2, note 552. The collapse of multiple social ranks into one corresponds to the collapse of multiple, *socially embodied* measures into the single measure of disembodied public reason, without social rank. Rawls's project, which begins from the vantage point of a "veil of ignorance" (Rawls, *Theory of Justice*, part 1, ch. 1, sec. 3, p. 12) and out of which citizens without a socially constituted history emerge, is a resume of a social order without rank.

[10] Montesquieu, *The Spirit of the Laws*, ed. Anne M. Cohler, Basia Carolyn Miller, and Harrold Samuel Stone (Cambridge: Cambridge University Press, 1989), part 4, book 20, ch. 1, p. 338.

aristocratic longing for glory. A world exhausted by war chooses a more pacific course.

> We have finally reached the age of commerce, an age that must necessarily replace that of war, as the age of war was bound to precede it. War and commerce are only two different means to achieve the same end, that of possessing what is desired. Commerce is . . . an attempt to obtain by mutual agreement what one can no longer hope to obtain through violence. . . . War then comes before commerce. The former is all savage impulse, the latter civilized calculation. It is clear that the more the commercial tendency prevails, the weaker must the tendency to war become.[11]

The taming of humanity that occurs in this second epoch is a consequence of more than just the victory of reason over glory, however. The collapse of multiple social ranks carries with it the burden and promise of human relations without predicates. The chasms among nations, social ranks, generations, and men and women are if not bridged, then at least *bridgeable* in principle, since differences among them have no durable foundation in nature.[12] Where the first epoch is characterized by rank and "pathos of distance," the second epoch is characterized by social equality and "fellow feeling."[13] Here, each human being is close enough to every other so that all suffering is noticed, and mutual sympathy is possible. Reason and commerce may attenuate and redirect the passion for glory, and render life orderly; but it is sympathy that finally *softens* humanity. In the second epoch—and this is one of its most wholesome achievements—concern and solicitude become possible.

The accomplishments and future prospects of the second epoch are not grand, but they are decent. Commerce cannot produce great men, but it can yield well-being for all. Sympathy and concern are no doubt pale affections in comparison to loyalty of the sort that rank inspires; but with loyalty comes cruelty as well, and the advantage of the paler affections is shown by this very conjunction.

[11] Benjamin Constant, "The Spirit of Conquest and Usurpation," in *Political Writings*, ed. Biancamaria Fontana (Cambridge: Cambridge University Press, 1988), part I, ch. 2, p. 53.

[12] See Smith, *Wealth of Nations*, vol. I, book I, ch. II, p. 18: "The difference of natural talents in different men is, in reality, much less than we are aware of; and the very different genius which appears to distinguish men of different professions, when grown up to maturity, is not upon many occasions so much the cause, as the effect of the division of labor."

[13] See Smith, *Theory of Moral Sentiments*, part I, sec. I, ch. I, paras. 2 and 3, pp. 8–9: "By our imagination we place ourselves in [another man's] situation, we conceive ourselves enduring all the same torments, we enter as it were his body, and become in some measure the same person with him. . . . His agonies, when they are brought home to ourselves, when we have thus adopted and made them our own, begin at last to affect us. . . . [T]his is the source of our fellow-feeling for the misery of others."

It is not too difficult to discern the kinship in this fable between the first, aristocratic epoch and what, in the *Republic*, is portrayed under the heading of timocracy.[14] In both cases, the ruling principle is honor. In both cases, too, the sons seek to imitate their fathers—as Polemarchus sought, without complete success, to do. Here the spirited, war-like element in the soul rules; the light of reason, which would cast doubt on the "conventions of the city"[15] is dim; and the appetites have not yet come to prominence. The fathers are firmly in command, and the sons follow in their stead. Wealth does not yet rule, but there are nascent signs of its coming prominence.[16]

Stable though this timocratic world may have appeared to be, it was unable to hold sway. Any number of explanations can be given for the calamity from which it could not recover: The Reformers undermined the hierarchy of the Roman Catholic Church by supplanting virtue with faith alone; scientists became suspicious of the vestiges of Aristotelianism, and sought a method that did not rely on the authority of others to vouchsafe their knowledge; the emergence of cities as autonomous centers of commerce undermined a mode of production predicated on landed property; the expansion of empires through conquest made possible global trade and economies of scale that destroyed the guild system, the idea of apprenticeship, and with it the stabilizing effects of prudential knowledge; and political revolutions—whether inspired by philosophical founders or not—extended the franchise and discredited long-standing notions of sovereignty and representation.

This list is by no means exhaustive. Neither these accounts nor others

[14] See, e.g., Tocqueville, *Democracy in America*, vol. II, part III, ch. 18, p. 618: "The medieval nobility reckoned military valor as the greatest of all the virtues. . . . [It] was born of war and for war."

[15] See Plato, *Republic*, Book V, 449c, where Adeimantus suggests to Socrates that "right needs to be defined, like everything else, in terms of the particular community in question." The "first wave" in Book V wrestles with just this question, under the guise of a conversation about the equality of the sexes. Socrates suggests to his interlocutors that without reason, there can be no basis of distinguishing what is good or bad within a particular city. The light of reason allows the philosopher to make distinctions that those who would wish to honor their city (and receive honors from it) fail to understand. See, in this regard, David Walsh, *The Third Millennium: Reflections on Faith and Reason* (Washington, D.C.: Georgetown University Press, 1999), ch. 2, p. 103: "The distortion of our world derives directly from our incapacity to deal with the boundary problems, and the latter is rendered inaccessible because the sense of what constitutes a boundary is crucially dependent on the revelation of transcendent Being."

[16] See Tocqueville, *Democracy in America*, vol. I, Author's Introduction, p. 10: "In proportion as new roads to power were found, the value of birth decreased. In the eleventh century, nobility was something of inestimable worth; in the thirteenth century it could be bought." Marx, too, would have concurred in the view that the aristocratic order concealed within itself forces that would later undo it.

of a different sort shall occupy us here, however, since our concern is to illuminate the extraordinary transformation to which history bears witness by rendering it, simply, in light of that portion of Plato's fable that traces the decline from timocracy to oligarchy. On this latter fabulous account, the *cause* of the transformation cannot be found in religious, scientific, economic, geopolitical, or intra-national facts, since these are the visible traces, as it were, of an *unconcealment* of a subsequent defective "type"—an unconcealment that was inevitable, because the timocratic fathers had given their sons a defective pattern on which to base their lives. It was, properly speaking, the unconcealment of this subsequent defective type that gave rise to the transformations and reconfigurations to which I have alluded above. The historical facts are but the shadows of the real transformation, whose cause was the emergence of the contradiction that lurked in the divided souls whose history we chronicle. The sons tried, but could not find the good in imitating their fathers—and not without reason, since the Good cannot be given mimetically, from father to son or from teacher to pupil. In time, this secret came out into the open; and the sons sought to comprehend this familial catastrophe through recourse to what I have here called the "fable of liberalism," in which the rulership of honor was rejected, and the sons set out on their own course, authorized by their certainty that mortal mimesis had failed them. And it had.

When oligarchy did emerge, as it had to in the absence of philosophy, all the fine distinctions that were made by the honor-loving father collapsed, only to be replaced by the single currency of money set forth by the oligarchic sons.[17] The sons, after all, wanted something more palpable than what the elusive fine points of honor could provide. Herewith, distinctions based on lineage, rank, peoples, and gods—all of which were the predicates of war and the manliness that is coterminous with it—were renounced.

In Plato's fable, this decision on the part of the oligarchic sons was *partially warranted*, for honor and manliness are not an adequate basis for justice, compelling as they surely are from a certain merely mortal vantage point. In their easy confidence, however, the oligarchic sons were blind to the ramifications of what they had done. Able to see the inadequacies of what ruled their fathers, they were nevertheless unaware of the deeper inadequacies to which the rule of wealth is subject. The

---

[17] Marx is helpful in illuminating this collapse. "The bourgeoisie, wherever it has got the upper hand, has put an end to all feudal, patriarchal, idyllic relations. It has pitilessly torn asunder the motley feudal ties that bound man to his 'natural superiors,' and left remaining no other nexus between man and man than naked self-interest, than callous 'cash payment'" ("Communist Manifesto," in *Marx-Engels Reader*, p. 475).

sons believed that they could avert war by deposing the honor-loving part of the soul and by enthroning *just this one appetite* for money. But once *one* appetite ruled, the other appetites that were kept in abeyance when honor ruled then pleaded their case to a sovereign that had neither wisdom (philosophy) nor shame (timocracy) to relegate them to their proper place. Formed as they were by their fathers and still under his tutelage, and notwithstanding their efforts to leave their inheritance behind, the oligarchic sons were inoculated from this democratic illness because they retained their honor-loving father's *habit* of keeping the appetites well-disciplined, and so could not see the imminent danger. In the souls of their offspring, however, were revealed appetites that in themselves only lay in wait. Here is the democratic soul.

It is beyond our purview here to consider evidence of the gross transformation from oligarchy to democracy that is perhaps now occurring, except to note that were we to undertake this task, we would have to keep firmly in mind the basis of the distinction between the two defective types: the rule of one appetite corresponds to oligarchy, while the rule of all the appetites we have when we are awake—the *equality of all* appetites, let us say—corresponds to democracy. (Might the fragmented, provocative, but ultimately helpless soul of post-modernity correspond to the shimmering iridescence of tyranny?)

Notwithstanding this distinction, however, these two types—oligarchic and democratic—are similar by virtue of having the common denominator of appetitive rule; and insofar as this is the case, they are both haunted, though to differing degrees, by the fear of death from which the philosopher and the timocrat, for different reasons, are inured. This fear of death, Socrates suggests, arises as a consequence of appetitive feasting, which binds the soul to the body in proportion as such feasting occurs.[18] The soul itself may wish for Eternity; but the soul bound firmly to the body understands eternity only under the auspice of the body living indefinitely. Death, therefore, must be staved off at all costs. For the appetitive soul, consequently, "self-preservation" is the highest good.[19]

We postpone, for a moment, the philosophic wager about the fear of

---

[18] See Plato, *Phaedo*, 116e–117a: "But Socrates, said Crito, I think the sun still shines upon the hills and has not yet set. I know the others drink the poison quite a long time after they have received the order, eating and drinking quite a bit, and some of them enjoy intimacy with their loved ones. Do not hurry; there is still some time. It is natural, Crito, for them to do so, said Socrates, for they think they derive some benefit from doing so, but it is not fitting for me."

[19] See Leo Strauss, *The Political Philosophy of Thomas Hobbes, Its Basis and Genesis*, trans. Elsa M. Sinclair (Chicago: University of Chicago Press, 1952), ch. VIII, p. 129: "[Hobbes's political philosophy can be characterized as a] movement away from honor as a principle to fear of violent death as a principle."

death, since that matter will be taken up in the section below on "The Socratic Wager." In the interim, and before turning to Tocqueville, let us briefly summarize our discussion of the rejection of the timocratic father by the oligarchic sons, for the purpose of more fully clarifying their joint misunderstandings. The oligarchic sons, we said, were correct in rejecting the *rulership* of honor, but failed to see that because justice requires "rendering each its due," the honor-loving part of the soul could not be subdued. Yet the account of the movement from the first to the second epoch offered in the fable of liberalism presumes that the principle of honor is not so much inscribed into the soul as it is *a historical artifact*, capable of being subdued or superceded as humanity progresses. The fable of liberalism supposes, in a word, that warfare can be eradicated because the honor-loving part of the soul will, in time, become an anachronism.[20] Manliness, on this account, is quaint, outdated, and an enemy of human progress. Commerce, not war, can rule; *just this one* appetite for wealth, not spiritedness, can save us. The oligarchic sons were certainly correct in rejecting the rule of honor, but in turning away from what is false they mistakenly thought that what they put in its place was true. Where the timocratic father thought that honor should rule, the oligarchic sons thought that honor had to be cast out and that the wealth had to be put in its place. Both the fathers and the sons were misguided. The fable of liberalism arises out of this configuration of misunderstanding.

The Tocquevillean Wager: Mimesis and the Mediational Site of Renewal

The particular rendition of the fable of liberalism that Tocqueville invokes now requires our consideration, in part because it is the fullest explication yet of this fable, in part because its very comprehensiveness may provide a remedy to the "configuration of misunderstanding," as I have called, out of which the fable arises. On the other hand, Tocqueville's thought may confirm that this misunderstanding is irresolvable within the categories of thought provided by the fable of liberalism, in which case the sort of account that I have offered of Plato's fable in the body of this work may prove more illuminating.

In Tocqueville's thought, the general contours of the historical argu-

---

[20] Nietzsche's critique of liberalism settles on just this point: "Must the ancient fire not some day flare up much more terribly, after much longer preparation? More: must one not desire it with all one's might? even will it? even promote it" (*Genealogy*, First Essay, sec. 17, p. 54).

ment we have thus far rehearsed remain intact, though the argument is augmented with, among other things, a theoretical insight about the importance of mediation. This insight has two distinguishable idioms: the first, sociological; the second, psychological. In its sociological idiom, Tocqueville's claim is that there must always be mediational bodies that stand between the one and the many; in its psychological idiom, Tocqueville's claim is that there must always be a node of experience, as it were, that stands between soliloquy and *they say*.

What I mean by these psychological nodal points I explain shortly, but at the moment I wish only to attend to the first, sociological expression of Tocqueville's insight about mediation, since it provides an immediate point of entry into the dispute between the timocratic and oligarchic types.

Like other iterations of the fable of liberalism, Tocqueville's historical typology is twofold, involving aristocracy, on the one hand, and democracy, on the other. Each is, in his words, "a distinct [kind] of humanity."[21] (In the terms of Plato's fable, again, the distinction we are tracing is between the timocratic and oligarchic type. Tocqueville conflates oligarchy and democracy in his fable, for reasons I hope to make clear shortly.) Different as the ages that give rise to these dissimilar kinds of souls may be, however, *in both ages* society is a three-tiered affair involving the one, the few, and the many. In the aristocratic age the form that this takes is straightforward: king, aristocrats, and peasants. But because rank disappears in democracy—or, to be less controversial, because the landed property class ceases to exist in democracy—the mediational layer must take a different form there. Instead of being based on rank of the sort that obtains in the aristocratic age, the mediational layer must be formed voluntarily,[22] since the aristocratic few no longer have any viable standing. There is, then, an "evacuation of the middle," so to speak, as aristocracy gives way to democracy, which only voluntary associations can fill. Without voluntary associations that gather the many together, the one (the state) grows more powerful,[23] the many become utterly isolated, and society becomes somnambulant. Human health

[21] Tocqueville, *Democracy in America*, vol. II, part IV, ch. 8, p. 704.

[22] See ibid., vol. I, Author's Introduction, p. 14: "Understanding its own interests, the people [in a democratic age] would appreciate that in order to enjoy the benefits of society one must shoulder its obligations. *Free associations of the citizens could then take the place of the individual authority of the nobles*" (emphasis added).

[23] This was Tocqueville's explanation for the emergence of Napoleon Bonaparte. The destruction of the aristocracy, without its replacement by voluntary associations, led to the concentration of power in the hands of the state. Once he assumed control, there was little or no opposition to his power, both in France and throughout Europe. See *Democracy in America*, vol. II, part IV, ch. 4, p. 675.

broadly understood requires a three-fold arrangement involving the one, the few, and the many, irrespective of the epoch.

The abolition of aristocratic class raises the obvious question of what happens to honor in the democratic age. Let us begin by asking *where* and *what*, in fact, is honor? In Tocqueville's account, honor is not located *in* a class of people, and so does not, strictly speaking, disappear in the democratic age, as classes tend to do. Nor is honor an aspect of a multifaceted soul, in which parts vie for ascendancy, as Plato's fable suggests. Rather, honor is an artifact of societies in which there are relatively stable social inequalities. Honor is the currency by which such inequalities are delineated.[24] In the democratic age, on the other hand, where there is increased social mobility, money, not honor, is the currency of choice.[25] With money, social inequalities are measured, *but not delineated*. Unlike money, honor cannot exist without relatively stable "social distance."

The democratic age brings with it the collapse of the social distance between classes and, therefore, an effective end to the idea of honor. Let us add to this two other considerations that bear on the collapse of the idea of honor: first, the moral vocabulary of the democratic age is that of self-interest, and the idea of honor cannot last long in an environment of strict, and sometimes stingy, calculation; second, the *carrier* of the idea of honor is the father, and his declining standing in the democratic family[26] makes it unlikely that the idea of honor can long survive.

This bleak conclusion about the future of the idea of honor in the democratic age is mitigated, however, by Tocqueville's reflections on the military, which lead in a diametrically opposed direction. Within the confines of domestic life, broadly understood, honor has little currency. The radii of deliberation in all of its forums emanate from self-interest,

---

[24] See ibid., vol. II, part III, ch. 18, p. 617: "Each of these associations [nations, classes or castes] forms, as it were, a particular species of the human race, and though they differ in no essential from the mass of men, they stand to some extent apart and have some needs peculiar to themselves. . . . Honor is nothing but this particular rule, based on a particular state of society, by means of which a people distribute praise and blame."

[25] See ibid., vol. I, part II, ch. 10, p. 406: "There is no sovereign will or national prejudice that can fight for long against cheapness"; ibid., vol. II, part III, ch. 17, p. 614: "Men living in democratic times have many passions, but most of these culminate in love of wealth or derive from it. That is not because their souls are narrower but because money really is more important at such times"; and p. 615: "In aristocratic nations money is the key to the satisfaction of but few of the vast array of possible desires; in democracies it is the key to them all."

[26] See ibid., vol. II, part III, ch. 5, p. 585: "In America the family, if one takes the word in its Roman and aristocratic sense, no longer exists." Consider, in this context, Socrates' observation that democracy is the regime of "boys and women" (Plato, *Republic*, Book VIII, 557d).

which is their self-evident center; and human life is oriented by commerce and the search for well-being. In this restless search for well-being, however, each competes with everyone else, which prompts some to look elsewhere than in the civil sphere for advancement. A few opt for "place-hunting" in the administrative apparatus of the government.[27] More opt for the military. In the democratic age, those who enter the military have their fortunes and standings yet to make, "which causes soldiers to dream of battlefields."[28] In the aristocratic age, by contrast, officers *already* possess a rank in society, and so have no need of military campaigns to establish their standing. Thus, the paradox: "[O]f all armies those which long for war most ardently are the democratic ones, but of all peoples those most deeply attached to peace are the democratic nations."[29] War, then, is an unanticipated and unintended consequence of equality itself.[30]

One of the cardinal tenets of the fable of liberalism, of course, is that as history progresses war is supplanted by commerce, until finally it is all but eradicated. Tocqueville's rendition of the fable, however, not only makes allowance for war, but suggests that rather than being an atavism that can almost be done away with, it is integral to democracy itself—not in the civil sphere, to be sure, but rather outside it, in the military.

It is worth noting that this spatial allocation, as it were, of the honor-loving aspect associated within the extra-civil domain of the military, has a sociological rather than psychological foundation. Tocqueville's account of military ambition in the democratic age contains no reference to the idea that the love of honor is inscribed in the human heart.[31] If the love of glory appears, then presumably it could be tempered or eliminated by altering social conditions—say, by making sure that there are plenty of opportunities for advancement in civil society.

---

[27] See Tocqueville, *Democracy in America*, vol. II, part III, ch. 20, p. 633: "To increase their comfort at the expense of the public treasury strikes them as being, if not the only way, at least the easiest and most expeditious by which to escape from a condition [of competition in civil society] which they no longer find satisfactory."

[28] Ibid., vol. II, part III, ch. 22, p. 648.

[29] Ibid., p. 647.

[30] Cf. Hobbes, *Leviathan*, part I, ch. xiii, para. 3, p. 75: "From this equality of ability ariseth equality of hope in the attaining of our ends. And therefore, if any two men desire the same thing, which nevertheless they cannot both enjoy, they become enemies." It is not differences among people that cause faction and war, but the fact that they are sufficiently alike each other in their tastes—but not in their judgments. It is this gap that justifies the need for an arbiter who stands over all.

[31] In his account of the American Indians, however, he suggests that a warrior, once civilized, never loses his desire for glory. See Tocqueville, *Democracy in America*, vol. I, part II, ch. 10, p. 319n., and pp. 331–32n. Democratic civilization, there, is a veneer on the surface of the aristocratic longing for glory.

The love of honor, then, makes an appearance in Tocqueville's rendition of the fable, but it is an exception, a paradoxical consequence of the general movement toward commerce and tranquility, of the ascendancy of a kind of humanity that knows nothing, really, of glory.[32] The iron logic of the fable of liberalism precludes Tocqueville from returning to the love of glory that characterized the first epoch, which is now but an anachronism. Yet he also seems unsatisfied by a world without it and troubled by the prospect that without war, humanity will be unable to renew itself.[33] Within the typology of Plato's fable, Tocqueville occasionally seems haunted by the thought that the oligarchic sons may not have made the "advance" over their timocratic fathers that they think they have.

We should not forget, however, that the burden of Tocqueville's project is to illuminate the manner in which the sons and daughters have broken with their aristocratic fathers. "We should not strive to be like our fathers," he says, "but should try to attain that form of greatness and of happiness which is proper to ourselves."[34] So, if not by honor and war, how then is society renewed and advanced on Tocqueville's account of the fable of liberalism?

The reflexive answer is, of course, commerce. And in an important sense, that is correct, though under Tocqueville's auspice the idea of commerce is thought through in terms of a larger theory of mediation, the gross features of which we have already considered. To be sure, he praises the Americans for their commercial spirit, but it is not an unmitigated good.[35] Commerce is not so much the *basis* of renewal as it is a visible and beneficent *effect* of local politics that draws the self out of itself and unleashes the sort of energy that only face-to-face relations can

[32] See ibid., vol. I, part II, ch. 9, p. 278, where the exploits of General Jackson are invoked as proof that the United States had no men who understand glory in the old, aristocratic sense.

[33] See ibid., vol. II, part III, ch. 22, p. 649: "I do not wish to speak ill of war; war almost always widens a nations mental horizons and raises its heart."

[34] Ibid., vol. II, part IV, ch. 8, p. 705. See also ibid., vol. I, part II, ch. 9, p. 285, where the Americans are said to "flee from the paternal hearth."

[35] Consider, e.g., Tocqueville's worries about blatant materialism (ibid., vol. II, part II, ch. 13, pp. 535–38; the development of a new aristocracy based on wealth (ibid., ch. 20, pp. 555–58; and the need for boundaries beyond which the accumulation of wealth should not be possible (ibid., part III, ch. 19, p. 630). Finally, it is worth noting that when Tocqueville discusses property rights, there is scarcely any mention of its relationship to productivity—a connection that is central, say, in the thinking of Locke. See John Locke, *Second Treatise of Government*, in *Two Treatises of Government*, ed. Peter Laslett (Cambridge: Cambridge University Press, 1988), ch. V, secs. 25–51, pp. 285–302. Tocqueville's concern is to show how practical experience with property rights renders the idea of rights in general *thinkable*.

generate. This is the reason why Tocqueville conflates oligarchy and democracy together: Robust commerce is the consequence of politics based on equality at the local level.

> The morals and intelligence of a democratic people would be in as much danger as its commerce and industry if ever a government wholly usurped the place of private associations. Feelings and ideas are renewed, the heart enlarged, and the understanding developed only by the reciprocal action of men one upon another.[36]

This idea, the very epithet of *Democracy in America*, will shortly bring us to the psychological nodes to which I referred at the outset of this section. First, however, let us continue along the sociological path we have taken thus far, and consider how the political institutions that robust commerce requires are produced and maintained.

In the democratic age, recall, voluntary associations must occupy the mediational space once occupied by men of rank during the aristocratic age. With the advent of the democratic age in Europe, however, this changeover did not occur, because aristocratic *habits of thought* that were anathema of democratic freedom still lingered.[37] In the absence of robust voluntary associations and local self-governance, political power became concentrated in the hands of the state, and commerce remained relatively anemic. In the United States, on the other hand, the political situation was reversed: Local government arose before the state,[38] and so was well instantiated before the state began to develop. The Puritans of the early seventeenth century, not the Founding Fathers of the late eighteenth century, were the real progenitors of the United States. They resolved the problem of the democratic age, which to the Europeans remained intractable. The commercial spirit of the Americans, consequently, dwarfed that of the Europeans.

We come now the linchpin of Tocqueville's analysis, on which the prospect for the future of democratic freedom in America and else-

---

[36] Tocqueville, *Democracy in America*, vol. II, part II, ch. 5, p. 515.

[37] See ibid., vol. I, Author's Introduction, pp. 12–13: "A new political science is needed for a world itself quite new. But it is just that to which we [Europeans] give least attention. Carried away by a rapid current, *we obstinately keep our eyes fixed on the ruins still in sight* on the bank, which the stream whirls us backwards—facing toward the abyss" (emphasis added).

[38] See ibid., vol. I, part I, ch. 2, p. 44: "In most European nations political existence started in the higher ranks of society and has been gradually, but always incompletely, communicated to the various members of the body social. Contrariwise, in America one may say that the local community was organized before the county, the county before the state, and the state before the Union."

where hangs: the relationship between founding events and subsequent conditions.

> Go back; look at the baby in his mother's arms; see how the outside world is first reflected in the still hazy mirror of his mind; consider the first examples that strike his attention; listen to the first words which awaken his dormant powers of thought; and finally take notice of the first struggles he has to endure. Only then will you understand the origins of the prejudices, habits, and passions that are to dominate his life. They whole man is there, if one may so put it, in the cradle. Something analogous happens with nations. Peoples always bear some marks of their origin. Circumstances of birth and growth affect all the rest of their careers.[39]

Whatever is established in the beginning endures. Patterns, established early on,[40] reproduce themselves over and over again, in their own image.[41] The good fortune of the Americans, Tocqueville suggests, is to have been the descendents of the Puritans, who themselves had the habit of forming associations—political and otherwise—of the sort that democratic freedom requires. For the Americans, mediating institutions were *familiar*, while in other countries with different historical origins, they were not.[42]

Tocqueville's analysis, then, is based on the idea that human beings are *mimetic* beings. Indeed, not only does this insight pertain to the Puritans and the happy legacy of democratic freedom to which the Americans are heir in the opening portions of volume 1 of *Democracy in America*, but it also pertains to the three peoples about which Tocqueville writes in the closing portions of that same volume: the American Indians, the African slaves, and the Russians.[43] In short, volume 1 of *Democracy in America* is about the beneficent, poignant, agonizing, and ominous implications of mimesis—past, present, and future.

Volume 2 of *Democracy in America*, written some five years later, has a very different cast to it. The opening chapter reveals the contours of an American "philosophical method" that is suspicious of anything whose

[39] Ibid., vol. I, part I, ch. 2, p. 31.

[40] Cf. Plato, *Republic*, Book II, 378d–e: "Whatever [young] minds absorb is likely to become fixed and unalterable."

[41] Cf. Plato, *Republic*, Book VI, 492b.

[42] Putnam, too, wrestles with this problem of path-dependency, in his study of Northern and Southern Italy. His findings prompted one civic leader from the South to proclaim: "This is a counsel of despair. You're telling me that nothing I can do will improve our prospects for success. The fate of the reform was sealed centuries ago" (Robert D. Putnam, *Making Democracy Work: Civic Traditions in Modern Italy* [Princeton: Princeton University Press, 1993], ch. 6, p. 183).

[43] For Tocqueville's discussion of the American Indians, see *Democracy in America*, vol. I, part II, ch. 10, pp. 321–39; for his discussion of slavery, see pp. 340–65; for his discussion of the Russians, see pp. 412–13.

reason for existence pertains to durability and inheritance.[44] This *anti-mimetic* disposition, as it were, we have encountered already in the oligarchic sons we described in our overview of the fable of liberalism. The pertinence of this anti-mimetic disposition throughout volume 2 should not be difficult to discern: Having dedicated no small effort in volume 1 to explaining why democratic freedom is vouchsafed by mediating institutions in America that owe their origin and maintenance to mimetic good fortune, the fateful question—treated equivocally by Tocqueville—is this: Which is more powerful, mimesis or the anti-mimetic disposition that is unleashed by the oligarchic sons? A perusal of *Democracy in America*, volume 2, part IV, will convince the reader of Tocqueville's foreboding apprehensions about which of the two will prevail.

The Tocquevillean wager, at least insofar as we have encountered it through a consideration of the sociological ruminations about mediation that inform his rendition of the fable of liberalism, is that democratic freedom is a matter of establishing mediating institutions, *which themselves will be maintained mimetically* once human beings have been properly introduced to them. Said otherwise, only mediating institutions can save us. Democratic freedom requires not philosophy, but rather "institution building."

Let us turn now to Tocqueville's analysis of what I earlier called the "psychological nodes" of the democratic age. There I suggested that democratic freedom requires a locus of experience, as it were, that stands between soliloquy and *they say*. To understand what is meant by these nodes, or loci, let us attend briefly to what Tocqueville thinks about the nature of authority in the democratic age.

> [In the democratic age] intellectual authority will be different, but it will not be less. Far from believing that it is likely to disappear, I anticipate that it may easily become too great and that possibly it will confine the activity of private judgment within limits too narrow for the dignity and happiness of mankind. I see clearly two tendencies in equality; the one turns each man's attention to new thoughts, while the other would induce him freely to give up thinking at all. . . . Thus it might happen that, having broken down all the bonds which classes of men formerly imposed on it, the human spirit might bind itself in tight fetters to the general will of the greatest number.[45]

In the aristocratic age, authority was vested largely in intermediary bodies, the consequence of which was that truth was not understood as ab-

---

[44] See ibid., vol. II, part I, ch. 1, pp. 429–33. Cf. Michael Oakeshott, "Rationalism in Politics," in *Rationalism in Politics and Other Essays* (Indianapolis, Ind.: Liberty Classics, 1991), pp. 5–42.

[45] Tocqueville, *Democracy in America*, vol. II, part I, ch. 2, p. 436.

stract, universal, and discernible by "reason," but was rather vested *in a name*.[46] In the democratic age, on the other hand, there are no such intermediary bodies, and so authority and truth change their location and character. They do not, however, disappear.

In the democratic age, the two nodal points where authority and truth lie are, in Tocqueville's words, "private judgment" and the "general will." Americans, he says, naturally suppose *two* things at once: Authority and truth are personal matters, unique to each individual, which are disclosed in the warp and woof of their own soliloquy, *and* that public opinion—what "they say"[47]—is the final authority and truth. The nodal point of soliloquy accords individuals the freedom to rehearse and stage endlessly their personal narratives without real interruption; the nodal point of "they say" emboldens individuals to rebuff the voice of conscience and condescend to the level of unreflective brutes. Neither one of these nodal points, which the democratic age produces, dignifies humankind nor renews civilization.

As might be expected in light of the centrality of mediation in Tocqueville's thinking, this intractable paradox can be attenuated only by the presence of a nodal point between "private judgment" and the "general will," that is, by a coherent locus of human experience that is neither utterly private nor comprehensively public. This locus is generated in the mediational space of associational life, in the face-to-face relations, where human beings must gather together for the purpose of addressing the problems of daily life.

> As soon as common affairs *are treated* in common, each man notices that he is not as independent of his fellows as he used to suppose and that to get their help he must offer his aid to them.[48]

Here, human beings are drawn out of themselves, gathered together as neighbors, and brought to "self-interest rightly understood,"[49] that sublime achievement of the democratic age that bridges the chasm between

---

[46] See ibid., vol. II, part I, ch. 2, p. 434: "[In the democratic age, mankind has] a very high and often thoroughly exaggerated conception of human reason." See also ibid., part III, ch. 21, p. 641: "For, taking the general view of world history, one finds that it is less the force of an argument than the authority of a name which has brought about great and rapid changes in accepted ideas."

[47] See James Fennimore Cooper, *The American Democrat* (Indianapolis, Ind.: Liberty Classics, 1956), p. 233: " 'They say,' is the monarch of this country. No one asks '*who* says it,' so long as it is believed that '*they* say it.' Designing men endeavor to persuade the public, that already 'they say,' what these designing men wish to be said, and the public is only too much disposed blindly to join in the cry of 'they say' " (emphasis in original).

[48] Tocqueville, *Democracy in America*, vol. II, part II, ch. 4, p. 510 (emphasis added).

[49] See ibid., vol. II, part II, ch. 8, pp. 525–28.

soliloquy and "they say." Without this nodal point of common affairs at the intermediate level, new ideas cannot coalesce from the "mental dust"[50] out of which a provisional consensus about authority and truth emerge, and human beings hold fast to the well-worn apparati of personal "narratives" and public platitudes.[51]

I said above that Tocqueville could be said to hold to the view that only "institutions can save us." Let us, however, dwell on what such a formulation entails psychologically, on what it tells us about this intermediary node of experience that is integral to his wager about the democratic age. I have, on a number of occasions here, mentioned that Tocqueville's real concern was the renewal of civilization. There is, of course, no corollary for "renewal" in Plato's fable, and this warrants our attention. In Plato's fable, as in Tocqueville's writing, there is attentiveness to the soul; and also an account of the "powerful [public] beast"[52] that is every bit as chilling as Tocqueville's. To this let us add that Plato's fable is concerned about the human tendency to be self-satisfied and, so, in its own way could be said to be offering the same sort of mediational alternative, whereby human beings are drawn out of themselves in face-to-face encounters with others, which roust them from their slumber.

The sort of encounter toward which Tocqueville directs our attention is not, however, a philosophical one. "Nothing is so unproductive for the human mind as an abstract idea," he says.[53] While we may certainly point out that in Plato's fable there is no real interest in *abstract* ideas, either (since abstractions are to be found in the world of coming-into-being-and-passing-away), this corrective in no way alters the difference between them: Tocqueville simply did not believe that philosophy was necessary to save democracy.[54] Nor is it the case that Tocqueville

---

[50] See ibid., vol. II, part I, ch. 1, p. 433.

[51] It is not simply a coincidence that the liberal/communitarian debate occurs in the United States during the Cold War and after the New Deal. Both events consolidated federal power and undermined mediational sites, without which we are left with *both* a caricatured understanding of the individual *and* a vacuous notion of community. Neither is adequate to the challenges of the democratic age. See Joshua Mitchell, *The Fragility of Freedom: Tocqueville on Religion, Democracy and the American Future* (Chicago: University of Chicago Press, 1995), ch. 5, p. 258: "Without [associations] we are condemned to oscillate back and forth between . . . an insular concrete personal life that is abstracted from community and a substantive community that abides only as an empty and dangerous, even if imaginative, abstraction; between the solemn impotence of self-enclosure and the euphoric identification with a national forum of politics that promises to fill the void in our souls but simply cannot."

[52] See Plato, *Republic*, Book VI, 493a–d.

[53] Tocqueville, *Democracy in America*, vol. II, part III, ch. 18, p. 617.

[54] Consider, among other things, Tocqueville's criticisms of the attempt by European thinkers to found democracy on philosophical ideas (ibid., vol. I, part II, ch. 9, p. 294; and his assessment of the impossibility of plumbing to first principles with philosophy (ibid., vol. II, part I, ch. 4, pp. 443–44).

thought that such face-to-face encounters were for the purpose of grand politics of the sort that provides a forum for human beings to show forth heroically in speech and in deed, against the backdrop of necessity.[55] Tocqueville's view was comparatively ordinary. Face-to-face encounters between human beings in these mediational fora make their world more expansive, broaden their horizons, unleash their energies—all so that they do not withdraw into themselves and broodingly shut out the world. Neither philosophy of the sort Plato's fable invites, nor noble politics in the Aristotelian sense, captivated Tocqueville's attention. On his reading, unless certain steps were taken, the end of history would be a time of resignation and stupor. Face-to-face relations between human beings, over "common affairs," draw them out of their soliloquies and renew their lives in and through their relations with those immediately around them.[56] Human beings *truly live*, he thought, only in the mediational space between soliloquy and "they say."

It would be incorrect to conclude, on the basis of this rather ordinary and institutional understanding of face-to-face encounters, that Tocqueville's own account of the fable of liberalism conforms entirely with its postulate that the second, oligarchic, epoch tames man and leaves him alone and unmoved, with calculating reason, a faculty that knows nothing of great longing,[57] as his only guide. Great longing—say, for Beauty—involves a pull from above, so to speak, of the sort that calculating reason, which, in *having* "preferences" itself *sits still*, and therefore cannot discern. That kind of longing, Tocqueville thought, would no longer be possible.[58]

While Beauty is not available to modern man, however, religion of a rather novel form finally is; and herein lays an important modification in Tocqueville's account of the fable of liberalism.[59] In the post-aristocratic

---

[55] Cf. Arendt, *The Human Condition*, ch. II, sec. 7, pp. 54–55: "[I]f the world is to contain a public space [which gathers men together and relates them to each other], it cannot be erected for one generation and planned for the living only; it must transcend the lifespan of mortal men. Without this transcendence into the potentially earthly immortality, no politics, strictly speaking, no common world and no public realm, is possible."

[56] I add here that Tocqueville thought that while the idea of rights may have originally had a religious justification, in this troubled time the only way to secure the idea was through the practical experience with political rights at the local level. See *Democracy in America*, vol. I, part II, ch. 6, p. 239. See chapter 2, section on "Rights and the Relativity of All Things."

[57] Cf. Nietzsche, *Thus Spoke Zarathustra*, Prologue, sec. 4, p. 17: "The time has come for man to set himself a goal. The time has come for man to plant the seed of his highest hope. His soul is still rich enough. But one day this soil will be poor and domesticated, and no tall tree will be able to grow in it. Alas, the time is coming when man will no longer shoot the arrow of his longing beyond man, and the string of his bow will have forgotten how to whir!"

[58] See Tocqueville, *Democracy in America*, vol. II, part I, ch. 17, pp. 482–87.

[59] See ibid., vol. I, part II, ch. 9, p. 295: "Eighteenth-century philosophers had a very simple explanation for the gradual weakening of beliefs. Religious zeal, they said, was bound to die down as enlightenment and freedom spread. It is tiresome that the facts do not fit this theory at all."

age, he thought, God would show Himself not through the carefully coordinated formalisms of the Church, but rather in an *unmediated* fashion—as is perhaps fitting for an epoch naturally disposed to be suspicious of mediation of any sort.[60]

> [In this new epoch, every man,] raising his eyes above his country, begins at last to see mankind at large, [and] God shows himself more clearly to human perception in full and entire majesty. [Under these circumstances] God's intervention in human affairs appears in a new and a brighter light.[61]

Notwithstanding the fact that human life in the post-aristocratic age is in one sense smaller than during the aristocratic age, because Beauty is foreclosed and calculative reason rules, in another more important sense human life is larger, because the luminous wonder and sublime consolation of religion shows forth in its unmediated glory—often under the guise of "Fundamentalism."[62]

But how, we may ask, can this new, unmediated, relationship to God be juxtaposed with that other naked fact about the post-aristocratic age, *viz.*, the fixation on money as the single measure?

This conjunction may seem incongruous for any number of reasons, not the least of which is that it is not immediately obvious how the technological advancements that attend the division of labor, extensive markets, and the pervasiveness of money as the currency of exchange can happily complement Christian religion, in the increasingly unmediated aspect it takes on in the post-aristocratic age. Tocqueville's argument, as brief as it is provocative, can be understood in the context of his comparison between Christianity and Islam.[63] The former, he says,

---

[60] See ibid., vol. II, part IV, ch. 2, p. 668: "The idea of secondary powers, between the sovereign and his subjects, was natural to the imagination of aristocratic peoples, because such powers were proper to individuals or families distinguished by birth, education, and riches, who seemed destined to command. Opposite reasons naturally banish such an idea from the minds of men in ages of equality." For a consideration of the multiple forms that religion may take in America in the future, see Joshua Mitchell, "The Trajectories of Religious Renewal in America: Tocquevillean Thoughts," in *A Nation under God?—Essays on the Future of Religion in American Public Life*, ed. R. Bruce Douglass and Joshua Mitchell (New York: Rowan & Littlefield, 2000), pp. 17–43, especially part II, sec. 2.

[61] Tocqueville, *Democracy in America*, vol. II, part I, ch. 17, p. 486.

[62] The term "fundamentalist" emerged in the early years of the twentieth century, as a consequence of the publication of a multi-volume series entitled *The Fundamentals: A Testimony to the Truth*, ed. R. A. Torrey (Los Angeles: Bible Institute of Los Angeles, 1917). Two of the important predicates of fundamentalism are sincerity and literalism, both of which are distinctively democratic idioms. Said otherwise, fundamentalism is a form of religion to be expected in the democratic age.

[63] See Tocqueville, *Democracy in America*, vol. II, part I, ch. 5, p. 445. An additional difficulty, he says, is the matter of scientific advancement. Christianity can accommodate

proffers only *general* specifications about the relations between the divine and the human economy. For that reason, when the modalities of mediation that characterize the aristocratic age begin to falter, there is no reason, in principle, that Christianity cannot be comprehended in different, less mediated, forms, of the sort that, say, the Reformers had in mind. Christianity emerged in the aristocratic age; but the *form* in which it appeared during that age did not constitute its essential features, which, again, were general, not specific. This, Tocqueville says, assures that "Christianity is destined to reign in this age, as in all others."[64] The post-aristocratic age is characterized by the absence of mediation, in *all* domains of human life: The naked currency of money strips away "the decent drapery of life" in the realm of exchange, no less than does the direct and unmediated experience of God strip away that "decent drapery" in the realm of religion. Juxtaposing money and God along the axis that separates things "secular" and things "sacred" misses what is really going on in the post-aristocratic age. The real issue is what happens to mediation. The love of money and the more direct experience of God are the visible markings of this new, unmediated post-aristocratic soul.

In Tocqueville's account of the fable of liberalism, then, the oligarchic sons are largely sustained—in the United States, at least—by mimetic good fortune. The habit of gathering together in mediational fora, bequeathed to them by their Puritan ancestors and precariously nurtured by the governmental apparatus of federalism, draws solitary individuals out of themselves and unleashes enormous energy, most of which "spills over" into commerce.[65] Commerce does, indeed, rule in this second epoch, but it is made possible in no small part by what Tocqueville called "local liberty,"[66] which is to say, by *democratic* participation at the local level. There is, therefore, no historical inevitability that the oligarchic sons will prevail, only the likelihood that they will do so if mediating institutions of the sort that are so precarious in the post-aristocratic age fill in the "evacuated middle" about which I spoke at the outset of this section.

---

it; Islam cannot. Notwithstanding Galileo's treatment by the Roman Catholic Church, Christianity, unlike Islam, proffers no scientific cosmology. The First Article of the Nicene Creed—*I believe in God the Father, Creator of Heaven and Earth*—is mute with respect to the features of the cosmos, their respective relationship one to another, as well as the manner in which, together or in part, they can be known; and so can accommodate a vast array of technological advancements.

[64] Tocqueville, *Democracy in America*, vol. II, part I, ch. 5, p. 445.

[65] See ibid., vol. I, part II, ch. 6, pp. 241–45.

[66] Ibid., vol. II, part II, ch. 4, p. 511.

Threatening this happy mimetic fortune, however, is the anti-mimetic proclivity of a misnamed philosophical method that would undermine local liberties in the never-ending search for efficiency, uniform rules, and rationality—all of which are impatient with the blunders that local liberty engenders.[67] Curious light is shed on this anti-mimetic proclivity by Appendix I, Y, of *Democracy in America*, which I iterate here nearly in its entirety.

> Men think that the greatness of the idea of unity lies in means. God sees it in the end. It is for that reason that the idea of greatness leads to a thousand mean actions. To force all men to march in step toward the same goal—that is a human idea. To encourage endless variety of actions but to bring them about so that in a thousand different ways all tend toward the fulfillment of one design—that is a God-given idea.[68]

Tocqueville is suggesting that this democratic impulse, which forever seeks to separate the wheat from the tares,[69] and which has no corollary in the Greek world, is in reality the outwork of *bad* Christian theology. The mystery of God's providence is His use of the imperfections of creation to bring about perfection *at the end of time*. Human beings in the post-aristocratic age, however, do not have the patience to wait. Whatever the *content* of their aspirations may be—an efficient state, uniform laws, public reason, and so on—the *spirit* behind it is thoroughly Christian.[70] Thus, the mimetic good fortune of the Americans may be undermined, ultimately, by a philosophic method that is itself the bastard offspring of Christianity—an irony of no small proportion in light of the fact that Christianity is the fertile ground out of which democratic freedom emerged.[71]

Tocqueville's wager, finally, is that *if* mediating institutions can be in-

---

[67] See ibid., vol. I, part I, ch. 5, p. 61: "A very civilized society finds it hard to tolerate attempts at freedom in a local community; it is disgusted by its numerous blunders and is apt to despair of success before the experiment is finished."

[68] Ibid., Appendix I, Y., pp. 734–35.

[69] See Matt. 13:24–30.

[70] See, again, Nietzsche, *Genealogy of Morals*, First Essay, sec. 9, p. 36: "It is the Church, and not its poison, that repels us."

[71] See Tocqueville, *Democracy in America*, vol. I, Author's Introduction, p. 10: "The ranks of the clergy were open to all, poor and rich, commoner and noble; through the Church equality began to insinuate itself into the heart of government"; ibid., part II, ch. 9, p. 287: "Every religion has some political opinion linked to it by affinity"; and ibid., vol. II, part I, ch. 3, p. 439: "All the great writers of antiquity were either members of the aristocracy of masters or, at the least, saw that aristocracy in undisputed possession before their eyes. Their minds roamed free in many directions but were blinkered there. *Jesus Christ had to come down to earth to make all members of the human race understand that they were naturally similar and equal*" (emphasis added).

stantiated and mimetically reproduced, and *if* the fugitive search for perfections of one sort or another can be averted by a theology that is cognizant of the mystery and *final* irresolvability of human suffering in a
partially broken world,[72] *then* human freedom may be saved and the future redeemed. A residue of honor, from the aristocratic age, still obtains
and is present on the borders of civil society, in the military. But it need
not pose a threat to the oligarchic sons and daughters, who are assured
of their standing by the march of history itself. In this victory, however, philosophy plays no part. Against the backdrop of a historical
movement that renders life evermore naked, lonely, and exposed, only
mediation—or rather, only the mimetic reproduction of vestigial mediational fora from the aristocratic age that remain: family, religion, munic-
ipal associations, and so on—can save us.

The Socratic Wager: Mimesis and the
Philosophical Practice of Death

From the vantage point of philosophy, neither the ruling principle of
honor nor of wealth, which delineate the two epochs specified in the fable
of liberalism, do justice to the mortal condition in shadowy times. To be
sure, the oligarchic sons are correct in rejecting mimesis of the sort that
their aristocratic fathers had in mind—what, in the *Republic*, is referred
to ironically as a "truly noble concept of education."[73] They are also correct in rejecting the rule of honor, since the noble (but not philosophic)
practice of death that war involves is defective. The question, however, is
whether the oligarchic sons understand the reason *why* both mimesis
and the timocratic practice of death are defective.

In Plato's fable, mimesis is defective because all merely mortal patterns
are "no measure at all"[74] in comparison to the divine pattern that illuminates the philosopher. The oligarchic sons properly reject mortal
patterns—think of Smith's dubiety about a system of production based
on apprenticeship—but mistakenly conclude from this contingent world
without durable mortal patterns that "markets," along with all that they
entail, are the most adequate response. Tocqueville's rendition of the fa-

---

[72] See ibid., vol. II, part I, ch. 8, p. 454: "Aristocratic nations are by their nature too
much inclined to restrict the scope of human perfectibility; democratic nations sometimes
stretch it beyond reason." See also Reinhold Niebuhr, "The Tower of Babel," in *Beyond
Tragedy: Essays on the Christian Interpretation of History* (New York: Charles Scribner's
Sons, 1951), pp. 27–46.

[73] Plato, *Republic*, Book III, 401d.

[74] Plato, *Republic*, Book VI, 504b–c.

ble of liberalism modifies this understanding in important ways, since he recognizes that commerce is impossible without mediational life. This position, in effect, reintroduces mortal patterns into the equation (sociological, not economic), because the ability to form associations depends on whether the habits necessary to do so have been passed down from generation to generation. This modification, however, does not absolve the predicament to which life that is not oriented toward the divine pattern is subject. It is an expedient measure, which averts the collapse of the oligarchic dream only for a time—as Tocqueville himself may have understood in the concluding chapters of *Democracy in America*.

Whether the oligarch seeks a justification for rejecting mortal patterns in the domain of *economics* (Smith) or seeks to reintroduce mortal patterns in the domain of *society* (Tocqueville), the rule of wealth—of one appetite alone—cannot long prevail. To be sure, there is considerable confusion and disagreement among liberals about this matter, with some arguing that markets must make *further* assaults against entrenched mimetic patterns, against "inefficiency," and others arguing that markets must not be allowed to undermine that amorphous set of mimetic patterns now called "social capital." But these debates misapprehend the deeper issue involved, namely, whether wealth has stature enough to be sovereign. The ambivalence toward mimesis exhibited by the oligarchic sons suggests that there is a contradiction in the inner workings of the sovereign that has been set up in their soul. For the moment, while the afterglow of the events of 1989 has not fully faded, the Tocquevillean disposition still has the upper hand: There is a great interest in nourishing "social capital" in regimes outside of the Anglo-American orbit whose social fabric is fragile. Yet after the stiff realization has settled in that not all nations have the historical antecedents—the mimetic inheritance—to generate social capital, we can be sure that the *other* oligarchic moment will once again assert itself, in the name of "efficiency."

In Plato's fable, however, this hardened trajectory will only deepen the rift between the rich and the poor[75] and, eventually, produce a countervailing reaction against the disciplines of the oligarchic sons, in the name of equality—of the right of every mortal model, every "life-style," to perdure. Since the desideration is not *who* rules and what visible structures obtain, but rather *what* rules in the soul,[76] this will mark the true onset of democracy. Oligarchy first undermines mimesis (Smith), and then looks to

---

[75] See Plato, *Republic*, Book IV, 422e–423a; Book VIII, 551d.

[76] See Emerson, "Circles," in *Selected Essays*, p. 404: "The key to every man is his thought. Sturdy and defying though he look, he has a helm which he obeys, which is the idea after which all his facts are classified. He can only be reformed by showing him a new idea which commands his own."

mimesis for support (Tocqueville). In any event, it cannot survive because oligarchy is an incoherent basis of rule, informed by the partially correct insight that mortal patterns given by the timocratic fathers are not enough. Today we stand on the threshold of *this* event. Denying the existence of a divine pattern, the oligarchic sons oscillate back and forth between rejecting mortal mimesis, which thrusts us ever deeper into the logic of markets, and all that they entail, or embracing mortal mimesis, which seeks to redeem oligarchy through the instantiation of institutions that even in the most salutary conditions may not be able to long endure against the onslaught of markets, as Tocqueville's own melancholy prognostication attests. In Plato's fable, of course, mimesis cannot save us—not, at any rate, the mortal sort of mimesis that institution building supposes. Only philosophy, which is attentive to the divine pattern, can save us.

Let us turn now to the practice of death. From the vantage point of the oligarchic sons, the practice of death brings to mind the war-like passions that their timocratic father championed. Indeed, the fable of liberalism supposes that the practice of death must be understood in these terms and no other: Death is an affair *of the body*, honored by the timocrat and abhorred by the oligarch. The former welcomes it for the sake of glory; the later censures it for the sake of commerce.[77]

Cessation of the body is, of course, the *only* way that death can be understood when reason's light is dim. In *this* respect, the difference between the timocrat and the oligarch is negligible. For our purposes here, we must remember that the death of the body that they both understand bears but a shadowy resemblance to the *philosophic* death about which we hear Socrates speak, which pertains to the soul. Herein lays the real chasm, in comparison to which the divergence between the timocrat and the oligarch is nearly unmeasurable.

Yet in this nearly unmeasurable divergence lies what I called, at the end of the section entitled "The Fable of Liberalism," above, "the configuration of misunderstanding" that gives rise to the fable of liberalism. In the light of Plato's fable, this misunderstanding may be characterized in the following way. The oligarchic sons, themselves unilluminated by the divine pattern, mismeasure their honor-loving fathers and, in casting out honor, lose sight of the spirited part of the soul, *which is the necessary precursor to philosophic death that is needed*. In Plato's fable, the soul *ruled* by honor is violent and unbridled, while the soul *without* honor is stingy and fearful. Neither is capable of philosophical death. The timocratic fathers are certainly mistaken that honor must rule; the oligarchic sons are even more misguided in attempting to banish honor altogether.

[77] See Hobbes, *Leviathan*, part I, ch. xiii, para. 9, p. 76.

The honor-loving part of the soul, however, cannot be banished by the sleight of hand that underwrites the fable of liberalism. Honor is neither a historical nor sociological artifact, as that fable suggests. Even when it is *shamed* into submission, the means by which it is silenced confirms its ineradicable presence—for shame is the very currency of honor. The honor-loving part of the soul is not an artifact; it is indigenous. Without it, the oligarchic sons, along with their democratic and tyrannical descendants, are haunted by the specter of death, all the while living in the condition of "lingering death"[78] that obtains in the world of coming-into-being-and-passing-away. Neither living nor dying, they seek refreshment where it cannot be found, until they themselves pass away.

The fear of death that haunts the oligarchic sons cannot be averted by denouncing the honor-loving part of the soul that invites death, nor, let us add, by their *hope* that death may be eliminated in the future, through advances of science that are both the cause and consequence of the love of wealth. Moreover, even if the death that is brought to mind by the honor-loving part of the soul *could* be banished, the insatiate appetites themselves would bring death near. Let us not forget that the spirited element of the soul emerges only in the "city in fever," when the appetites show themselves under the guise of unboundedness. The oligarchic sons, it is true, still believe that such unboundedness will not befall them; but we have seen elsewhere[79] that they lack the antidote to forestall this from occurring. In a bounded world, appetitive transgression is the precursor to war and to death.

> Like cattle they graze, fatten, and copulate. Greed drives them to kick and butt one another with horns and hoofs of iron. Because they are insatiable, they slay one another. And they are insatiable because they neglect to seek real refreshment for that part of the soul that is real and pure.[80]

Try as they may, then, the oligarchic sons cannot escape the proximity of death that prompted them to reject their timocratic father in the first place. And now, having renounced honor, they have no remedy for death's sting. What matters their Midas touch if they cower in their castles of gold?

Those souls located on the honor-loving side of this "configuration of misunderstanding" are quick to point out—as, say, Rousseau did—that war is a constitutive activity of human affairs and that it is at no small cost that the oligarchic sons renounce honor.[81] True though this certainly

---

[78] Plato, *Republic*, Book III, 406b.
[79] See chapter 2, section on "Oligarchy," p. 82–89.
[80] Plato, *Republic*, Book IX, 586b–c.
[81] See Rousseau, *First Discourse*, part II, para. 43, p. 19: "What, then, precisely is at issue in this question of luxury? To know what matters most to Empires, to be brilliant and

is, the objection in no way ascends to the level of philosophic insight, which understands the honor-loving part of the soul to be a necessary propaedeutic to the practice of death, rightly understood, but nothing more. The oligarchic sons make a grave mistake in setting up the appetitive part of the soul as sovereign; but returning the honor-loving part of the soul to the throne is equally ill advised.

In Plato's fable, neither wealth nor honor should rule; but neither should wealth be shunned nor honor emasculated, as those on *this mortal side* of philosophy are wont to do, some siding with wealth, others with honor. The fable of liberalism establishes an antinomy between wealth and honor that subsists only for those who know nothing about the philosophic practice of death. Without this practice of death—which is generated by the seed of appetitive transgression, nourished in the soil of spiritedness, but brought to full flower only by philosophy—"there can be no end to troubles . . . in our cities or for all mankind."[82] Justice, after all, entails "rendering each its due." Illuminated by the light of the Good, philosophic reason is able to rule and grant what is proper to both the honor-loving and appetitive parts of the soul. Short of that, this "tale that has been saved and not lost,"[83] this fable of Plato's that points beyond lingering death, will be supplanted by the lesser contest we witness today, to which the fable of liberalism bears witness. Neither wealth nor honor, however, can provide what is needed. While we may hope, as Polymarchus did in the opening passages of the *Republic*, that what we have inherited in the way of love of honor or of wealth is adequate, the wager of Plato's fable is that in truth only philosophy can save us.

---

short-lived, or virtuous and long-lasting. I say brilliant, but with what lustre? A taste for ostentation is scarcely ever combined in one soul with a taste for the honest. No, minds debased by a host of futile cares cannot possibly ever rise to anything great; and even if they had the strength, *they would lack the courage*" (emphasis added).

[82] Plato, *Republic*, Book VI, 473d.
[83] Plato, *Republic*, Book X, 621c.

BIBLIOGRAPHY

Arendt, Hannah. *The Human Condition*. Chicago: University of Chicago Press, 1958.

Aristotle. *Metaphysics*. Trans. W. D. Ross. In *The Complete Works of Aristotle*, ed. Jonathan Barnes.

———. *Nicomachean Ethics*. Trans. W. D. Ross. In *The Complete Works of Aristotle*, ed. Jonathan Barnes.

———. *Poetics*. Trans. I. Bywater. In *The Complete Works of Aristotle*, ed. Jonathan Barnes.

Athanasius. *On the Incarnation*. Trans. A Religious of C.S.M.V. Crestwood, N.Y.: St. Vladimir's Orthodox Theological Seminary, 1993.

Augustine, *City of God*. In *The Fathers of the Church*, ed. Roy Joseph Deferrari. New York: Fathers of the Church, 1950.

———. *Confessions*. Trans. Henry Chadwick. Oxford University Press. 1991.

———. *The Trinity*. Trans. Edmund Hill. New York: New City Press, 1991.

Bacon, Francis. "The New Organon, or True Directions Concerning the Interpretation of Nature." In *The New Organon and Other Writings*, ed. Fulton H. Anderson. New York: Macmillan, 1960.

Barnes, Jonathan, ed. *The Complete Works of Aristotle*. 2 vols. Princeton: Princeton University Press, 1984.

Benhabib, Seyla. *Democracy and Difference: Contesting Boundaries of the Political*. Princeton, N.J.: Princeton University Press. 1996.

Blumenberg, Hans. *Work on Myth*. Trans. Robert M. Wallace. Cambridge, Mass.: MIT Press, 1985.

Blundell, Mary Whitlock. *Helping Friends and Harming Enemies*. Cambridge: Cambridge University Press. 1991.

Brann, Eva T. H. "The Music of the *Republic*." *St. John's Review* 39, nos. 1 and 2 (1989–90): 1–103.

Buber, Martin. *I and Thou*. Trans. Ronald Gregor Smith. New York: Charles Scribner's Sons, 1958.

Burke, Edmund. *Reflections on the Revolution in France*. Ed. J.C.D. Clarke. Stanford, Calif.: Stanford University Press, 2001.

Calvin, John. *Institutes of Christian Religion*. Ed. John T. McNeill. Philadelphia: Westminster, 1960.

———. "Commentary on the Epistle of Paul the Apostle to the Romans." In *Calvin's New Testament Commentaries*, ed. David W. Torrance and Thomas F. Torrance. Grand Rapids, Mich.: William B. Eerdmans, 1995.

Caputo, John D. *The Mystical Element in Heidegger's Thought*. New York: Fordham University Press, 1978.

Connolly, William. *Identity/Difference*. Ithaca, N.Y.: Cornell University Press, 1991.

Constant, Benjamin. "The Spirit of Conquest and Usurpation." In *Political Writings*, ed. Biancamaria Fontana. Cambridge: Cambridge University Press, 1988.

Cooper, John M., ed. *Plato: Complete Works*. Indianapolis, Ind.: Hackett, 1997.

Cooper, James Fennimore. *The American Democrat*. Indianapolis, Ind.: Liberty Classics, 1956.

Dawkins, Richard. *The Selfish Gene*. New York: Oxford University Press, 1976.

Derrida, Jacques. "Plato's Pharmacy." In *Dissemination*, trans. Barbara Johnson. Chicago: University of Chicago Press, 1981. Pp. 62–171.

Descartes, René. *Discourse on the Method*. In *The Philosophical Writings of Descartes*, trans. John Cottingham, Robert Stoothoff, and Dugald Murdoch. 2 vols. Cambridge: Cambridge University Press, 1985. Pp. 111–51.

———. *Meditations on First Philosophy*. In *Philosophical Writings*. Pp. 37–43.

———. *Rules for the Direction of the Mind*. In *Philosophical Writings*. Pp. 7–78.

Emerson, Ralph Waldo. "An Address to the Senior Class in Divinity College." In Emerson, *Essays and Lectures*. Pp. 73–92.

———. "Circles." In *Essays and Lectures*. Pp. 403–14.

———. "Compensation." In *Essays and Lectures*. Pp. 285–302.

———. *Essays and Lectures*. New York: Library of America, 1983.

———. "Self-Reliance." In *Essays and Lectures*. Pp. 259–82.

Fanon, Franz. *The Wretched of the Earth*. New York: Grove, 1963.

Foucault, Michel. *Discipline and Punish*. Trans. Alan Sheridan. New York: Vintage, 1995.

Frazier, Nancy. *Justice Interruptus. Critical Reflections on the "Post-Socialist" Condition*. New York: Routledge. 1997.

Freud, Sigmund. *Civilization and Its Discontents*. Ed. James Strachey. New York: W. W. Norton, 1989.

Girard, Rene. *Violence and the Sacred*. Trans. Patrick Gregory. Baltimore: The Johns Hopkins University Press, 1977.

Gray, J. Glenn. *The Warriors: Reflections on Men in Battle*. New York: Harper & Row, 1970.

Gray, John. *Two Faces of Liberalism*. Cambridge, U.K.: Polity, 2000.

Habermas, Jürgen. *Between Facts and Norms*. Trans. William Rehg. Cambridge: MIT Press, 1996.

———. *Moral Consciousness and Communicative Action*. Trans. Christian Lenhardt and Shierry Weber Nicholson. Cambridge: MIT Press, 1990.

———. *Theory and Practice*. Trans. John Viertel. Boston: Beacon, 1973.

Hand, Judge Learned. *The Spirit of Liberty*. Ed. Irving Dillard. New York: Alfred A. Knopf, 1960.

Hegel, G.W.F. *Early Theological Writings*. Ed. Richard Kroner. Philadelphia: University of Pennsylvania Press, 1971.

———. *The Phenomenology of Spirit*. Trans. A. V. Miller. Oxford: Oxford University Press, 1977.

———. *The Philosophy of History*. New York: Dover, 1956.

———. *Reason in History*. Trans. Robert S. Hartman. Indianapolis, Ind.: Bobbs-Merrill, 1953.

Heidegger, Martin. *An Introduction to Metaphysics*. Trans. Ralph Manheim. New Haven: Yale University Press, 1959.

———. *Being and Time*. Trans. John Macquarrie and Edward Robinson. New York: Harper and Row, 1962.

———. "The Essence of Truth." In *Martin Heidegger: Basic Writings*. New York: Harper & Row, 1977. Pp. 113–41.

———. "Letter on Humanism." In *Martin Heidegger: Basic Writings*. New York: Harper & Row, 1977. Pp. 193–242.

———. "Nur Ein Gott Kann Uns Retten." *Der Speigel* 30, no. 23 (May 31, 1976): 209.

———. "Plato's Doctrine of Truth." In *Philosophy in the Twentieth Century*, ed. William Barrett and Henry Aiken. New York: Random House, 1962. Vol. 3, pp. 251–70.

———. *The Question Concerning Technology*. Trans. William Lovitt. New York: Harper & Row, 1977. Pp. 3–35.

Hennis, Wilhelm. "In Search of the 'New Science of Politics.'" In *Interpreting Tocqueville's Democracy in America*, ed. Ken Masugi. Savage, M.D.: Rowan & Littlefield, 1991. Pp. 27–62.

Hirschman, Albert O. *The Passions and the Interests*. Princeton: Princeton University Press, 1977.

Hobbes, Thomas. *Leviathan*. Ed. Edwin Curley. Indianapolis, Ind.: Hackett, 1994.

Horkheimer, Max, and Theodor W. Adorno. *Dialectic of Enlightenment*. Trans. John Cumming. New York: Continuum, 1987.

Hume, David. *A Treatise of Human Nature*. Oxford: Oxford University Press, 1978.

Inglehart, Ronald. *Culture Shift in Advanced Industrial Society*. Princeton: Princeton University Press, 1990.

———. *Modernization and Postmodernization*. Princeton: Princeton University Press, 1997.

Irigaray, Luce. *I Love to You*. Trans. Alison Martin. New York: Routledge, 1996.

Jüngel, Eberhard. *Theological Essays II*. Trans. Arnold Neufeldt-Fast and J. B. Webster. Edinburgh: T&T Clark, 1995.

Kant, Immanuel. "Idea for a Universal History from a Cosmopolitan Point of View." In *On History*, ed. Lewis White Beck. New York: Macmillan, 1963. Pp. 11–26.

———. "Perpetual Peace." In *On History*, ed. Lewis White Beck. New York: Macmillan, 1963. Pp. 85–135.

Kierkegaard, Søren. *Philosophical Fragments*. Ed. V. Hong and Edna H. Hong. Princeton: Princeton University Press, 1985.

———. *Purity of Heart Is to Will One Thing*. Trans. Douglas V. Streere. New York: Harper & Row, 1956.

———. *The Sickness unto Death*. Trans. Howard V. Hong and Edna H. Hong. Princeton: Princeton University Press, 1980.

Kuhn, Thomas. *The Structure of Scientific Revolutions*. Chicago: University of Chicago Press, 1962.

Kymlicka, Will. *Multicultural Citizenship*. Oxford: Oxford University Press. 1995.

Levinas, Emmanuel. *Totality and Infinity*. Trans. Alphonso Lingis. Pittsburgh: Duquesne University Press, 1969.

Livius, Titus. *History of Rome*. Trans. Canon Roberts. London: J. M. Dent & Sons, 1905.

Locke, John. *Second Treatise of Government*. In *Two Treatises of Government*, ed. Peter Laslett. Cambridge: Cambridge University Press, 1988.

Luther, Martin. "The Freedom of a Christian." In *Luther's Works*, Edited by Helmut Lehmann. Philadelphia: Fortress Press. 1967. Vol. 31.

———. "Heidelberg Disputations." In *Basic Theological Writings*, ed. Timothy F. Lull. Minneapolis, Minn.: Augsburg Fortress, 1989.

———. "Lectures on Galatians." In *Luther's Works*, vol. 27.

MacIntyre, Alasdair. *After Virtue*. Notre Dame: Notre Dame University Press. 1984.

MacPherson, C. B. In *The Theory of Possessive Individualism*. Oxford: Clarendon, 1962.

Madison, James. "Federalist No. 10." In *The Federalist Papers*, ed. Robert Scigliano. New York: Random House, 2000. Pp. 53–61.

———. "Federalist No. 51." In *The Federalist Papers*, ed. Robert Scigliano. New York: Random House, 2000. Pp. 333–35.

Mandeville, Bernard. *The Fable of the Bees*. Indianapolis, Ind.: Liberty Classics, 1988.

Manent, Pierre. *The City of Man*. Princeton: Princeton University Press, 1998.

Marx, Karl. "The Communist Manifesto." In *The Marx-Engels Reader*, ed. Robert Tucker, pp. 473–500.

———. "Economic and Philosophic Manuscripts of 1844." In *The Marx-Engels Reader*, ed. Robert Tucker, pp. 66–125.

———. "The German Ideology." In *The Marx-Engels Reader*, ed. Robert Tucker, pp. 147–99.

———. Letter to Friedrich Engels of August 2, 1862. In *Marx-Engels Correspondence*, trans. George Hanna. Moscow: Progress, 1955.

Maslow, Abraham H. *Towards a Psychology of Being*. New York: Van Nostrand Reinhold, 1982.

Mill, J. S. "On Liberty." In *On Liberty and Other Essays*, ed. John Gray. Oxford: Oxford University Press, 1991.

Mitchell, Joshua. *The Fragility of Freedom: Tocqueville on Religion, Democracy and the American Future*. Chicago: University of Chicago Press, 1995.

———. *Not by Reason Alone: Religion, History, and Identity in Early Modern Political Thought*. Chicago: University of Chicago Press, 1993.

———. "The Trajectories of Religious Renewal in America: Tocquevillean Thoughts." In *A Nation under God?—Essays on the Future of Religion in American Public Life*, ed. R. Bruce Douglass and Joshua Mitchell. New York: Rowan & Littlefield, 2000. Pp. 17–43.

Montesquieu, Baron de. *The Spirit of the Laws*. Ed. Anne M. Cohler, Basia Carolyn Miller, and Harrold Samuel Stone. Cambridge: Cambridge University Press, 1989.

Nasr, Sayyed Hossein. *Knowledge and the Sacred*. New York: Crossroad, 1981.

Niebuhr, Reinhold. *The Nature and Destiny of Man.* 2 vols. New York: Charles Scribner's Sons, 1964.

———. "The Tower of Babel." In *Beyond Tragedy: Essays on the Christian Interpretation of History.* New York: Charles Scribner's Sons, 1951. Pp. 27–46.

Nietzsche, Friedrich. *Beyond Good and Evil.* Trans. Walter Kaufmann. New York: Random House, 1966.

———. *The Gay Science.* Trans. Walter Kaufmann. New York: Random House, 1974.

———. *The Genealogy of Morals.* Trans. Walter Kaufmann. New York: Random House, 1967.

———. "Homer's Contest." In *The Portable Nietzsche,* trans. Walter Kaufmann. New York: Viking Penguin, 1968. Pp. 32–99.

———. *Thus Spoke Zarathustra.* Trans. Walter Kaufmann. New York: Penguin Books, 1968.

Oakeshott, Michael. "Political Philosophy." In *Religion, Politics and the Moral Life,* ed. Timothy Fuller. New Haven: Yale University Press, 1993. Pp. 138–55.

———. "Rationalism in Politics." In *Rationalism in Politics and Other Essays.* Indianapolis, Ind.: Liberty Classics, 1991. Pp. 5–42.

Plato. *Apology.* Trans. G.M.A. Grube. In *Plato: Complete Works,* ed. John Cooper. Pp. 17–36.

———. *Euthyphro.* Trans. G.M.A. Grube. In *Plato: Complete Works,* ed. John Cooper. Pp. 1–16.

———. *Gorgias.* Trans. Donald J. Zeyl. In *Plato: Complete Works,* ed. John Cooper. Pp. 791–869.

———. *Laches.* Trans. Rosamond Kent Sprague. In *Plato: Complete Works,* John Cooper. Pp. 664–86.

———. *Laws.* Trans. Trevor J. Saunders. In *Plato: Complete Works,* ed. John Cooper. Pp. 1318–616.

———. *Phaedo.* Trans. G.M.A. Grube. In *Plato: Complete Works,* ed. John Cooper. Pp. 49–100.

———. *Phaedrus.* Trans. Alexander Nehamas and Paul Woodruff. In *Plato: Complete Works,* ed. John Cooper. Pp. 506–56.

———. *Philebus.* Trans. Dorothea Frede. In *Plato: Complete Works,* ed. John Cooper. Pp. 398–456.

———. *Platonis Rempublicam.* Ed. S. R. Slings. Oxford: Oxford University Press, 2003.

———. *Protagoras.* Trans. Stanley Lombardo and Karen Bell. In *Plato: Complete Works,* ed. John Cooper. Pp. 746–90.

———. *Republic.* Trans. Richard W. Sterling and William C. Scott. New York: W. W. Norton, 1985.

———. *Sophist.* Trans. Nicholas P. White. In *Plato: Complete Works,* ed. John Cooper. Pp. 235–93.

———. *Statesman.* Trans. C. J. Rowe. In *Plato: Complete Works,* ed. John Cooper. Pp. 294–358.

———. *Symposium.* Trans. Alexander Nehamas and Paul Woodruff. In *Plato: Complete Works,* ed. John Cooper. Pp. 457–505.

———. *Theaetetus*. Trans. M. J. Levett. In *Plato: Complete Works*, ed. John Cooper. Pp. 157–234.

Polanyi, Michael. *Meaning*. Chicago: University of Chicago Press, 1975.

———. *Personal Knowledge*. Chicago: University of Chicago Press, 1958.

———. *The Study of Man*. Chicago: University of Chicago Press, 1958.

Putnam, Robert D. *Making Democracy Work: Civic Traditions in Modern Italy*. Princeton: Princeton University Press, 1993.

Rawls, John. *A Theory of Justice*. Cambridge, Mass.: Harvard University Press, 1971.

Ricoeur, Paul. *The Symbolism of Evil*. Boston: Beacon, 1967.

Rorty, Richard. *Philosophy and Social Hope*. New York: Penguin, 1999.

Rousseau, Jean-Jacques. "Discourse on the Origin and Foundations of Inequality among Men." In *The First and Second Discourses*, ed. Victor Gourevitch. Cambridge: Cambridge University Press, 1997.

———. *Emile*. Trans. Allan Bloom. New York: Basic Books, 1979.

———. "Whether the Restoration of the Sciences and the Arts Has Contributed to the Purification of Morals." In *The First and Second Discourses*, ed. Victor Gourevitch. Cambridge: Cambridge University Press, 1997.

Sahlins, Marshall. *Stone Age Economics*. Chicago: Aldine-Atherton, 1972.

Smith, Adam. *The Theory of Moral Sentiments*. Ed. D. D. Raphael and A. L. Macfie. Indianapolis, Ind.: Liberty Classics, 1982.

———. *Wealth of Nations*. Chicago: University of Chicago Press, 1976.

Strauss, Leo. *The City and Man*. Chicago: Rand McNally, 1963.

———. "The Dialogue between Reason and Revelation." In *The Rebirth of Classical Political Rationalism*. Chicago: University of Chicago Press, 1989.

———. "Jerusalem and Athens: Some Preliminary Reflections." In *Studies in Platonic Political Philosophy*, ed. Thomas Pangle. Chicago: University of Chicago Press, 1983. Pp. 147–73.

———. *The Political Philosophy of Thomas Hobbes, Its Basis and Genesis*. Trans. Elsa M. Sinclair. Chicago: University of Chicago Press, 1952.

———. *Studies in Platonic Political Philosophy*. Ed. Thomas Pangle. Chicago: University of Chicago Press, 1983.

Taylor, Charles. *The Ethics of Authenticity*. Cambridge: Harvard University Press, 1991.

———. *Multiculturalism: Examining the Politics of* Recognition. Princeton: Princeton University Press, 1994.

———. *Sources of the Self*. Cambridge, Mass.: Harvard University Press, 1989.

Tocqueville, Alexis de. *Democracy in America*. Ed. J. P. Mayer. New York: Harper & Row, 1969.

———. Letter to Madame Swetchine, January 1, 1856. In *Selected Letters on Politics and Society*, ed. Roger Boesche. Berkeley: University of California Press, 1985.

Torrey, R. A., ed. *The Fundamentals: A Testimony to the Truth*. Los Angeles: Bible Institute of Los Angeles, 1917.

Tucker, Robert, ed. *The Marx-Engels Reader*. New York: W. W. Norton, 1978.

Voegelin, Eric. *The New Science of Politics*. Chicago: University of Chicago Press, 1952.

———. *Plato*. Baton Rouge: Louisiana State University Press, 1957.

Walsh, David. *The Third Millennium: Reflections on Faith and Reason*. Washington, D.C.: Georgetown University Press, 1999.

Weber, Max. *The Methodology of the Social Sciences*. Trans. Edward Shils and Henry Finch. New York: Free Press, 1949.

———. "Politics as a Vocation." In *From Max Weber*, ed. H. H. Gerth and C. Wright Mills. New York: Oxford University Press, 1946. Pp. 77–128.

———. *The Protestant Ethic and the Spirit of Capitalism*. Trans. Talcott Parsons. New York: HarperCollins, 1991.

———. "Science as a Vocation." In *From Max Weber*, ed. H. H. Gerth and C. Wright Mills. New York: Oxford University Press, 1946. Pp. 129–56.

Young, Iris Marion. *Democracy and Inclusion*. Oxford: Oxford University Press, 2000.

INDEX

NEW FORUM BOOKS

New Forum Books makes available to general readers outstanding original interdisciplinary scholarship with a special focus on the juncture of culture, law, and politics. New Forum Books is guided by the conviction that law and politics not only reflect culture but help to shape it. Authors include leading political scientists, sociologists, legal scholars, philosophers, theologians, historians, and economists writing for nonspecialist readers and scholars across a range of fields. Looking at questions such as political equality, the concept of rights, the problem of virtue in liberal politics, crime and punishment, population, poverty, economic development, and the international legal and political order, New Forum Books seeks to explain—not explain away—the difficult issues we face today.

James Hitchcock, *The Supreme Court and Religion in American Life: Volume 1, The Odyssey of the Religion Clauses; Volume 2, From "Higher Law" to "Sectarian Scruples"*

Christopher Wolfe, ed., *That Eminent Tribunal: Judicial Supremacy and the Constitution*

David Novak, *The Jewish Social Contract: An Essay in Political Theology*

Joshua Mitchell, *Plato's Fable: On the Mortal Condition in Shadowy Times*